66

Old Ford

34

R. Lee

Moor Field

Stepney

Cornhill

Fenchurch

Redcliff

Blackwall

Brook

Wall

Over ey

Southwark

Rother hithe

Isle of Dogs

Canutes Trench

Bermondsey

River Thames

STREET

ington

ington

130

Greenwich

Camberwell

Deptford

Blackheath

Peckham

29 Denmark Hill

Nun head

108

hampion Hill 125

198

Quaggy

Hern Hill

88

Dulwich

Ravens B.

Forest Hill

102

162

INSIDER'S
LONDON

RICHARD BAKER

PICTURES *left to right*
- Cutty Sark
- St Paul's Church, Covent Garden
- St Pancras Church, Euston Road
- Southwark Bridge

INSIDER'S LONDON
Designed and produced by Parke Sutton Limited, 8 Thorpe Road, Norwich NR1 1RY
for Jarrold Colour Publications, Barrack Street, Norwich NR3 1TR
in association with the British Tourist Authority, Thames Tower, Black's Road, Hammersmith, London W6 9EL

Printed in Great Britain
Text typeface 10pt ITC Galliard Roman

INSIDER'S
LONDON

RICHARD BAKER

PICTURES *left to right*
- Madame Tussaud's
- Sarah Siddon's grave, St Mary's Church, Paddington
- J P Guivier and Co
- Blackfriars Pub, Queen Victoria Street
- Cleopatra's Needle
- Star and Garter Home, Richmond

CONTRIBUTORS

AUTHOR
Richard Baker

EDITOR
Michelle Jarrold

DESIGN
Geoff Staff

RESEARCH
Jan Tavinor

PHOTOGRAPHS
John Brooks, Alan Guttridge, Neil Jinkerson

CONTENTS

PRELUDE

Of all the great cities of the world, London must be one of the most difficult to know. It has been thrown together by 2000 eventful years of history, and its shape owes little – all too little, some would say – to the vision of the town-planner. Edinburgh's New Town, the Ring which embraces the ancient heart of Vienna, the 'etoile' of Paris, the geometrical layout of Manhattan: all these are the result of a concerted attempt to impose a pattern on urban living. But the average Englishman is an anarchist at heart, and when this quality is coupled with commercial enterprise, the result is a capital city which has countless interesting features but an elusive personality. G.K. Chesterton commented neatly on this question, as on so many others, when he compared the British and French capitals. 'London', he said, 'is a riddle. Paris is an explanation.'

Stand in the middle of Waterloo Bridge and look around. To the west is the Palace of Westminster where the mother of parliaments assembles and the majestic face of Big Ben tells the world the time. Look southwards and you will see the concrete bunkers which house the National Theatre and the Queen Elizabeth Hall. On the eastern side, the spires of the Wren churches which used to punctuate the City skyline so tactfully, and even the dome of St Paul's itself, are overwhelmed by vast twentieth-century tower blocks. That is the architectural jungle which is London today. Many deplore it,

of course, but others find it exciting; and much has mysteriously survived in the onward rush of the present century.

'London', said Disraeli, discussing another aspect of its diversity, 'is a nation, not a city.' Indeed, with the racial mix to be found in the capital today, you could say it was many nations. This helps to give the city its infinite human variety. What's more, this former capital of a great empire is not so much a single community as a series of villages, each with its own identity and commanding its own loyalty. The City of London, the square mile which houses one of the world's three greatest financial centres, is a village on a global scale, where the inhabitants hobnob in pubs, clubs and restaurants much as they would in a village inn. Mayfair and Belgravia are villages with streets of village shops, which just happen to have the famous department store Harrods not too far away. Blackheath, Hampstead, Chiswick and Soho are renowned for their village atmospheres – that's what attracts people to them – and areas like Clapham, Islington and Kentish Town, Wapping, Limehouse and Greenwich all have marked individual characters and their own committed adherents. If there happens to be a football team in the district, such as Tottenham Hotspur, Chelsea, Arsenal or Crystal Palace, they earn their support partly because they are just very famous village teams. In addition, if you have lived – and worked – in London for a lifetime as I have done, then you will have your own personal vision of the city, coloured by your own interests and experience.

I was born in Willesden, one of the older villages of north-west London; very old indeed, if you take into account the fact that King

Athelstan granted the manor of Willesden to the monks of St Athelstan around AD 940. I wasn't aware of that as a boy, but I did like trains and it calls for no great leap of historical imagination to visualise modern Willesden growing at a fierce pace around Willesden Junction station. In the nineteenth century, Willesden's population multiplied itself more than a hundred times. But although I started life in Willesden, moving at the age of three to a small terrace house in nearby, newly developed Kensal Rise, it was really in Paddington that 'my London' began.

Paddington was once the ancient settlement of 'Padda's people', whoever Padda was, and mushroomed, like Willesden, when the railways came. The large station built in 1854 as the terminus of Brunel's Great Western Railway was the heart of Paddington, a name associated with transport in more ways than one. In 1829 a coachbuilder called George Shillibeer introduced London's first bus service from Paddington Green; in fact his vehicles were called 'shillibeers' until the same man also patented a new type of funeral carriage under his own name, after which it was thought preferable

In this early twentieth-century photograph, Platform One at Paddington is filled, not with weary commuters, but with crowds waiting for the Windsor Garden Party or Henley Regatta special trains.

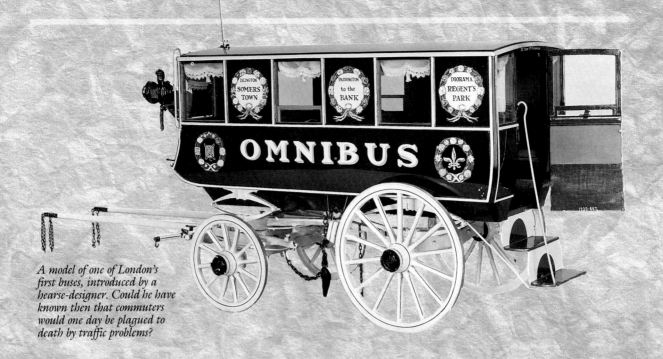

A model of one of London's first buses, introduced by a hearse-designer. Could he have known then that commuters would one day be plagued to death by traffic problems?

to adopt the Latin 'omnibus', as a means of distinguishing road vehicles for the living.

So I had Mr Shillibeer to thank for my regular Saturday morning penny bus rides in the early 1930s to visit my grandmother in Paddington. She lived in a four-storey Victorian terrace house with a basement. Well, she lived in the basement and let the rest to a variety of tenants. There was a reserve policeman, a 'special', and his wife on the ground floor. They had a small daughter called Margaret Mary, black haired and beautiful, who appealed to me greatly. There was an elderly mother and her middle-aged daughter in two rooms on the first floor and on the two floors above them a young unmarried music teacher, Gertrude Holmes. Miss Holmes's kitchen was in the attic. Above the sink was a skylight, and if you stood on a chair you could peer out and get a marvellous view of London, a view all the more exciting at night when the lights from the West End were reflected on the clouds. I'm not sure how I persuaded Miss Holmes to let me look out of her skylight. Perhaps it was a quaint way of rewarding me for doing well at the piano lessons which I started with her at the age of seven.

After these piano lessons, which were often punctuated by sharp raps on the knuckles with a pencil when scales did not go according to plan, I often used to spend the remainder of the weekend with my grandmother, sleeping in a little room at the back of the house. I have a great affection for London's domestic gardens, usually small and hemmed in by brick walls. My grandmother's plot was not very well cared for, but it did have a pretty lilac tree whose blooms I could see out of my bedroom window, and the smell of lilac to me will always be redolent of London in the spring.

My grandmother's name was Emily and I called her Amy. She was a plucky Irishwoman who had survived the break up of an unhappy marriage; my mother was her only remaining child, for Amy had lost another daughter and her small son in the appalling 'flu epidemic which followed the First World War. This tragic bereavement worked, I now believe, to my advantage, for Amy decided to lavish on me all the affection she had felt for her own son. She was eager to introduce me to London, and on Saturday afternoons and evenings (some-times for longer periods in the school holidays)

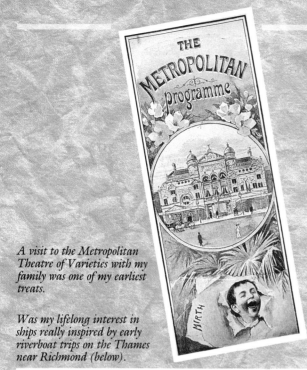

A visit to the Metropolitan Theatre of Varieties with my family was one of my earliest treats.

Was my lifelong interest in ships really inspired by early riverboat trips on the Thames near Richmond (below).

we would explore it together. She was far from affluent, but it was wonderful what two people on a weekend jaunt in London could do in those days for half a crown (12½p in present-day money).

For six old pence you could get into the World News Cinema in Praed Street (near Paddington Station) which provided one of my favourite Saturday afternoon treats. Not because a future television newsreader was already showing marked interest in current affairs, but because news cinemas invariably made up their hour-long programmes with Mickey Mouse, Donald Duck and Laurel and Hardy.

Amy enjoyed music, and was very keen that I should 'be a credit to her' where Miss Holmes was concerned, but her musical tastes, in keeping with her limited income, did not rise much above listening to the band in the park and in the Embankment Gardens. One great merit of the gardens was that they were near the river. The Thames in its upper and lower reaches held infinite fascination for me, and an expedition on a Mears steamer to Richmond or Greenwich was the perfect holiday treat. This was even more the case if such an outing was followed, as it very occasionally was, by a visit to a theatre, sometimes to the Palladium, the Holborn Empire or the famous Metropolitan Theatre of Varieties in the Edgware Road.

If Amy's tastes in music and theatrical entertainment were unpretentious, she aspired to refinement in other ways. She loved to read about the royal family and members of the aristocracy and talked about them as if she knew them personally. We often visited the big shops together. Thanks to Amy, I acquired champagne tastes at an early age with no prospect whatever of gratifying them. It was she who gave me to understand that eating sandwiches in public was not quite the thing to do, and I always resisted doing so when my parents suggested we should take sandwiches on a family outing. In the event, of course, greed always overcame etiquette and I usually consumed more than anybody else.

Other early memories include my father taking me to the Proms at the Queen's Hall, exploring the South Kensington museums, going to Richmond, Kew and Hampstead Heath, and cruising down the river on the Eagle steamers to Clacton or Margate for our summer holidays. But there was very little money to spare in our family, as my father was often out of work in his trade as a plasterer, so it was left to my grandmother to add an occasional touch of luxury to our lives.

The London I have come to know as an adult is haunted by memories of the London I saw in childhood. When I went into Buckingham Palace early in 1969 to prepare my commentary for the television coverage of President Nixon's visit to the Queen, I remembered how I'd stood outside the railings with Amy to watch the changing of the guard, speculating as Christopher Robin did, when he 'went down with Alice' in A.A. Milne's poem, about what the King and Queen were doing inside at that moment. When firewatching during the war on the roof of the Royal Naval College at Greenwich, where I was training to be a naval officer, or much later when I found myself in a similar position on the roof reporting on the knighting of Sir Francis Chichester by the Queen, my mind went back to river expeditions when we were young, the magic of which was greatly enhanced if we were allowed to go back on the launch to Tower Pier after dark.

As one who queued many a time for the gallery to see Gilbert and Sullivan at Sadler's Wells Theatre or the Golders Green Hippodrome, I still marvel at being able to walk through the artists' entrance at the Royal Albert Hall to introduce the Last Night of the Proms or the Festival of Remembrance; and it was with a vision of the old Queen's Hall in Langham Place clearly before my eyes that I described for television the opening nights of the re-modelled Royal Festival Hall, the Queen Elizabeth Hall and the Barbican. Thanks to my broadcasting work I've been able to get an insider's view of many a place I saw from the

Exuberant concert-goers at the Royal Albert Hall share one of my earliest musical memories, the Last Night of the Proms.

outside as a child: St Paul's and the Guildhall in the City, Westminster Abbey, St James's Palace, Lloyds and the Stock Exchange, the Royal Opera House and Covent Garden, to name but a few. In this way my own idea of London has grown up too.

Coupled with this personal image of the capital is the knowledge that has come to me, like any other Londoner, from books, from hearsay and tradition. Behind and beyond the rapidly changing facades of the eighties, there's a city that's been here for centuries, with its kaleidoscope of character and occupation, aspiration and ambition. Though too much has gone of the old London, a lot remains, and it is still possible to sense the feeling of the past when exploring the city of the present day.

I decided to set this book in a musical framework, partly because so much of my working life has been spent in or near the musical world. But there's a special reason too for picturing London as 'a theme with variations'. Elgar's famous *Enigma Variations* is a wonderful portrait gallery of the composer's friends. But there's more to it than that – at least according to Elgar, who was fond of riddles. Tantalisingly

he wrote: 'The enigma I will not explain – its "dark saying" must be left unguessed; further, through and over the whole set another and larger theme "goes" but is not played'. This statement has teased countless critics and music lovers over the years. Was Elgar referring to some general theme such as friendship? Was the stated musical theme itself a variation on some very well known tune such as the national anthem or 'Auld Lang Syne'? The riddle has never been resolved. Nor can any one person hope to unravel the enigma of London. That remains.

Meanwhile I take here as my theme the London we see today, with its high-tech, high-rise blocks, its maze of new developments both good and bad, its crowded streets and high-pressure lifestyle. The variations on this theme are my vivid memories of a London from days gone by, interwoven with the London of the more remote past which still casts its haunting shadow over the more impersonal metropolis of the late twentieth century.

The superb interior of St Paul's Cathedral, one of London's best-loved landmarks.

WATER MUSIC

As long as I can remember, I have been drawn to the sea and, since Old Father Thames in the well known ditty 'keeps rolling along, down to the mighty sea', London's river too has always appealed powerfully to my imagination. I have to confess that as a boy it was the lower river which chiefly attracted me, with its docks and cranes and dirty, busy warehouses. There I could see the big ships with as many as three funnels being inched out of Tilbury Docks on their way to furthest India or the Far East, and I would ask myself in puzzled wonder, with Rudyard Kipling, 'Oh, where are you going to, all you big steamers?' By comparison the Upper Thames with its punts and launches seemed very tame.

But it's not only small boys from Willesden Green who love the River Thames, that liquid thread which runs through the whole history and geography of London. Kings and queens have used it as a ceremonial highway and as a source of pleasure over the centuries. According to a well-established legend, it was through an invitation to compose music for a royal river party that Handel won his way back into favour with King George I – he had walked out on the future king when he was Elector of Hanover in order to come to London to seek his fortune. But it seems there is no truth in this romantic story about the origins of Handel's 'Water Music', for the king had too high an opinion of the composer's genius to dispense with his services – even temporarily – out of injured pride.

In a despatch dated 19th July 1717, a foreign envoy at the court of King George reported the day's proceedings as follows:

Some weeks ago the King expressed a wish to Baron von Kilmanseck to have a concert on the river, by subscription, like the masquerades this winter which the King attended assiduously on each occasion. Baron Kilmanseck resolved to give the concert on the river at his own expense, and so the concert took place the day before yesterday. The King entered his barge at about eight o'clock with the Duchess of Bolton, the Countess of Godolphin, Madame de Kilmanseck, Madam Vere and the Earl of Orkney, gentleman of the King's Bedchamber who was on guard.

By the side of the Royal Barge was that of the musicians to the number of 50 who played all kinds of instruments, viz. trumpets, hunting horns, oboes, bassoons, German flutes, French flutes à bec, violins and basses, but without voices. This concert was composed expressly for the occasion by the famous composer Handel, native of Halle, and first composer of the King's music. It was so strongly approved by H.M. that he commanded it to be repeated, once before and once after supper, although it took an hour for each performance.

The evening party was all that could be desired for the occasion. There were numberless barges, and boats filled with people eager to take part in it. In order to make it more complete, Mad. de Kilmanseck had made arrangements for a splendid supper at the pleasure house of the late Lord Ranelagh at Chelsea on the river, to where the King repaired an hour after midnight. He left there at three, and at half past four in the morning H.M. was back at St James'. The concert has cost Baron Kilmanseck £150 for the musicians alone.

This contemporary account of perhaps the most famous musical party in history omits to tell us whether the king was in a fit condition for the conduct of state business the morning after. However, he clearly enjoyed his outing on the River Thames in the company of his

favourite mistress, Madame Kilmanseck; and perhaps there was added relish in the thought that Handel's glorious aquatic concert had been paid for by the lady's husband.

The River Thames has no doubt been a source of pleasure to Londoners ever since the city's foundation. It has also been indispensably useful. London in fact would not be where it is if there hadn't been two small areas of river gravel around present-day Cornhill and Ludgate Hill. On them, not long after Julius Caesar landed in the British Isles in AD 43, the Romans built a settlement near the lowest fordable point on the river which was also the tidal limit at that time. Why they gave the settlement the name Londinium is uncertain, but it may have been derived from a Celtic word meaning 'wild' or 'fierce'. At all events Londinium grew rapidly in its strategic riverside setting and by the second century was among the five biggest cities in the known world.

In succeeding generations, city men have been sensible enough to rate the value of London's river very highly. There are two stories at least that suggest the Thames meant more to them in former times than the favour of their monarch. The sixteenth-century chronicler John

The larger ships don't go far up the river, but smaller craft still cruise its length. Immune from traffic jams, the Thames now offers a convenient way of getting from one place to another.

Stow relates that when a city alderman heard how Queen Mary, in her displeasure against London, had decided to remove the parliament to Oxford, 'this plain man demanded whether she meant also to divert the river of Thames from London or no? And when the gentleman had answered "no", "then", quoth the alderman, "by God's grace we shall do as well at London whatsoever become of the parliament".' A similar tale is told about King James I, who threatened to remove his court to Windsor when the City refused him a loan. Then, according to the historian James Howell, the Lord Mayor replied: 'Your majesty hath power to do what you please, and your City of London will obey accordingly; but she humbly desires that when your Majesty shall remove your Court, you would please to leave the Thames behind you.'

The importance of the river as London's great commercial highway has declined in recent years now that big ships usually come no further up the Thames than Tilbury, but it is very much in use again as a means of public transport, immune as it is from traffic jams. The erection of the Thames Barrier at Woolwich Reach to prevent London being flooded by a tidal wave is a wary twentieth-century salute to the continuing power of the river, and as for its capacity to give enjoyment, that remains as great as ever. Indeed the river is a great deal more pleasant than it once was. I have an almost nostalgic memory of the overpowering smell the water used to give off at Woolwich, but London is much better off without it; and the lower river is now clean enough for fish to have returned in large numbers.

The Thames Barrier at Woolwich is London's acknowledgement of the unpredictable power of its river.

Hampton Court (right), where the initials of Henry VIII and Anne Boleyn entwine (above) in a permanent reminder of their short-lived marriage.

The outings I used to enjoy as a child with my family took us sometimes as far up the river as Hampton Court, the great country residence west of London that was begun in 1514 by the mighty Cardinal Wolsey. However, his king, Henry VIII, was mightier. Wolsey fell, and Hampton Court became a royal palace.

Twickenham was another place that we used to visit. It had become very fashionable in the seventeenth and eight-eenth centuries: Alexander Pope occupied a villa there, although its once-famous grotto is now used as a passage under the road between two sections of a modern school. Horace Walpole settled in a cottage close by and enlarged it until it became a unique mixture of mansion and castle called Strawberry Hill. This Gothic masterpiece attracted many tributes which no doubt flattered Walpole. In a letter, the great man quoted with approval these

Alexander Pope's Twickenham villa is no more, but his grotto (below and below, left) is now a subterranean passage linking two school buildings.

lines written in 1755 by William Pulteney, Earl of Bath:

> Some talk of Gunnersbury,
> For Sion some declare,
> Some say, that with Chiswick House
> No villa can compare;
> But all the beaux of Middlesex
> Who know the country well
> Say that Strawberry Hill, that
>   Strawberry Hill,
> Doth bear away the bell.

A century later, Edward Fitzgerald also recorded his admiration for what he called this 'toy of a very clever man'. He was saddened to see 'the rain coming through the roofs, and gradually disengaging the confectionery Battlements and cornices'.

On the river itself, there was the famous Twickenham ferry, which inspired a Victorian ditty by Theo Marzials:

> O-hoi-ye-ho, Ho-ye-ho, Who's for the
>   ferry?
> (The briar's in bud, the sun going
>   down)
> And I'll row ye so quick and I'll row ye so
>   steady
> And 'tis but a penny to Twickenham
>   Town.

Strawberry Hill (below and right) was transformed by Horace Walpole from a cottage into a castle.

Twickenham Ferry, inspiration for one of many Victorian river-songs.

There was quite a vogue for river songs in Victorian times, reflecting the popularity of the river as a pleasure resort then. That popularity was no less marked in Edwardian days and in the twenties, when the strains of the Charleston would float across the river from many a punt equipped with a wind-up gramophone. They often had discreet awnings too, thus providing a twentieth-century equivalent of the barge in which King George I glided along the Thames, accompanied by his beloved, and serenaded by the music of Handel.

I once had to interview the comedienne Beatrice Lillie for a television programme at her home on the Upper Thames, and she elected to give the interview in a punt. When I arrived, the awning was stretched over the punt and Miss Lillie was nowhere to be seen. So I knocked on the awning framework and enquired 'Is Miss Lillie about?' 'About what?' came the voice from inside. 'It's about this interview' I said. 'About time!' replied the star, 'Come aboard!' Upon which she flung the awning aside, I stepped carefully into the punt, and the interview began.

Most of our childhood excursions up the Thames took us no further than Richmond. The pleasure of going there by boat from, say, Westminster Pier was so great that I was even prepared to overcome a strange childish inhibition and eat sandwiches among the crowds that surged, as they still do today, along the river bank at weekends. The invasion must often have been resented by those who live in the town. In May 1920 Virginia Woolf noted in her diary: 'Richmond on a fine Saturday afternoon is like a lime tree in full flower – suppose one were an insect sitting on the flower. All the others swarm and buzz and burble. Being residents we don't of course.'

No sign of the 'swarm and buzz and burble' of visitors in this peaceful corner of Richmond Park in spring.

Like Hampton Court and Twickenham, Richmond is full of royal associations. Edward I built a palace there in the thirteenth century, and it was Charles I who enclosed Richmond Park as a hunting ground. But Richmond has long been a resort for humbler folk too. The painter Benjamin Haydon, writing in 1816, defined the three summits of human happiness as, first, 'the consciousness of having done your duty', second, 'success in great schemes' and third, 'a lovely girl who loves you in the dining room of the Star and Garter at Richmond, sitting, after dinner, on your knee, with her heavenly bosom palpitating against your own'. The Star and Garter inn got its name from Richmond's royal connections, referring as it does to the insignia of Britain's prime order of knighthood, the Order of the Garter. Deservedly more famous today is the Royal Star and Garter Home which was built on the site of the old inn. The present building, designed by Sir Edwin Cooper, was opened by King George V and Queen Mary in 1924 as a hospital and home for disabled ex-service people. It still fulfils that function, though its expertise is now more widely available to the community; anyone who has served in the forces at any time is eligible for treatment. I have visited the Star and Garter Home on more than one occasion and, although the building is somewhat too cavernous and monumental for my liking, the staff and residents make it both inspiring and friendly.

The Star and Garter Home crowns Richmond Hill, a famous viewpoint long celebrated by poets, among them James Thomson who exclaimed in 'The Seasons':

> Heavens! What a goodly prospect spreads around,
> Of hills, and dales, and woods, and lawns, and spires,
> And glittering towns, and gilded streams, till all
> The stretching landscape into smoke decays!

There must have been something of a misty pall over London in 1727, though surely not as much as in the days before the Clean Air Act, when people used to refer to the city simply as 'the Smoke'.

One of the best ways to appreciate the River Thames and its influence upon London is, of course, to take a trip down the river to Greenwich, a trip that, for the first part at least, follows in the path of history. For Queen Elizabeth I's body was taken by river from Richmond to Westminster Abbey for burial almost 400 years ago.

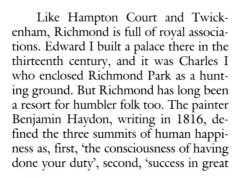

The Star and Garter Home, Richmond (below) is a lasting and practical tribute to disabled British servicemen.

Kew Gardens (right) have now virtually recovered from the devastation caused by hurricane-force winds in October 1987.

Moving on down the river Kew Gardens, on the right, is a reminder of the mother of King George III, for it was she who in 1759 founded the Royal Botanical Gardens. Then, in 1841, Queen Victoria bestowed on the nation what was to become the most famous collection of plants in Europe. Considerable damage

(Left and below) The 'des. res.' riverside village of Strand-on-the-Green, near Kew Bridge. The watercolour view from the river is by T.H. Lambert.

was caused at Kew by the hurricane of 16th October 1987, but the gardens have all but recovered and are worth much more than a passing glance from a river launch. On the left is the square and imposing Syon House, where the first Duke of Northumberland commissioned Robert Adam to redesign the interior in 1762. Adam based the decor of one room on Diocletian's palace at Spalato and adorned it with twelve green marble columns dredged up from the River Tiber.

As the River Thames swings round under Kew Bridge, the attractive riverside village of Strand-on-the-Green comes into view. Its fine houses and pleasant setting make it a very desirable – and expensive – place to live. Further downstream Mortlake marks the finish of the Oxford and Cambridge Boat Race, a national institution that began in 1829 as the result of a private challenge. Crews from the two ancient universities compete over a four and a quarter mile course, rowing upstream from Putney to Mortlake. A for-

midable test of stamina and skilful training, it used to engender fierce rivalry throughout the land, regardless of whether people had a personal attachment to either university. Light and dark blue favours were sold in millions, and in my schoolboy days you had to declare yourself firmly either 'Oxford' (dark blue) or 'Cambridge' (light blue). I seem to remember I was consistently for the Light Blues, though I had no idea that one day I would find myself studying by the banks of the Cam. General enthusiasm for the race seems to have waned in recent years, and partly thanks to television coverage the bridges and river banks are not as packed as they once were with eagerly committed spectators.

The bridges of Paris have merited a popular song to themselves, and some of the Thames bridges too are worthy of celebration. More or less in the middle of the boat race course is Hammersmith Bridge, a grand piece of gilded Victoriana now valued, as it should be, as an

Captured on canvas by Walter Greaves (1846–1930), spectators crowd Hammersmith Bridge on Boat Race Day. Like me, perhaps many would have been Cambridge supporters without quite knowing why.

The graceful lines of Hammersmith Bridge, cobweb-fine against the evening sky.

historical monument, though the weight of modern vehicles has caused trouble at times to the suspension design of 1887, and heavy lorries are now forbidden. Further down towards Westminster is another elegant suspension bridge, the Albert Bridge. Built in 1873 by the man who designed the roof of the Albert Hall, R.M. Ordish, it was the last toll bridge

The Albert Bridge was built by the man who designed the Albert Hall's roof – though you'd never know from their contrasting styles.

across the Thames. Still nailed to one of the toll booths is the warning: 'All troops must break step when marching over this bridge.' The fact that the bridge still stands has been attributed by hostile critics to the British tendency to be always out of step.

Albert Bridge has long been a noticeable landmark at Chelsea, but it has to compete for attention now with one of London's most spectacular residential developments of recent years at Chelsea Harbour. Here, those who possess them can moor their yachts alongside their houses, in sharp contrast to the numerous people who make their homes in the large collection of picturesque barges moored near Battersea Bridge.

Cadogan Pier, Chelsea, marks the upriver end of another famous boat race. This one dates back to the year 1716 when Thomas Doggett, comedian and joint manager of Drury Lane Theatre, offered a coat and badge, from then on known as Doggett's Coat and Badge, 'to be rowed for by six watermen that are out of their time within the year past'. It's a tough race, over four and a half miles

The spectacular redevelopment of Chelsea's waterfront means high-rise accommodation for those who like to keep their feet – however remotely – on the ground (right). Others prefer the houseboats moored near Battersea Bridge (below).

from London Bridge to Chelsea, and has to be rowed with the tide, but at the time when the tide is strongest. The race is now supervised by the Fishmongers' Company, but the number of qualified competitors is limited, for there are nothing like the numbers of professional watermen on the river that once existed. It's been estimated that at the end of the sixteenth century some 40,000 people were employed on the river, and that about 2000 wherries provided public transport. When coaches became popular, this trade suffered badly, and in a pamphlet of the 1620s called 'The World runs on Wheels', John Taylor, the 'water poet', bitterly attacked what he called 'this infernal swarm of trade-spillers who have so overrun the land that we can get no living upon the water'. But watermen continued to work on the river in large numbers long after that. There were some 9000 of them in 1822, and even now there are still many families who belong by tradition and upbringing to a life of work on the Thames.

When Thomas Doggett founded his watermen's boat race, Chelsea was still a riverside village, although King Charles II had already established there the Royal Hospital for old and disabled soldiers in a building designed by Christopher Wren and completed in 1694. This is still the home of the Chelsea Pensioners who can always be guaranteed to raise a warm-hearted cheer when they appear at public occasions dressed in their scarlet uniforms. Once famous for buns and porcelain, Chelsea has won renown more recently as the home of many distinguished artists and literary figures, including such nineteenth-century artists as Turner, Whistler, Rossetti, Carlyle and Wilde. A less happy historical association is revealed by the shiny surface of the riverside parapet near Chelsea: it has been worn smooth by the bottoms of convicts as they sat in chains waiting to be transported to Botany Bay.

Just by the side of Chelsea Bridge are Ranelagh Gardens, on the site of the house where King George I had supper

Looking towards the Albert Bridge from the Embankment at Chelsea. The parapet in the foreground was worn smooth by convicts who sat awaiting transportation to Botany Bay.

during his water music expedition, and where subsequently a very popular public pleasure garden was established. On the other side of the river is Battersea Park. Here, during the summer of 1951, I had more than one night out at the large-scale pleasure garden and funfair that were established as part of the Festival of Britain.

Passing by Battersea Power Station, soon to be transformed into a leisure centre, the river turns north and we begin to enter its grandest stretch. Vauxhall Bridge heralds the change. Each of the stone piers on which the steel arches rest is embellished with a pair of statues, one facing upstream and the other down. The four upstream statues represent Engineering, Pottery, Architecture and Agriculture, while downstream more intellectual pursuits are illustrated: Fine Arts, Local Government, Science and Education. Thus the traveller by boat is prepared for the splendours of the national centre of political power, the Houses of Parliament. But before going under Vauxhall Bridge it would be a pity not to spare a special glance for the figure representing architecture. She holds a representation of St Paul's Cathedral, known to watermen as 'Little St Paul's on the Water'.

Vauxhall Bridge may be a familiar sight to Londoners, but how many have spotted the figures that decorate it, such as this one holding a small version of St Paul's.

Ranelagh Gardens near Chelsea Bridge (above), once a popular venue for musical entertainments.

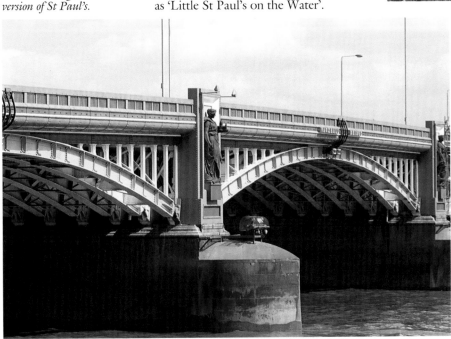

Coming up to Lambeth Bridge, it's worth pointing out the stone pineapples that crown the pillars at the entrances to the bridge. In the sixteenth and seventeenth centuries sailors returning to America from the West Indies would hang pineapples on their doorknockers as a sign of welcome. The King Pine was first presented to King Charles II by John Rose, the successor to the plant-hunter and gardener John Tradescant (c.1570–1638) who among other achievements imported the Rosa Acicularis from Russia and had the familiar house-plant *Trades-cantia* named after him. People interested in such matters should not miss the Tradescant Museum established in the nearby church of St Mary-at-Lambeth near the Archbishop of Canterbury's London home, Lambeth Palace.

Lambeth Bridge (above and left) boasts a surprising array of stone pineapples.

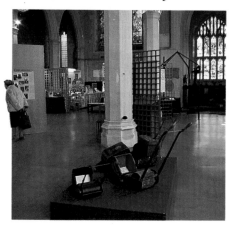

The Tradescant Museum (above) honours John Tradescant, plant-hunter and gardener. The Knot Garden (right) is in the museum's grounds.

A contemporary engraving (above) shows the Houses of Parliament on the morning after the 1834 fire; (below) the splendid interior of Westminster Hall.

Big Ben weighs a formidable 13½ tons.

The Houses of Parliament might not stand where they do on the opposite bank between Lambeth and Westminster Bridges if it hadn't been for the Duke of Wellington. After the old Palace of Westminster was burned down in 1834, there were proposals to replace it with a new building in Green Park or on the present site of Buckingham Palace. But the duke thought the Houses of Parliament should never be in a position where they could easily be surrounded by a mob, and as this was the time when the working-class Chartist movement was gaining strength, his advice was heeded. Charles Barry's magnificent Gothic edifice went up between 1837 and 1857, with the River Thames providing a ready-made moat along one side.

The clock tower of the Houses of Parliament is generally known as Big Ben, but the name actually applies to the great bell which chimes the hours inside it. Weighing 13½ tons, it was cast in 1858 and bestowed immortality on Sir Benjamin Hall, who happened to be First Commissioner of Works at the time.

By far the most ancient part of the Palace of Westminster is Westminster Hall, built by William Rufus, son of William the Conquerer, in 1097. This magnificent chamber has been the scene of many notable historic events – the abdication of King Edward I, the deposition of Richard II, and the trial of King Charles I for treason to name but a few. Sir Thomas More was tried here too, as were the Earl of Essex in 1601 and Guy Fawkes, four

years later, after his abortive terrorist enterprise. Many people will remember, like me, the solemn splendour of the scene early in 1965 when Sir Winston Churchill lay in state in Westminster Hall and thousands of us waited all night to pay homage in a long queue that snaked across Waterloo and Westminster Bridges. From Westminster, Sir Winston's body was transported in a solemn waterborne cavalcade to St Paul's Cathedral for his funeral service, and afterwards back by river to Waterloo Station, from where he was carried by train to his final resting place at Bladon. Seen all round the world on television, it was an inspired use of London's river as a ceremonial highway, and it spoke eloquently of the end of an era in more ways than one. The riverside cranes which were made to bow their heads in salute – the same cranes which had serviced the ships and busy warehouses of the Pool of London in days gone by – now also belong to the past.

However varied the quality of debate in the House of Commons may have been, Sir Winston was content nonetheless to regard it as 'the best club in Europe'; as for the House of Lords, Churchill's deputy Prime Minister during the Second World War, Clement Attlee, was less complimentary. 'It is', he said, 'like a glass of champagne that has stood for five days.'

The story of Westminster Bridge has been rather more stimulating. It was opened in 1863 with a twenty-five gun salute to mark the number of years of Queen Victoria's reign. This noisy event took place at a quarter to four in the morning, the precise hour of the queen's birth. The old bridge which stood on the site from 1750 was made to a great extent from magnesian limestone, and a certain Dr Ryan, familiar with purgative medicines, once pointed out that in the unlikely event of the bridge being 'covered with water and sulphuric acid, it would be converted into Epsom Salts'. Westminster

Churchill's coffin leaves Tower Pier aboard the launch **Havengore** *on 30th January 1965.*

The opening of Westminster Bridge (above) must have caused quite a stir back in 1863. The South Bank complex (below) has evolved from the 1951 Festival of Britain into today's major cultural site.

Bridge has had an impact on many: Boswell boasted that he once made love on the bridge; the poet George Crabbe nearly threw himself off it; and John Clare was astonished at the number of unaccompanied ladies he met on it late at night – he was later informed that they were 'girls of the town'. In 1802 the view from the bridge in the early morning inspired Wordsworth's famous declaration that 'earth has not anything to show more fair'.

Just downstream of the bridge is Westminster Pier, a busy junction for the river's passenger traffic, opposite which stands the imposing mass of County Hall, former home of the now defunct London County, and Greater London, Councils. Further along is the cultural conglomeration of the South Bank: the Royal Festival Hall, Queen Elizabeth Hall, Purcell Room, Hayward Gallery, National Film Theatre and, on the other side of Waterloo Bridge, the National Theatre. In 1951, the South Bank site was the main attraction of the Festival of Britain, dominated by the Skylon which was brilliantly lit up at night, the Dome of Discovery, the old Shot Tower and the newly completed Festival Hall. At the time it seemed exciting, but the Festival had little real effect on the drabness of those post-war years.

The plaque (above) commemorates the hazardous journey of Cleopatra's Needle (below) to London.

During my boyhood excursions on the Thames, it was the features of the north bank at this point that intrigued me. Cleopatra's Needle, covered with hieroglyphics three and a half thousand years old, I found very romantic. This trophy of imperialism was presented to Britain in 1819 by the viceroy of Egypt, Mehemet Ali, but not set up on the newly created Victoria Embankment until 1878, after a sea journey that cost six sailors' lives. A reminder of where the river bank once was can be seen in the gardens near Charing Cross station where my grandmother and I used to listen to the band, and at the foot of some time-worn steps down from Buckingham Street is the seventeenth-century York Gate, which at one time gave access to the river.

York Gate (left), now situated a few hundred feet from the river, used to provide direct access to the Thames.

Downstream of Waterloo Bridge, which 'streaks across the river like an elegant greyhound', my youthful excitement always grew, because then came the first glimpse of seagoing ships. Alongside the eight foot thick granite embankment walls were Captain Scott's *Discovery,* the former sloop *Wellington,* now the floating Livery Hall of the Honourable Company of Master Mariners, and two vessels belonging to the London Division of the Royal Naval Reserve, HMS *Chrysanthemum* and HMS *President.* The RNR has now transferred its London headquarters ashore, which to an old RNR man seems a pity. It was pleasant to drink a gin and tonic in the wardroom of *President* and allow the gentle motion of the river to transport my imagination to the sea. Without the aid of gin, that was how I felt

One of the ships that fired my boyish imagination, the **Wellington.** *The first stone of Blackfriars Bridge is laid in 1760 (below).*

as a boy when I saw these four ships, long retired from active service and attached by heavy chains to their inland moorings.

Blackfriars Bridge was probably the widest river bridge in Britain until the great motorway bridges came along. It was enlarged to its present width to accommodate trams in the early years of the present century, but in its original form it dates back over 200 years. There was at first a halfpenny toll to cross it, an

Blackfriars Bridge today (left), and (above) one of the tollgates that caused so much trouble 200 years ago.

Ryland's engraving (above) shows the original Southwark Bridge in 1818.

imposition so resented that the toll house was burned down. Happily the government of the day heeded the warning and made access on to the bridge free. Southwark Bridge is referred to by Dickens in *Little Dorrit* as 'the iron bridge', for it was constructed of three cast-iron arches. It had a romantic opening ceremony by lamplight in the middle of the night in 1819, but was replaced by the present, more prosaic bridge in 1921.

A pleasant place to have a drink or a meal is an old Southwark riverside inn, the Anchor, from which there is a grandstand view of the river and the City beyond. By the inn door are bollards, placed there originally to prevent carts from mounting the pavement. There were many of these in London at one time, made from the business ends of sawn-off cannons, with the cannon ball left in the mouth of the cannon, fixed in position by lead. The ones outside the Anchor are early examples of cast iron bollards which were made to resemble the sawn-off cannon, even down to their imitation cannon balls. They bear the inscription 'Clink 1812' and stand in Clink Street. The name of this street is a reminder of one of several prisons that once existed in Southwark, namely the Clink Prison, a private one belonging to the powerful bishops of

The bollards outside Southwark's Anchor pub (left) and Tower Hill (above) aren't real cannon-barrels, though many around London used to be.

London Bridge in 1597 (above) looked nothing like its present-day descendant (below).

Winchester. It's also a reminder of the term 'Liberty of the Clink' which refers to an area around Winchester House then outside the jurisdiction of the city. It conferred an immunity which had the important effect of attracting outspoken theatre people, among them William Shakespeare, to Southwark. Here was the famous Globe Theatre, currently being recreated by Sam Wanamaker after many years of persistent lobbying and fund-raising.

The river then flows under London Bridge. I happen to be a Freeman of the City of London, and one day I really must exercise my theoretical right to drive sheep across the bridge. This spot marks the very heart of London's history. The Romans probably built a pontoon bridge here around AD 50; then there was the amazing bridge that took thirty years to build in the twelfth century. Eventually it had nearly 200 houses standing on it and was 'comparable in itself to a little city'. The ghastly habit of displaying the heads of executed offenders on the bridge seems to have started in 1395, and about two centuries later the heads were utilised in particularly gruesome fashion. A number of Germans employed in the Mint fell sick from inhaling fumes from the molten metal, and were told that the cure was to drink from the skull of a dead man. Accordingly they were given the right 'to take off the heads upon London Bridge and make cups thereof, whereof they drank and found some relief, though the most of them died'.

When the bridge was finally de-molished in the early nineteenth century, small bits of it were taken away and used elsewhere: for example, you can see stones from the arches at Adelaide House, King William Street and some of the iron rail-ings in St Botolph's churchyard, Bishops-gate. The bridge that replaced it – a masterpiece of engineering by John Ren-nie – has now itself been replaced, but Rennie's bridge still exists. It was im-ported free into the United States as 'a genuine large antique' in 1973 and re-erected at Lake Havasu City, Arizona,

where it has become the centre of a flourishing enclave of anglophilia.

Between London and Tower Bridges is the Upper Pool of London. Once the bastions of Tower Bridge, that massively imposing gateway to London's river, used to open frequently – much to the frustra-tion of road traffic trying to cross it – to admit ships to the Upper Pool. It was a scene of ceaseless activity, with ships moored alongside the ancient fish market of Billingsgate on the north bank and Hay's Wharf on the south. Hay's Wharf has now been partly reconstructed into a

Heavy traffic on London Bridge is obviously nothing new (left). A ship leaving the Upper Pool of London stops the traffic on Tower Bridge—a common sight at the beginning of this century (above).

Dockland redevelopment such as at Hay's Wharf has changed the face of the waterfront.

Hay's Galleria brings a new kind of commerce to the waterfront.

One of the Eagle steamers that used to make daily journeys from city to coast.

shopping precinct known as Hay's Galleria – a sample of the drastic changes which have come to this part of the Thames since the departure of waterborne commerce.

One great ship still to be seen in the Upper Pool is HMS *Belfast*, one of the last and largest of the cruisers of the Royal Navy. She will never go to sea again, but at her mooring off Hay's Wharf, she is a potent reminder of days gone by for old sailors like me, and attracts many younger visitors too. With their great guns, ships like *Belfast* were the seagoing equivalent in their day of the Tower of London, the massive fortress begun by William the Conqueror in the eleventh century to dominate what was even then a busy city.

Tower Pier alongside the Tower itself is a place for me of many memories. There as a child I several times embarked with huge excitement on one of the Eagle steamers, the large paddle boats which took passengers daily down the river to the resorts of Southend and Clacton on the Essex shore and Margate and Ramsgate in Kent. As a family we spent enjoyable holidays in both Clacton and Margate, but to me the most interesting part was the journey by river there and back. I had a youthful fantasy that I was the captain of the *Crested Eagle*, and in this role (though I don't think anyone was aware of it) I used to 'come alongside' friends' houses and 'take them on board for the daily passage to school'.

The first great event of those river journeys to the seaside was the opening of Tower Bridge for us. The original thousand-ton bascules were replaced by a hydraulic mechanism which could open the bridge in ninety seconds, and woe betide any road vehicle which failed to stop when signalled to do so. In December 1952, a number 78 bus found itself at the point of no return when the bridge began to open. The driver decided to accelerate and jumped the three-foot gap to the other side. The brave chap was given a medal and ten pounds from public funds. Tower Bridge is still opened from time to time, for example to admit warships on ceremonial visits to London, and I well remember the Royal Yacht coming

Tower Bridge (left) cost £80,000 to build, and was designed to harmonise with the nearby Tower of London. The photograph, taken before it opened in 1894 (right), clearly shows the towers' solid steel internal framework.

St Katharine's Dock (below) now provides temporary moorings to ships from a bygone age.

through in May 1960 to take Princess Margaret and Lord Snowdon away on honeymoon after their wedding. There was some delay in the couple's arrival, and on television Richard Dimbleby was left to fill in interminably with his customary resource about the scene in the Pool of London.

Immediately after Tower Bridge is the Lower Pool. In times gone by this too presented a busy scene, with small freighters alongside or moored in the river, loading or unloading into barges. St Katharine's Dock, abandoned by working ships, is now an assembly point for craft preserved from the past. Its World Trade Centre is another example of the transformation of old warehouses into attractive modern buildings, with moorings for yachts right in the heart of the city.

Wapping, on the north bank of the river, has long been associated with crime and punishment. Here was Execution Dock where the bodies of pirates were suspended in the river on chains; Captain Kidd, hanged here in 1701, was one of the most notorious of these maritime offenders. In former times the River Thames had a versatile assortment of evildoers. There were the 'river pirates' who would cut a ship adrift from its moorings and remove the contents when it went

An eighteenth-century pirate prepares to die at Execution Dock (above). The founder of the Marine Police is commemorated (right) in St Margaret's Church, Westminster (below, right). St Katharine's Dock (below), its warehouses refurbished, provides inner-city moorings for modern pleasure-craft too.

aground later downstream; the 'light horsemen' who stole from ships by night; the 'heavy horsemen' with large pockets built into their clothes to carry stolen items; the 'lumpers' who threw stolen objects overboard; and the 'mudlarks' who picked them up from the mud at low tide. In fact it was such tideway robbery that led to the construction of enclosed docks: following the West India Dock Act of 1799, the largest system of wet docks in the world was constructed in east London.

The reorganisation of the docks happened to some extent as the result of research by Dr Patrick Colquhoun who estimated that almost a third of river workers in the late eighteenth century were either thieves or receivers of stolen property. This remarkable man can also be credited with the idea of policing the river. An inscription on his memorial tab-

let in St Margaret's Church, Westminster, tells us that he founded the Marine Police by which means, we are assured, 'the morals of the river labourer materially improved'. The Thames Division of the

Metropolitan Police still has its headquarters in Wapping; with the aid of a friendly magistrate I was once taken out on one of their patrols, and most interesting it was, though we failed to apprehend any villains.

Sailors and stevedores generally had a taste for liquid refreshment, and this taste was always catered for in Wapping, which today still has colourful riverside pubs such as The Prospect of Whitby (now a rather elaborate haven for tourists). Across the river at Rotherhithe there's another picturesque old inn, the Mayflower, which stands on the site of a sixteenth-century tavern said to have been patronised by the Pilgrim Fathers. From Wapping to Rotherhithe runs the world's first underwater tunnel, constructed by Sir Marc Brunel and his son Isambard between 1825 and 1843. Hailed as a brilliant engineering achievement in its day, though financially it was a total failure, it now carries the East London Underground line.

The river turns quite sharply southwards towards Greenwich which is at the southern end of a loop in the river. Passing Limehouse, once the scene of east London's colourful Chinatown, the river flows by Millwall on the western side of the Isle of Dogs, so-named perhaps because the royal dogs were once exercised here, or maybe it was formerly the Isle of Ducks. The latter name would be fitting

The only floating police station in the world is home of the River Police at Waterloo Bridge.

The ever-popular riverside pub, The Prospect of Whitby (below, left) is across the river from the present-day Mayflower (below).

now, for much of the area consists of water, contained within the West India and Millwall dock system.

Just before Greenwich is Deptford on the southern shore. It's worth a mention here as this is where Henry VIII's navy was fitted out and Sir Francis Drake was knighted by Queen Elizabeth I in 1581 after his circumnavigation of the globe. It was with that event in mind and using the same sword, that the present Queen knighted Sir Francis Chichester in the open courtyard of the Royal Naval College at Greenwich in 1967. He had sailed his 53 foot ketch *Gipsy Moth IV* up the Thames after completing his single-handed trip around the world in 274 days. The whole event was striking and colourful, but as I remember the most surprising impression was created by the bright red trouser-suit worn by Lady Chichester when she disembarked from *Gipsy Moth* for the ceremony.

Now *Gipsy Moth IV* is ashore for ever at Greenwich, alongside the *Cutty Sark*. This fastest and most famous of the tea clippers has a figurehead showing a woman wearing a chemise, for the ship

Cutty Sark and her chemise-clad figurehead.

Britons watched on television as Queen Elizabeth knighted Francis Chichester, whose **Gipsy Moth IV** *is moored alongside – and dwarfed by –* **Cutty Sark***. It was the first time such a ceremony had been televised.*

takes her name from a similar garment worn by the witch in Robert Burns' poem *Tam o'Shanter*, where it is described as a 'cutty sark'. The present skipper of the *Cutty Sark* has a small collection of saluting guns, and one day when I was on board he decided to fire a salute to a passing vessel he thought worthy of his respect. The noise came as a great surprise, not only to myself, but also to the crowds of schoolchildren and others milling around the quayside.

This river exploration began at Hampton Court, one monument to the power of King Henry VIII, and ends where another of his favourite palaces stood. Here, at Greenwich Palace, Queen Mary and Queen Elizabeth I were born, but during the commonwealth the buildings were used as a biscuit factory and fell into neglect. The present magnificent group of buildings was begun during the reign of King Charles II. Sir Christopher Wren was the chief architectural influence, though several other architects had a hand in the work before the ensemble was finally completed in the early nineteenth century. A Seamen's Hospital was founded here in 1695 by William and Mary to match the hospital for former soldiers at Chelsea. It is now the Royal Naval Staff College and I was one of thousands of reserve officers who spent a period of

training here during the Second World War. I clearly remember what a hazard to shipping my fellow students and I must have been when we practised ship-handling on the river in small wooden minesweepers kept there for the purpose!

Greenwich Hospital, seen from the west in a 1786 engraving (above) which echoes the splendid buildings of the Royal Naval Staff College, Greenwich (below).

Greenwich today is alive with interest to lovers of ships and the sea, for here is the splendid National Maritime Museum, and on top of the hill in Greenwich Park is the former Royal Observatory, standing on the Greenwich Meridian, the line of zero longitude. In earlier times, every ship in the river would have an eyeglass trained on the bright orange ball which is hauled to the top of the mast every day just before one o'clock and allowed to slide down again precisely on the hour. The ceremony is still carried out, though I fancy few ship's chronometers take their time from it these days.

In 1988 the P&O shipping line celebrated its 150th anniversary with an evening at Greenwich. Her Majesty the Queen was on board one of P&O's cruise ships, the 20,000 ton *Pacific Princess*, moored immediately opposite the Royal Naval College. I was involved in a great spectacle of sound and light carried out to music. A laser beam from the top of the Observatory simulated the Greenwich Meridian, and a huge firework display over the river provided the finale to the strains of *Rule Britannia*. The effect, in a setting so deeply imbued with naval history, was both spectacular and moving.

Though the Royal Observatory left London in 1950 for the cleaner air of Sussex, its former home – and the Greenwich Meridian – still attracts visitors.

Returning to those little paddle steamers of my boyhood, my family and I would continue down the Thames, past Woolwich, Gravesend and Tilbury, watching the ships growing ever larger as we approached the sea. Moving with heavy grace among them would be the sailing barges (still frequently seen in the thirties), criss-crossing the estuary. Here the Thames is still fringed by miles of desolate mud flats which, to me, have a certain romance of their own.

From Greenwich it's possible to make one's way along the foot tunnel under the Thames, to the Isle of Dogs.

Here the scene has changed beyond recognition in a short space of time. Great new buildings have gone up and old ones have been adapted as newspaper offices and television studios, shops and homes, while old ships have been towed into the docks to serve as restaurants. Through it all runs the Docklands Light Railway, whose little red and blue robot trains carry people to and from the City. From the Isle of Dogs, it's possible to see the new transatlantic skyline of London, a stark contrast to the 'liquid history' that is the River Thames.

No sign now on the Isle of Dogs of the windmills that once drained its marshes.

PERPETUUM MOBILE

The popularity of Johann Strauss and his orchestra was such that they were in demand all over Europe and at a farewell concert in April 1861 – just before they left Vienna for a summer season at a resort near St Petersburg – Strauss introduced his latest novelty. It was a 'musical jest' called 'Perpetuum Mobile' which had no end: the conductor has to put a stop to things by calling out 'and so on, and so on'. The piece symbolises the incessant demands made on the orchestra not only on the concert platform but in terms of travel – demands which then, as now, no doubt presented plenty of problems to the itinerant musician.

The relatively small scale of Roman London meant that getting about on foot was not a problem.

Various solutions to the problem of getting around London have been tried over the centuries, but as the city has grown, perpetual motion has been more and more difficult to sustain. Even today, going on foot is sometimes much the best way of getting from A to B. Certainly it was on the morning after the great hurricane of October 1987, when there was no public transport available in central London, and I found the only way to reach Broadcasting House from the City was to walk. Of course a four mile stroll on a sunny morning did no harm, and I could have reflected that I was doing no more than millions of Londoners have had to do when they were without the price of a fare in their pockets.

Going by 'Shank's mare' or by 'Walker's bus' was how most people moved about in Roman London, although the colonisers used horses, and those who were rich enough were even carried around in a litter. This was a light carriage body with shafts fore and aft, between which either horses or men provided the motive power. Litters were still in use in Tudor times, when closed carriages began to appear on the roads. One of Raleigh's former sea captains started public transport when he introduced the two-seater

hackney coach (which took its name from the French *haquenée*, an ambling nag). This new development was seen as a threat by the Thames watermen, but they were powerless to prevent road transport from developing in a city which was spreading ever further away from the riverbank.

The sedan chair (named after the French town of Sedan, where it originated) came along in 1711. This was a sophisticated kind of litter: a padded box, protected

These villainous-looking characters were some of London's earliest taxi-drivers, carrying their passenger in a sedan chair.

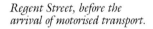

Early snuffers for putting out the link-boy's torch – at St James's Square (above) and the Welsh Office, Whitehall (right).

Regent Street, before the arrival of motorised transport.

from the weather, in which the passenger could sit in relative comfort, suspended on poles on either side, enabling the device to be carried by two men. On dark nights, the equipage would be preceded by a link-boy carrying a blazing torch, which would be extinguished on arrival in a conical snuffer – one of these can still be seen in St James's Square.

It's easy to think of traffic jams as a prerogative of modern times, but chaos on the roads was common in Victorian London. It's been estimated that by the end of the century there were some 300,000 horses in the capital, producing four to five hundred tons of manure to be cleared from the streets every day. When it rained, there were frequent accidents caused by horses falling on the slippery roads. The huge carts used for the transport of goods would park two or three deep for hours at a time. Heavy traffic on the move kept to the centre of the road, with coachmen and cabbies trying to overtake, for it was not until the late nineteenth century that it became customary to drive on the left.

It was an expensive business to own your own carriage (a brougham, horse and coachman could cost £200 a year), and such was the time and labour involved in maintaining it and grooming the horses that it could often not be used more than once a day. Many people chose therefore to hire carriages from one of the 140 or so 'jobmasters' – men who became rich by meeting this requirement of the market.

This open-topped bus was travelling London's streets in about 1905 . . .

For the general public, London versions of the stage coach started coming into operation in the late eighteenth century, plying to places like Greenwich, Croydon and Ealing. George Shillibeer, who introduced the first London omnibus in 1829, copied the name from the vehicles he had seen in France. A certain Monsieur Omnès sold tickets for a public vehicle service at his shop in Nantes, and adopted as his motto a Latin phrase which provided a convenient pun on his name: *omnes omnibus* or 'all for all'. The word 'General' appeared on the side of the London buses when I was a very small boy. This again had French origins, for the London General Omnibus Company was established in Paris in 1855 as the Compagniè Générale des Omnibus de Londres. The buses I remember from the late twenties and early thirties mostly had open top decks, and the front seat on top was highly desirable to a small boy, if rather less so to his ageing grandmother, trailing slowly up the stairs behind him. Waterproof aprons were provided for upper deck passengers if it rained but they did not give very much protection and if there was a heavy downpour, there was suddenly great pressure on the limited accommodation inside. However, there

are few better ways of seeing London than from the top of an open-decked bus, and tours around London in vehicles like this are a popular feature of the tourist scene today.

The London General Omnibus Company did not have things all its own way on the streets of London. For a time it had a serious rival in the London Road Car Company, as the writer Compton Mackenzie recalled. He remembered 'what fun it was to ride on the top of a Road Car bus armed with peashooters and shoot up the passengers on the outside of a General, while the drivers raced one another along the Hammersmith Road'. But the General survived such opposition to pass under the control of the London Passenger Transport Board in 1933.

I'm still fond of a bus ride. It has a companionable feeling about it, though I'm no more addicted to a densely packed bus in the rush hour than the essayist Robert Lynd, who wrote: 'if gaol were anything like the inside of a motor bus with standing room for five only, no man who was not either mad or a born criminal would risk being sent there'. However, such discomfort does not compare with the positive dangers of travelling on

In 1905, when an undergraduate at Oxford, Maurice Hare wrote a limerick inspired by the theory of predestination. It ran as follows:

There once was a man who said 'Damn!'
It is borne in upon me I am
An engine that moves
In predestinate grooves,
I'm not even a bus, I'm a tram.

He composed those lines when the London County Council was about half-way through the process of electrifying 120 miles of tramways around London; but the tram had come to the capital over forty years earlier when it was realised that horses could haul far greater and more profitable loads over smooth-railed tracks than was possible over uneven road surfaces. It was an American, aptly named George Francis Train, who persuaded the London authorities to allow him to lay experimental tram lines in 1861. Horse trams weren't an immediate success, but a decade later they were much in demand in the less affluent areas, not least because they were obliged by law to provide special workmen's tickets at half price in the morning and evening rush hours.

The first electric tram began running on 4th April 1901, using overhead wires to carry the electricity supply. These were cheap but unsightly, so when the London County Council began to electrify trams in the same year, they decided on a more expensive system for central areas, with conductor rails below the road surface.

Riding on trams always seemed to me an adventurous business, partly because they tended to sway like a ship at sea. But by the early thirties, they were already on their way out and being replaced by trolleybuses, or 'trackless trams' as they were called at first. These had a pair of trolleys running along overhead power lines, and since they used rubber tyres like ordinary buses, they gave a very smooth ride except when the trolleys jumped off the overhead wires, as they sometimes did at junctions. Then the conductor would have to get off and manoeuvre his trolleys back on to the wires with ropes attached to them for that purpose. I enjoyed many trolleybus rides as a boy with my family

. . . while the later motorised version is still popular with sightseeing visitors. Nowadays, though, you have to supply your own waterproofing.

some of the early buses. The vehicles of the Vanguard Motor Bus Service from London to Brighton, which started operating on 30th August 1905, were so designed that if the bus approached a stop on a steep hill, the crowd of passengers on the back stairs waiting to jump off could cause the whole bus to tip up like a rearing horse.

because in the evening it was possible to buy very cheap runabout tickets which enabled us to go many miles for next to nothing.

Trams and trolleybuses have long since departed from the streets of London but it is still possible to see part of an old tram tunnel in the underpass which connects Waterloo Bridge with Kingsway. It was opened in 1905, when Maurice Hare wrote his limerick, and there's a pair of doors under Waterloo Bridge which mark the former entrance to the tunnel. They serve as a reminder of a scheme proposed by a Royal Commission on London Traffic in the early part of this century. The proposal was to create a complete subterranean tramway system running east to west and north to south under London, but as that would have duplicated the existing underground railways, the idea was soon dropped. However, it has points of resemblance to the notion of creating fast underground routes through the capital on the lines of the Parisian RER, a suggestion which is still under serious consideration.

A tramcar emerges from the Kingsway tunnel in the summer of 1929. Despite ambitious plans for a subterranean network, Kingsway was to remain Britain's only tram tunnel.

The modern London taxi is descended from the hackney coach which first made its appearance in the London streets in the early seventeenth century. So successful was the hackney that as early as 1654, Parliament found it necessary to reduce the number of such vehicles plying for hire in London and Westminster to 300. In the early nineteenth century, the hackney gave way to the 'growler' and the

Was this handsome hansom as hard to hail as some of today's London cabs?

Cabmen's shelters: in Acacia Road, St John's Wood, from an 1875 engraving (above); Warwick Avenue, W9 (top right); Chelsea Embankment, SW3 (bottom right).

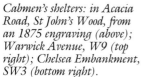

'cab', another import from France where it was known as the 'cabriolet de place'. Both were drawn by single horses, but whereas the cab had two wheels and accommodated two passengers under a hood, the growler had four wheels and could accommodate a third passenger alongside the driver. In 1834 Joseph Hansom patented an English version of the cab which became highly popular and by 1900 there were 25,000 hansom cabs on the streets of the capital. Light and elegant in appearance, they were dubbed 'the gondolas of London' by Disraeli, and their romantic connotations were reflected in verse by the poet Richard Le Gallienne. Seeing them in the Strand one night, with their twin oil lamps flickering in the dark, he wrote:

Like dragonflies the hansoms hover
With jewelled eyes to catch the lover.

Queen Victoria bought her own hansom for £200 in 1887, and Sherlock Holmes found them invaluable when in pursuit of a suspect; indeed he went so far

as to tip a driver half a sovereign in *The Hound of the Baskervilles*. However, from the turn of the century the number of hansoms declined rapidly, though they were still to be seen occasionally as late as 1927.

In Victorian times, cabmen had a reputation for heavy drinking, and as this could lead to some pretty wild driving, the Cabmen's Shelter Fund was set up in 1875. The object was to supply cabmen 'with a place of shelter where they can obtain good and wholesome (i.e. non-alcoholic) refreshment at very moderate prices'. At their peak there were 64 such shelters sited on cab ranks around London, but now only a dozen remain. The legal restraints on drinking and driving, let alone the professionalism of the modern cabbie, have made them reminders of a bygone age.

London's first motor cab was available for hire in 1904 and today there are some 15,000 of them. Most are now radio-controlled, and while this is convenient in some ways, it has made it much more difficult to hail a taxi in the street or

to find one on a rank at a station. When I need one, all too often they seem to be speeding on their way to some remotely delivered summons.

Travelling by private car is not to be recommended in central London, particularly during rush hours. There is insufficient off-street parking for the estimated one million or so cars which try to come into London in the course of a day, parking meter bays are inadequate in number and the advent of clamping with all its dire inconvenience has made the motorist in central London feel like a threatened species. Perhaps that's what he has to be, if movement is to be maintained at all on the city's streets. Often it is more practical (but dangerous too) to ride a push bike, and many colourfully dressed characters make their way to and from

work in this fashion, sometimes wearing a haversack to contain their city clothes and carrying a smart briefcase in a basket on the handlebars.

The heroine of a story by Rose Macaulay defines the bicycle as 'the nearest approach to wings permitted to men and women here below', and to me it certainly is a much more attractive mode of transport than the motor bike. These days bikes of both kinds are to be seen in great profusion on the London streets, employed on various urgent errands. A new race of intrepid messengers has appeared on the scene, attempting to beat the clock as best they can. I understand their need to move quickly, but I wish the motorised variety would refrain from terrorising the hapless pedestrian as often as they do.

The forerunner (forebiker?) of the motorcycle courier, a telegraph messenger poses proudly (above, left). Push-bikes are more sophisticated now (above) and still one of the quickest ways of getting around London.

Picturesque Little Venice is a quiet and little-spoilt part of London.

One way to escape these hazards is to travel by water. Waterbuses ply regularly on the River Thames, and a novel way of going from Paddington to the London Zoo is by canal. The network of canals in Paddington led both Robert Browning and Lord Byron to liken the area, rather fancifully, to Venice; and in the years since the Second World War, Little Venice has become a desirable residential

The 'company and barges' celebrating the opening of the Paddington Canal on 10th July 1801.

area whose inhabitants have included the artists Lucien Freud and Feliks Topolski. The Paddington Canal was opened with great celebrations in 1801, and nineteen years later the Regent's Canal extended the range of such waterways. They were intended primarily for commercial traffic, though they also seem to have been used for pleasure trips from an early date: one popular canal jaunt for Londoners in days gone by was from Paddington to Uxbridge.

Motorised boats and barges make travel by canal an easy matter these days, but it was once a much more laborious

T.H. Shepherd's watercolour shows commercial barges near the entrance to the Islington Tunnel on Regent's Canal (above). Regent's Canal has twelve locks: this one is at Camden (below).

Trippers aboard the Paddington to Uxbridge packet, 1801.

Regent's Canal is still used by pleasure-craft. This one is about to go under one of its forty bridges.

business. On open stretches, barges would be towed by horses using the tow paths which still run alongside most canals. Underground sections were more of a problem. There's a canal tunnel a thousand feet long, constructed by Nash between 1812 and 1820, which runs beneath Islington in north London, and through this barges were originally propelled by navvies who would lie on their backs and push against the ceiling of the tunnel with their feet.

The Railway Age reached London in the 1830s. The first line ran on a four mile continuous viaduct from London Bridge to Greenwich, and the first of the great London railway termini, those cathedrals of the Industrial Revolution, was opened at Euston in 1837. The old Euston Station was a magnificent structure with a portico flanked by four huge Doric columns, and inside there was a great hall of imposing proportions in Roman-Ionic style. Such grandeur was thought by the directors of the London and Birmingham Railway to be justified by the importance of the link between the capital and one of the country's most flourishing provincial centres, though when the line started operating in 1838, it took more than five hours to travel the 112 miles from London to the capital of the Midlands. The first mile or so of the journey was up a steep incline to Camden Town, and the trains were dragged up the slope by a seemingly endless rope some 5000 yards long and three inches thick. Incoming trains had their engines detached at Camden Town, and the coaches travelled down the slope under the control of the brakeman. The engines were stored in a remarkable circular structure, the Round House, which later became a warehouse and factory and in more recent times it has served as a centre for the performing arts. In 1964, the Round House became the home of Centre 42, a group whose name derived from Resolution 42 of the Trades Union Conference which signalled greater trade union involvement in the arts, but it is now empty and its future remains uncertain.

Passengers arrive at the entrance to Euston Station, the London terminus of the London-Birmingham railway, in 1838.

The Docklands Light Railway, opened in August 1987, will eventually join the Underground network. Shortage of land-space has meant elevated sections; this one is near Heron Quays.

The pit ponies which used to shunt wagons through tunnels under the Euston line were stabled underground. Grilles were set into the road above to provide their only source of light.

system operated by a steam-driven fan. This railway was not intended for passengers, but the story goes that soon after it opened, a lady in a crinoline was sucked along it. One hopes she was delivered safely at the other end.

Victorian prudery took many forms. Naked piano legs had to be decorously concealed, the steel structure of Tower Bridge had to be clad in stone to make it look as much like the Tower of London as possible, and St Pancras Station was designed to resemble a castle. As for the new-fangled underground railway, the trains were thought to constitute an unwarranted intrusion into respectable residential life, so in Leinster Gardens, Bayswater, a short terrace was completed with dummy house-fronts, in order to screen the railway from public view.

The first underground railway was not far below the surface, but in 1870 the earliest passenger-carrying 'tube', the 'Tower Subway' – operated by cable – came into operation. The first electric tube was the City and South London Railway which ran from King William Street in the City to Stockwell from 1890. Since then London's underground system has expanded enormously, but it seems now to be nearing the limit of its capacity, as rush hour travellers realise only too well. However, some modernisation and

expansion is occurring, particularly in the Docklands area, and a brand new tunnel, just under a mile long, will carry an extension of the Docklands Light Railway into the heart of the City at King William Street.

Railways apart, there's a hidden world under the streets of London that few people ever see. There is, for example, the complex of tunnels and vaults near the Round House known as the Camden Catacombs. British Rail uses them now for storage, but once they were stables for horses and pit ponies used for shunting railway wagons. The extent of the catacombs can be traced from the distinctive cast-iron grilles set at intervals into the road surface to provide a source of light for the horses below.

Harrods in Knightsbridge has its own system of private tunnels and subways running between the main store in Knightsbridge and its warehouse in Trevor Square. Frosty Way leads to the deep-freeze rooms; Wine Cellar Close is self-explanatory, and the Lock Up is for the reception of unsuccessful shoplifters. Harrods has its own underground transport system too: a fleet of green electric trolleys which run more or less silently to and fro under Brompton Road.

Below some London churches are interesting crypts, many of them survivors from medieval times. St Paul's has the most famous crypt, but perhaps one of the most useful was at St Stephen's Walbrook. In the mid-sixties, it was rediscovered by the founder of the Samaritans, the Rev Chad Varah, who cleared it out and equipped it as the Samaritans' telephone operations room. St John's, Smith Square, near the Palace of Westminster, and now a concert hall, has a magnificent crypt which serves as a restaurant and bar for members of the audience. The old *News of the World* building in Carmelite Street was erected over a vaulted crypt, once described as a gem of its kind, that probably dates back to the fourteenth century. It was used for years as a coal cellar, but has now been conserved and repositioned during the course of the redevelopment. Vestiges of a vault which belonged to another of London's ancient monastic establishments can also be seen under a famous Fleet Street inn, the Cheshire Cheese, which was built a hundred years after the dissolution of the monasteries in the sixteenth century.

The Adelphi Arches run forty feet down from Charing Cross Station to the Savoy Hotel; they were originally wine cellars and coal vaults and can still be seen today. Below the modern buildings of the Ministry of Defence there's another interesting wine cellar, once part of Cardinal Wolsey's Whitehall Palace. When an underground citadel was constructed below the ministry just after the Second World War, the cellar was moved in its entirety on rollers, a quarter of an inch at a time for forty-three and a half feet. Two years later, after the excavations were completed, it was restored to its original position by the same laborious method.

The catalogue of London's cellars could be indefinitely extended, but I'll just mention one more. This is the Chancery Lane Safe Deposit, where many important confidential papers and other items have been stored since the depository opened in 1884. It was bombed and flooded during the Second World War, and safes whose owners could not be traced were opened up. Inside one was a pair of Edwardian frilly lace knickers, bearing a label with the intriguing inscription 'My life's undoing'.

Though the Cheshire Cheese was built after the dissolution of the monasteries the original vaulted cellar remains (left). The News of the World *building in Carmelite Street has gone, but redevelopment of the site will leave the crypt beneath it virtually unchanged (below).*

OVERTURE AND BEGINNERS

My obsession with the sea was matched from a very early age by a compulsive fascination with the theatre, and this feeling has remained with me. There's nothing I enjoy more than appearing in a stage entertainment, preferably in one of the many beautiful old theatres which still exist in many parts of Britain. I love the atmosphere backstage, I admire the efficiency of stage crews who cope unfussily with whatever lighting and setting problems may be involved, I like brewing up a cup of tea in the dressing room between rehearsal and performance, and I am very disappointed if I don't hear over the PA system the traditional calls prior to the performance, culminating in 'Overture and Beginners, please!' at five minutes to curtain-up.

When I was a small boy, my practical father made me a toy theatre out of an old tea chest, and this we laboured to make as much like the real thing as possible. Of course in those days I did not realise that I was fortunate enough to live in the city with the richest and most varied theatrical tradition in the world. In my limited experience, theatres always had footlights and crimson velvet curtains, so that is what my theatre had to have. My grandmother embroidered on the curtains the golden letter 'E', for the name we chose for our theatre was the 'Elite' – nothing if not superior. The footlights were powered by batteries which had already seen service in an aunt's old-fashioned hearing aid, and we had quite elaborate scenic arrangements. I spent long hours attempting to make small dolls fly across the stage, because the first professional entertainment I saw was *Peter Pan*.

We went several times in the early 1930s to see Sir James Barrie's masterpiece with Jean Forbes-Robertson in the leading role: she played it for eight consecutive years from 1927 to 1934. She was the daughter of Sir Johnston Forbes-Robertson, one of the capital's leading actor-managers in his day, and I used to imitate her actions, to the extent of trying to fly off a staircase. Under the influence of Barrie's play, I certainly saw myself for long periods as Peter, and Margaret Mary, the small girl who lived in my grand-mother's house, was cast as Wendy. Our romance was furthered by frequent visits to Peter Pan's statue in Kensington Gardens.

Peter Pan was performed every Christmas in those days at the London Palladium. Built in 1910 on the site of Charles Hengler's circus, it was designed by Frank Matcham, who created many of the finest theatres in the country. There was telephone communication between the boxes, and an elegant palm court built of Norwegian granite behind the stalls. The Palladium opened with a variety bill, and as the home of the Royal Command Performances, it remains the most famous variety theatre in the world, though it has also presented many other long-running shows.

The first pantomime I saw was at the Lyceum Theatre just off the Strand. These were very long and very elaborate affairs with spectacular stage effects. Printed in the programme was a 'Synopsis of Scenery' which listed the innumerable set-changes, and when the final 'walk-down' had taken place at the end of the story, it was followed by a traditional harlequin-ade. The characters of Harlequin, Columbine, Pantaloon and the rest, which

Jean Forbes-Robertson as Peter Pan (below, left). I turned out to be not as good at flying as she was. The London Palladium, where Peter Pan was once regularly performed is still the world's premier variety theatre (below).

originated in the Italian *commedia dell' arte*, had become immensely popular in London in the eighteenth century, so much so that rival theatre managers competed fiercely with each other to present the most attractive harlequin entertainments. The custom persisted into the 1930s.

Apart from the programme, the thing to do at the Lyceum was to purchase a 'book of words'. This enabled me to read the text of the pantomime, only this was rather difficult to follow on account of the ad libs of the comedians. Another thing which impressed me was the fact that a large section of the Lyceum's roof was opened during the interval. Since I was always taken to a matinée, the gap invariably revealed daylight, and I longed to go in the evening and see stars through the ceiling.

The pantomimes were produced by the Melville brothers who ran the Lyceum for thirty years from 1910. Since the war it has been a dance hall when it has not been 'dark', and it has only rarely been used for theatrical entertainments – some matinées of *Pinocchio* in the sixties and more recently some unforgettable performances of the mystery plays presented by the National Theatre. The future of the Lyceum is currently very uncertain; if the name disappears it will remove a potent reminder of one of the most famous English theatrical figures, Sir Henry Irving, who reigned over the Lyceum for nearly three decades with Ellen Terry as his leading lady.

Irving was a riveting actor and a man of contradictions. He was, wrote Ellen Terry, 'quiet, patient, tolerant, impersonal, gentle, close, crafty, incapable of caring for anything outside his work'. He lived during the period of his greatest fame on the first and second floors of a house in Grafton Street, among 'the confusion and neglect of order in which the artistic mind delights'. His study was kept in perpetual twilight with curtains drawn over the windows of stained and leaded glass. But whatever his eccentricities were, he contrived to make the theatre respectable at a time when puritan prejudice against the stage was still strong, and he

The first actor to be knighted for services to the theatre, Sir Henry Irving (right, with Ellen Terry), lived in 'confusion and neglect' at 15a Grafton Street (below).

was the first actor to be knighted for services to the theatre in the Birthday Honours of 1895.

When I went to the Lyceum in the 1930s, my grandmother pointed out another very interesting theatre on the corner of the Strand and Aldwych, the Gaiety, which continued to exist until 1939. Now only a tablet remains on the wall of a bank to recall what was for many years the home of musical comedy in London.

In the year before he died, 1869, Dickens saw his last play at the old Gaiety, *Uncle Dick's Darling*. The young Henry Irving was in the cast, and Dickens correctly predicted a great future for him. Twenty years later, in 1889, Irving, now firmly installed at the Lyceum, crossed swords with the management of the Gaiety. George Edwardes had just taken over, and had put on a succession of popular skits, including one on the Victor Hugo play *Ruy Blas*. In this, Fred Leslie did an impersonation of Irving which was reported to the great man himself. He was

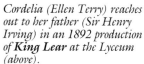
Cordelia (Ellen Terry) reaches out to her father (Sir Henry Irving) in an 1892 production of **King Lear** at the Lyceum (above).

The Gaiety Theatre, dominating the junction of The Strand and The Aldwych in 1913 (left).

Marie Elba and Jeanne Douste as Hansel and Gretel at Daly's Theatre, December 1894 (below).

*I once sat through two performances of **Pagliacci** in one day at Kilburn's Gaumont State (above). A sweeping staircase leads from its marble-columned foyer (below) into the auditorium.*

not amused and wrote to Leslie: 'I see that in your new burlesque I am put by you into woman's clothes, and I hope you will at once withdraw such an exhibition. Whether or not you are doing this by your manager's desire I cannot tell, but it seems to me no consideration should tempt an artist to such an act.'

It is good to recall that peace finally prevailed in the relations between the Gaiety and Lyceum. When Edwardes closed the old Gaiety in 1903 before opening a new theatre nearby, Irving, whose reign at the Lyceum had just ended, not only attended the last night, but made a graceful speech on stage. 'I have just dropped in', he said, 'as an old neighbour of thirty years standing who used to carry on a different kind of shop over the way. In a few weeks Mr Edwardes will open the doors of the new Gaiety to a flood of popularity and prosperity which I am sure will keep him and the company and the public in the highest good humour for many years to come.'

This indeed proved to be the case, for Edwardes was a manager of genius, with the rare gift of knowing what the public wanted before they knew themselves. In 1892 he put on what's usually called the first musical comedy. *In Town* opened at the Prince of Wales Theatre, though it transferred in the following year to the Gaiety. There followed a long series of similar shows, many with 'girl' in the title, for Edwardes thought, not without reason, that there was magic in the word. *The Runaway Girl*, *The Shop Girl*, *The Country Girl* and *The Quaker Girl* were all staged by Edwardes either at the Gaiety, or at the theatre he built in Cranbourn Street for the American impresario Augustin Daly. George Edwardes later took over Daly's Theatre himself, where he staged the first London performances of Humperdinck's *Hansel and Gretel* in 1895, and later, in 1907, *The Merry Widow* with Lily Elsie. Edwardes had an eye for propriety as well as female beauty; the beautiful 'Gaiety girls' he chose for the chorus were expected to respond with discretion to the hordes of 'mashers' who crowded round the stage door, and a number of them made aristocratic marriages. Those who worked for the tall and handsome George generally fell for his charm, and there was affection as well as respect in their voices when they spoke of him simply as 'the Guv'nor'.

Daly's survived Edwardes to witness the runaway success of *The Maid of the Mountains* in the First World War, but during the twenties its popularity waned. James White, the ex-bricklayer who bought the theatre for £200,000, lost a great deal of money there and the theatre was involved in the financial crash which led to White's suicide in 1927. Ten years later Daly's was pulled down and Warner's cinema was erected on the site.

In the thirties, 'going to the pictures' was a great family outing. The trick was to get in for sixpence as early as possible, start off in the cheapest seats which were always at the front, and then move back to the more expensive seats under cover of darkness. This could sometimes be accomplished at the grandest of our local cinemas, indeed even at one of the most opulent ever built, the Gaumont State at Kilburn. Designed by George Coles, it had seating for 4004 people and foyers of

immense grandeur. The programmes were also huge with two feature films, news and cartoons plus an ambitious stage show. One week this consisted of a complete performance of Leoncavallo's one-act opera *Pagliacci*, and I stayed to see it through twice, sitting patiently in the cinema from lunchtime until eight o'clock at night.

Such was the popularity of film-going in the London of that period that the Gaumont State had several rivals in

The exterior of the Granada in Tooting barely hints at the Moorish-inspired opulence of the auditorium within.

size. There was the Granada in Tooting, which had almost exactly the same capacity and was opulently decorated in the Moorish style of Granada in Spain. The fine Odeon at Hammersmith, now a very successful venue for pop concerts, was considered the architectural masterpiece of Robert Cromie and survives as a monument to art deco. Biggest of all was the Trocadero at the Elephant and Castle, which opened in 1937, like the Gaumont State. With 5000 seats it was at the time the largest cinema in the world.

Survivors from the great days of the picture palaces include another pop concert venue, the Rainbow Theatre, formerly the Astoria, at Finsbury Park. Here audiences are still greeted by 'an illuminated fountain from a Moorish harem, complete with goldfish', while in the auditorium there is a rich mix of styles, from the Baroque to wall friezes depicting Bengali scenes.

Many cinemas have been pulled down; others have been sub-divided into smaller units, or have become bingo halls.

Pictured in 1932, the Trocadero (above) was designed by the same architect – George Coles – as the Gaumont State.

The magnificent foyer of the Rainbow Theatre, Finsbury Park, formerly the Astoria (right).

Eclectic style: the Carlton, Islington, is now a bingo hall (below).

Memorial to William Friese-Greene (above) in Highgate Cemetery and (below) the man himself.

One cinema to undergo conversion into a bingo hall was the Carlton at Islington with its exceptionally diverse decor: the exterior was Egyptian, with bulbous columns, papyrus leaves and pyramidal forms, while the foyer was classical Greek.

It is tempting to claim that cinematography was invented in London, but the facts do not really support such a notion, in spite of the activities of William Friese-Greene, whose inscription on his memorial in Highgate Cemetery reads 'His genius bestowed on humanity the boon of commercial kinemaphotography of which he was the first inventor and patentee'.

Friese-Greene (real name William Green), a photographer from Bath, is said to have been the first person to show moving pictures when, in 1890, he ran a brief sequence shot at Hyde Park Corner at No. 20, Brooke Street, Holborn. But there now seems to be doubt that he ever did so, and Patent No. 10131 of 21st June 1889, on which Friese-Green's claim as a pioneer rests, describes his projector much less clearly than his motion picture camera. The word cinematography derives from a machine called the *cinématographe* patented by the French Lumière brothers in 1895, though the technique was being developed in a number of countries at the same time. But the fact remains that Friese-Green did work on his ideas for many years in collaboration with Mortimer Evans and spent £10,000 of his own money in bringing them to fruition. However significant or otherwise his

287 Kennington Road, SE11, where Charlie Chaplin (below, right, as the little tramp) spent part of his childhood.

contribution to the early cinema was, it is ironic that he should have died almost a pauper, in view of the countless millions that have been made out of the industry which grew out of ideas such as his.

One of the first people to make a large fortune in films and become a world movie star was born in south London. There's a plaque at 287 Kennington Road, SE11 recalling that 'Charlie Chaplin (1888–1978) lived here'. The circumstances were depressing, for Charlie's mother had been taken away to a lunatic asylum, and the boy lived with his father, his father's mistress and their child in two rooms. 'Although the front room had large windows', Chaplin recalled in his autobiography, 'the light filtered in as if from under water . . . the wallpaper looked sad, the horse-hair furniture looked sad, and the stuffed pike in the glass case that had swallowed another pike as large as itself – the head sticking out of its mouth – looked gruesomely sad.'

How we all loved the sad comedian on the screen when we were small. My family and I saw him at the cinema, of course, and sometimes enjoyed fragments of his films on the little 9.5 millimetre reels we used to hire for projection on the hand-operated Pathé projector we had at home. I used to try and show the films on a screen erected within my model stage, thus combining the rival attractions of the cinema and theatre. Whatever the show, it was quite essential to operate the crimson velvet curtains. I also tried to synchronise the films with music on the wind-up gramophone, an early incursion of music into my life.

The year 1896 saw the beginning of news on the screen when a Hatton Garden diamond merchant, Robert Paul, reproduced pictures of the Derby in the Alhambra Music Hall on the evening of the race. He continued to provide 'living pictures' at the Alhambra for four years, and extended his activities to other music halls, sometimes travelling twenty miles or more to visit eight of them on the same evening. In 1906 'Hale's Tours' began at 165 Oxford Street. Here the small audience sat in a 'railway carriage' and were given the illusion of travel by watching projected landscapes go by.

My grandmother took me at an early age to one of the most famous and successful of London's music halls, the Metropolitan Theatre of Varieties in Edgware Road. Built in 1862 on the site of the White Lion inn, which had a music room at the back, it was typical of many theatres of a similar type which opened in London around that time. Another was the Bedford at Camden Town, where the wife of the famous murderer Dr Crippen, Bella

Elmore, once appeared in a lowly place on the bill. It was to be the favourite theatre of one of the greatest of the music hall stars, Marie Lloyd, and attracted the

The Metropolitan was demolished in 1963 to make room for a flyover. This example (left) of their publicity material dates from 1879; I saw Gracie Fields there about fifty years later.

Robert Paul, diamond merchant and supplier of 'living pictures' to London's music halls.

'The Chapel on the Green', Collins' Music Hall, was so successful in the 1870s that it was also known as 'the little goldmine' (far left). Sam Collins only survived the opening of his music hall by three years (left).

interest of the painter W.R. Sickert. From his lodgings in Islington, Walter Sickert would also frequent Collins' Music Hall on Islington Green. Collins' had been converted from the Lansdowne Arms into a theatre in 1862 by a former chimney sweep, Sam Vagg, who made his name on the stage as Sam Collins. He was famous for his Irish songs such as *Limerick Races* and *The Rocky Road to Dublin*, and gave his theatre a reputation for such clean jokes that it became known as 'the Chapel on the Green'. Collins' was to welcome most of the great music hall stars before it finally closed in 1958, but Sam survived there for only three years. He died in 1865 at the age of 39.

The inimitable Dan Leno takes on the role of a butcher for this song.

Not surprisingly, many music hall performers in those days died young. The exacting demands of their profession often meant that they would appear at a number of theatres on the same night, each of which would offer up to twenty star turns (the term 'star' derives from the music hall). And what characters they were, each with their own highly developed skills. There were trapezists and acrobats, trampolinists and dancers, but above all there were the character comedians. Marie Lloyd, Gus Elen, Alex Hurley and Albert Chevalier, pearliest of the pearly kings, epitomised the spirit of London. There was Harry Tate with his rotating moustache, Harry Champion, belting out songs like *Boiled Beef and Carrots* at tremendous speed, and the fabulous Nellie Wallace, with her suggestive humour and cheeky hats. Dan Leno was always the inimitable Dan Leno, and although Little Tich might adopt a variety of roles from a jockey to a fireman, his diminutive size and outsize boots gave him an unmistakable identity.

'In its heyday', wrote W. Macqueen Pope, 'the music hall represented the type of entertainment most loved by the masses. It was gay, raffish, carefree. Its themes were fully understood and appreciated by the multitude, for they dealt with their own emotions, their own troubles, their own raw humour. The music hall gave people songs they could join in singing . . . it may be said to have supplied this country with the folk songs of an era. Nothing was restrained, nothing was sophisticated: it was all high spirits, and every day was a Bank Holiday.'

By the time I went to the Met in the early thirties, the music hall was well past its peak as a medium of entertainment yet major stars could still attract packed houses, as was the case when Gracie Fields topped the bill during a special week to mark the reopening of the theatre after redecoration. Variety bills were usually given twice nightly, and as a very special treat I was once taken to the second house to see Gracie Fields. Her voice could have carried her to success in opera, and her most popular song, *Sally in Our Alley*, displayed her top notes admirably. I well

The audience leaves the Theatre Royal, Stratford East, after an early Theatre Workshop production. No evidence that any of them received the squashed-tomato treatment there, as I once did.

remember preferring her moments of Lancashire comedy, in particular when she portrayed the girl who'd been asked to take her harp to the party but nobody asked her to play. Gracie Fields occupied the whole first half of the programme; the second was devoted to a revue called *Beauties of the Night*. I don't remember much about this except that there were glimpses of statuesque nudes from time to time.

Scantily clad females in rigid postures formed part of a music hall bill I saw in the early fifties at the Theatre Royal at Stratford in east London. This was just before the theatre was taken over as the home of Joan Littlewood's highly influential Theatre Workshop, and it was having a hard struggle to survive. I remember sitting in the front row of the dress circle and realising the top of my head was getting wet. When I touched my hair I understood why. Someone in the front row of the gallery above had been squeezing a tomato and had obviously derived more amusement from dropping the con-

Theatre Royal, Stratford East, today.

The Old Vic. In 1830, Edmund Kean was paid £100 for two nights' appearances in this auditorium.

tents on my head than from watching *Great Treasures from the World of Art* on the stage, as depicted by those motionless nudes. I'm not altogether surprised that the East End audience had to be reprimanded from the stage on the night of the Theatre Royal's opening on 17th December 1884. Perhaps the play *Richelieu* did not command their undivided attention either. Since the Theatre Workshop days, however, the fine old house has continued to thrive under an enlightened management and with enthusiastic support from the district and further afield.

More serious theatre-going began for me at the Old Vic in Waterloo Road, when my mother took me to see a memorable production of Shakespeare's *A Midsummer Night's Dream* in the late thirties complete with Mendelssohn's incidental music. The part of Puck was played by a juvenile John Mills, and the whole experience impressed me deeply, the more so since I had just made my own stage début at my all-boys school playing a lady-in-waiting to Hyppolita in the same play.

We had a tenuous family connection with the Old Vic. My mother worked as an unpaid temporary secretary to Lilian Baylis there in the First World War, and as a change from these duties she was occasionally invited to take part in crowd scenes. In *Julius Caesar* the crowd had to select their costumes from a great heap in the Green Room, and my mother was delighted when she came across a rather elegant white robe edged with gold. Wearing this, she was waiting in the wings to go on when a panic-stricken dresser was heard enquiring if anyone had seen Miss Thorndike's costume. My mother had inadvertently adorned herself in the clothes Sybil Thorndike was to wear as Portia and had to disrobe there and then.

I related this story to Dame Sybil Thorndike on one occasion, and she reacted with her characteristic warmth. The last time I met her was when I went to record a radio interview with her in her flat in Chelsea. It was towards the end of her life and she was not in the best of health. In fact on the morning I arrived, she had just fallen out of bed. I was all for postponing the interview, but at her insistence I was invited into the flat. When I reached the bedroom, there she was, still on the floor, but her humour had not deserted her. As her companion and I lifted her up she said: 'Oh thank you, Richard. Thank you for coming to the aid of a fallen woman!'

At an early age I learned with admiration of the achievements of Lilian Baylis at the Old Vic, and of her aunt Emma Cons before her. This redoubtable reformer (the first woman member of the London County Council) bought the freehold of the theatre in 1880. Until that date it had enjoyed a chequered career since its opening as the Royal Coburg in 1818. Renamed the Royal Victoria in 1833, it was a home for melodrama of the most bloodcurdling kind, and the audiences seem to have been as rough as the plays. During a stampede which followed a false fire alarm in 1858, sixteen people lost their lives.

Emma Cons drastically changed the image and intention of the 'Old Vic', as it was affectionately known. She opened it as a temperance amusement hall, naming it the Royal Victoria Hall and Coffee Tavern. She put on vocal and orchestral concerts, scenes from Shakespeare, and in 1900, her first opera, *The Bohemian Girl*. In 1912, Lilian Baylis took over, establishing a regular Shakespeare season under the leadership of Ben Greet, Lewis Casson and Sybil Thorndike. Throughout the twenties and thirties Lilian Baylis brought to the Old Vic all the best young actors of the day, including John Gielgud, Laurence Olivier, Alec Guinness and Ralph Richardson. It was for me a moving

Lilian Baylis (right), who so terrified the young Ralph Richardson, used to fry her supper in her box at the Old Vic (below). The theatre where 'the Lady' established a permanent Shakespearean company in 1914.

moment to stand on the stage of the Old Vic with Sir Ralph Richardson in 1983, when we were making a television documentary about the refurbishment of the theatre. Sir Ralph told me how terrifying it had been to appear on that stage in his youth, well aware that 'the Lady', as Lilian Baylis was known, would be watching every move, or rather listening to every word. She used to sit through performances in a stage box with the curtains drawn, and there, in the early days at least, she used to fry her supper on a gas ring. The smell was very noticeable from the stage and must have been oddly distracting for anyone attempting to deliver the great lines of the immortal bard.

It is impossible to exaggerate the importance of the Old Vic under Lilian Baylis in the subsequent history of the theatre in London, and her influence has been ever more widely felt since her death in 1937. In 1963 the Old Vic became the first home of the National Theatre, thus bringing to fruition at last an idea which commanded the support of David Garrick in the eighteenth century and was subsequently championed by George Bernard Shaw, Harley Granville-Barker and William Archer among others. But the National could not survive for long in the limited space of the Vic, and after a series of exciting seasons it started operations in 1976 in its new headquarters on the South Bank. Unattractive from the outside, the complex houses three fine auditoria of varying sizes and superb foyer spaces which are exciting features of the building. As might be expected from an institution which claims to represent the best in world drama, and which has to be supported with substantial amounts of public money, the National has been beset with controversy, but there's no doubt that it works – and works well.

The director at the time of the move to the South Bank was Peter Hall, who had taken over the previous year from the first director, Laurence Olivier. And it was Hall who in 1960 had had the vision to establish a London base for the Royal Shakespeare Company at the Aldwych Theatre, in former days the home of the famous Aldwych farces. This radical new role for the Aldwych proved prodigiously successful, so much so that the Royal Shakespeare Company was later offered a permanent home at the new Barbican Arts Centre in the City.

When I was presenting the BBC-TV arts programme, *Omnibus*, in 1983, I was given the chance to relive youthful dreams by trying out Peter Pan's flying harness at the RSC Theatre in the Barbican. This is an uncomfortable business which puts great pressure on the vital organs – how actors can remember lines and look ethereally happy when suspended in this way is a mystery to me.

Both the Barbican and the National Theatre are near the sites of London's first theatres. The pioneer was the actor James Burbage who in 1576 built The Theatre in Shoreditch. The Curtain, also in Shoreditch, followed soon after, as did the Blackfriars Playhouse, not far from the present-day site of the Mermaid Theatre, opened at Puddle Dock by Bernard Miles in 1956. The first proposal to build a theatre on the Mermaid site was made in 1616, but the City authorities refused permission on the grounds that the actors might be tempted to steal from the royal wardrobe nearby.

The new Mermaid Theatre, Puddle Dock. Its concrete roof rests on old warehouse walls four feet thick.

It was the severe jurisdiction encountered by the players in the City that drove them across the river to seek freedom of speech and action in the 'Liberty of the Clink' at Southwark. There the Rose was built in 1586, the Swan and the Globe in the 1590s and the Hope in 1613. But the troubles of the actors were not over. The Swan probably borrowed its name from one of the Southwark brothels, which may have been the reason why a local Justice of the Peace, William Gardener, declared in no uncertain terms his desire to 'pluck down' the Swan. Theatre people, especially if they speak their minds, have never been on the best of terms with the powers that be.

One of the Swan's playbills, outlining the plot of **England's Joy,** a 1602 production. It's the only playbill to have survived from this period.

The Globe was built in 1599 with materials taken from The Theatre in Shoreditch. Most of Shakespeare's plays were performed there by a company which played at the Blackfriars Theatre in the winter. In 1613, during a performance of *Henry VIII*, the old Globe burned down. There were no casualties, although one man 'had his breeches set on fire, that

would perhaps have broiled him if he had not, with the benefit of a provident wit, put it out with Bottle-Ale'. The theatre was quickly rebuilt and survived until it was closed by the Puritans in 1642. For many years the American actor Sam Wanamaker has led a campaign to reconstruct the Globe Theatre near its original site on Bankside, and work finally began on the project on Shakespeare's birthday in 1988. It's hoped that the International Shakespeare Globe Centre, with facilities

The first actress to appear in pyjamas on the British stage did so at the Globe theatre, Shaftesbury Avenue.

for the study as well as the performance of Shakespeare, will be completed in 1992.

The Globe Theatre in Shaftesbury Avenue is one of the most interesting theatres in the West End. Designed by W.R. Sprague for the actor Seymour Hicks and the American impresario Charles Frohman, it opened in 1906 with a musical comedy called *The Beauty of Bath*. A few years later, the landlord threatened to sue when he discovered that

The Adelphi, not far from where George Bernard Shaw lived for a time.

Frohman had installed a lift in the theatre without his permission. So Frohman decided to board the first liner sailing for England from New York. It happened to be the *Lusitania* which was torpedoed by a German submarine, and shortly before the ship went down, it's said that Frohman turned to a friend and quoted a line from *Peter Pan*: 'to die will be an awfully big adventure'.

*One of the Globe's most successful productions was its 1949 staging of **The Lady's Not For Burning,** with John Gielgud as Thomas Mendip, Nora Nicholson as Margaret Devize and Pamela Browne as Janet Jourdemayne.*

Peter Pan's creator, Sir James Barrie, born at Kirriemuir in Scotland, moved into a third floor flat at No. 3 Robert Street just off the Adelphi in 1911. At the corner of the terrace opposite him lived George Bernard Shaw, and the two playwrights used to toss biscuits or cherry stones across the street at each other's windows when either of them had a guest he thought the other would like to see. While living there, Shaw wrote some of his greatest plays including *Pygmalion*, the basis of *My Fair Lady*.

I saw this masterpiece of Lerner and Loewe at the Theatre Royal Drury Lane under somewhat unusual circumstances. A friend of mine from Cornwall, a Falmouth man with a heart of gold who was an ardent amateur singer and fisherman, happened to be in London and asked if I could get seats for *My Fair Lady*. I managed this, thanks to the good offices of the actor who was playing Professor Higgins at the time, Charles Stapley, who invited us to come for a drink in his dressing room after the show. The star dressing room at Drury Lane is extremely grand, but my friend was not in any way abashed. 'I thought you sang quite well', he said in his broad Cornish accent. 'Would you like me to send you a box of mackerel?'

The cast of *My Fair Lady* donated a silver punch bowl and ladle to be used on the occasion of the consumption of the Baddeley cake by the resident company each year. This is a tradition that arose from the generosity of a pastry cook turned actor, Robert Baddeley, who died in 1794. He left £100 which was to be invested, so that the interest could then be spent on a cake to be eaten in the Green Room on Twelfth Night every year.

The Theatre Royal, Drury Lane: The Monarch's Box.

The Theatre Royal Drury Lane is probably richer in tradition and legend than any other theatre in London. Robert Baddeley appeared at Drury Lane during the time when the playwright Richard Brinsley Sheridan was manager. Among his leading ladies were Sarah Siddons and Dorothy Jordan. Mrs Jordan attracted the interest of the Duke of Clarence, King George III's son, who paid her, it was said, £1000 a year. When the king told his son that this sum should be halved, Clarence repeated the remark to the actress. Mrs Jordan sent for a Drury Lane playbill and pointed to the words at the bottom which read: 'No Money Returned After the Rising of the Curtain'.

This London theatre was also witness to another royal upset: George III had a public argument with his eldest son, the Prince of Wales, in the foyer of the Theatre Royal; in fact he physically belaboured him. Consequently the management decided it would be wise to keep the antagonists apart in future, which is why the Lane has a Prince of Wales box as well as a monarch's box and why one entrance to the auditorium is labelled 'King's Side'

The Theatre Royal, Drury Lane: The Prince of Wales's Box.

Garrick's villa in Richmond where the great English actor held 'memorable night fêtes'.

and the other 'Prince's Side'. Each of the royal boxes has an elegant retiring room behind it, and when they are not required by members of the royal family, who generally prefer to sit in the stalls or circle, they can be used by members of the public.

Going back to the Theatre Royal's humble beginnings, the first theatre to be constructed on the site opened in 1663. Two years later, the orange-seller Nell Gwynne made her stage début there at the age of fifteen. When Charles II saw her speak the prologue to *Tyrannic Love* in 1669 he determined to make her his mistress. It's said that he founded the Chelsea Hospital under her beneficent influence.

After a fire, Christopher Wren re-built the theatre in 1672. This building witnessed the attempted assassination of the future King George II in 1716, and riots in 1737 when footmen were refused free entry to the gallery. One of the greatest English actors, David Garrick, who had been rejected by the Drury Lane

management as a young man, began his management of the theatre in 1747, which was to last almost thirty years. Apart from his genius as an actor in both comic and tragic roles, Garrick was a reformer who, for the first time, banished privileged members of the audience from the stage, and instituted stage lighting concealed from the public. He had town houses in Southampton Street and the Adelphi and a villa at Richmond, where he gave memorable 'night fêtes'. These were sometimes attended by Dr Johnson, who remarked 'Ah, David, it is the leaving of such places as these that makes a death bed terrible'. On the lawn of the garden, reached by a tunnel under the road, there still stands a temple to Shakespeare, whose leading roles were so famously interpreted by Garrick. The memory of the great actor is also perpetuated in the Garrick Theatre and at the Garrick Club in Garrick Street. The membership still includes many members of the entertainment profession as well as writers, artists,

Dan Leno as Mother Goose (above) in a Drury Lane production in 1904. His ghost is still said to haunt the dressing rooms. A controversial play staged at the Haymarket (below) in 1737 led to an Act of Parliament that controlled performances there for over 200 years.

publishers, politicians and lawyers, and it houses a fine collection of theatrical portraits and memorabilia, many of them connected with Garrick.

In 1794 Richard Brinsley Sheridan replaced Wren's theatre with a new building and this new theatre was destroyed by fire in 1809. The blaze could be seen from the House of Commons, where Sheridan sat watching it as he sipped a glass of port. When someone asked him why he was sitting there so calmly, Sheridan remarked 'Surely a man may take a glass of wine by his own fireside?'

A show is said to be assured of a long run if the ghost of a man in grey appears in the dress circle. He's thought to be the person whose bones were found with a knife in the ribs behind one of the theatre walls in 1840, soon after the theatre was rebuilt. The spirit of Dan Leno, who

frequently appeared at Drury Lane in pantomime, is said to revisit the dressing rooms from time to time.

Another fine Theatre Royal, the one in the Haymarket which was built on the site of an earlier theatre by John Nash in 1820, is said to be haunted by the ghost of J.B. Buckstone, who ran the theatre from 1853 to 1878. His appearance is also said to be an augury of success and he generally haunts the dressing rooms, although in 1964 he was seen by a stage manager on the stage itself.

The old 'Theatre in the Hay' had an eventful history in the eighteenth century. In 1737 Henry Fielding presented a play called *The Historical Register* which was thought so outrageously disrespectful of Prime Minister Walpole, that the Lord Chamberlain was charged henceforth with the responsibility for approving all

plays before they were performed. His censorship of the theatre lasted 231 years until 1968, when the act establishing it was repealed. These days the Haymarket is very far from subversive, indeed until recently it was the only London theatre where God Save the Queen was still played at every performance.

Perhaps the best loved of the Haymarket's theatre managers was Herbert Beerbohm Tree. During his reign from 1887 to 1896, Oscar Wilde's *A Woman of No Importance* and *An Ideal Husband* were first produced. There's a story about a meeting of the two men in the street outside the theatre one morning. Wilde said he admired the red silk lining inside Tree's top hat. 'In that case,' said Sir Herbert, 'I see I must give it you.' Expecting to receive the hat, Wilde was delighted; but all he got was the lining, which Tree ripped out and deposited in the astonished playwright's hands before hurrying on his way.

Fire regulations have dictated that the Regency fireplaces in the Haymarket's dressing rooms be blocked off, but the mantels are still there (left). The royal retiring room (below) is just behind the royal box.

In 1897 Tree made such vast profits from the run of *Trilby* that he was able to build Her Majesty's Theatre on the other side of the Haymarket. Under its copper dome he established his private apartments and here he gave dinner parties known as 'Sir Herbert Tree's At Domes'.

He also established a dramatic school attached to the theatre which was to become the Royal Academy of Dramatic Art. Just before he died, the theatre saw the opening of the prodigiously successful *Chu Chin Chow* which ran for 2238 performances.

Her Majesty's Theatre, over the road from the Haymarket, under whose copper dome Sir Herbert Beerbohm Tree regularly gave dinner parties.

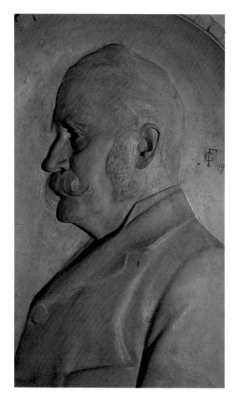

The final word goes undoubtedly to a playwright who found his greatest fame in collaboration with a musician, and that is Sir William Schwenck Gilbert. Born in 1836 at No. 17 Southampton Street, he was soon afterwards kidnapped and ransomed by his parents for £25 – a scenario which sounds like an episode from one of the prodigiously successful Savoy operas that he was to produce with Sir Arthur Sullivan. On the profits of those operas Gilbert bought a splendid house at No. 39 Harrington Gardens in South Kensington which, remarkably for those days, was equipped with telephone, central heating and a bathroom on every floor. He ended his life in 1911 at a rambling mansion called Grimsdyke in Harrow, where he died in an ornamental lake, trying to rescue a lady guest from drowning.

Gilbert's wit expressed itself in repartee which could be extremely cutting. One day, beneath the portico of the Haymarket Theatre, he was approached by a red-faced man who mistook him for a commissionaire. 'Call me a cab!' commanded the stranger. 'Very well', replied Gilbert, 'You're a four-wheeler.' 'What the devil do you mean, sir?' asked the gentleman. 'Well', said Gilbert, who was about to enter his own carriage, 'you asked me to call you a cab. But I could never call you hansom.'

Grimsdyke, Harrow (above), where W.S. Gilbert ended his days. He left an estate worth double that of his collaborator, Sir Arthur Sullivan. The alabaster portrait of Gilbert (top, left) is at Grimsdyke.

LONDON SYMPHONY

Our word symphony derives from the Greek words for 'sound' and 'together', and the sounds to be heard in the streets of London have themselves inspired a number of symphonic works, such as Elgar's *Cockaigne* overture and the *London Symphony* of Vaughan Williams. As for London's importance as a centre for the creation and performance of music, that has never been greater than it is at the present time. Every musical artist of renown wants to be heard in London; the city boasts a great variety of musical venues and a vast reservoir of musical talent which supplies, for example, more major orchestras than any other city in the world.

I count myself fortunate to have been born when this twentieth-century musical renaissance in London was already well under way. In the mid-twenties, when I arrived on the scene, the Proms were flourishing and, by the time I was old enough to be interested, opera and ballet were available at Sadler's Wells at a price I could afford. This was thanks to the extraordinary Lilian Baylis, a lady who occupies almost as important place in the story of London's twentieth-century musical progress as she does in the sphere of the classical theatre. It should never be forgotten that the English National Opera grew out of Sadler's Wells Opera, and that the Royal Ballet is the successor of Sadler's Wells Ballet. Both were the result of the construction by Lilian Baylis of a new Sadler's Wells theatre in 1930.

That idea was first mooted in 1925 when the actress Estelle Stead suggested to 'the Lady' the notion of expanding her missionary work at the Old Vic to north London. With the help of an influential committee chaired by the Duke of Devonshire, Miss Baylis raised funds for the purchase of the decayed Sadler's Wells theatre at Islington, and there she made up her mind to establish a second home for the Old Vic Shakespeare and Opera Companies. Ballet began to feature in these visions for the future in 1926 when a very determined young woman called Ninette de Valois was engaged at £1 a week to arrange dances for the plays at the Vic, on the understanding that she would get the chance to do something more substantial when the chance arose.

All this brought renewed promise for the future to a place long associated with musical entertainment in London's history, for the origins of Sadler's Wells date back to 1683.

Workmen for a surveyor of the highways called Richard Sadler were then excavating for gravel on the country footpath from Clerkenwell to Islington when they came across an old well. When it was opened up, some curious stonework was discovered: the well was identified as having once belonged to the Priory of Clerkenwell, and it had, in the Middle Ages, been associated with miraculous properties. Before long Dr Morton, later Physician-in-Ordinary to King William III, was recommending patients to try it with the result that soon five or six hun-

Despite recession and financial crises, the Old Vic continued to stage drama throughout the 1930s.

'Old' Sadler's Wells in 1813 (left), when it was sometimes known as the Aquatic Theatre. Nautical dramas were staged here, complete with real water. 'New' Sadler's Wells (below) opened in 1931, after years of fund-raising by Lilian Baylis. The Royal Ballet started life here as the Sadler's Wells Ballet Company.

dred people were visiting the well every morning. They were advised to drink the water warm – a quarter of a pint of scalding milk to three pints of the water. From four to ten glasses a day were prescribed, with a stroll after each second glass, so the visitors had some time to spare. Canny Richard Sadler provided amusement for them in a Musicke-House he had constructed on the site. With its rope dancers, jugglers and other similar performers it attracted not only the patrons of the waters, but a more general audience of 'strolling damsels, half-pay officers, peripatetic tradesmen, tars, butchers and others that are musically inclined.'

In the mid-eighteenth century the Musicke-House and its stone-built successor acquired a respectable reputation for drama. The great clown Joseph Grimaldi appeared there in 1781 when he was not quite three years old, and in 1801 little Master Carey made his entrance on the stage: the world was to know him as Edmund Kean. In 1804 under the management of Charles Dibdin, a large glass-sided tank was installed on the stage and Sadler's Wells became the home of 'aquatic drama', starting with the spectacular *Siege of Gibraltar*, complete with naval

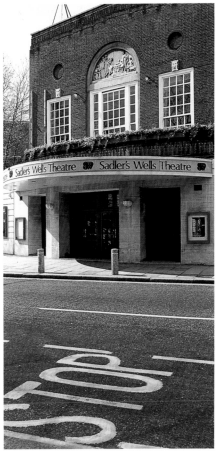

bombardment. After that there was a notable period under the actor Samuel Phelps, who produced thirty-four of Shakespeare's plays, followed by a period of sad decline. The theatre became successively a skating rink, pickle factory and boxing arena, though it did serve for a time as 'a house of melodrama' before finally closing in 1906.

The late twenties saw Lilian Baylis relentlessly raising funds for the construction of her new theatre: never afraid to ask her audiences at the Old Vic for money, she did so every time she made a curtain speech. But while she was admired by many, she also aroused resentment in some quarters. One magazine of the time wrote of her: 'The Old Vic represents her kindly spirit towards the poor of the Surrey side; and now this warm-hearted woman wishes to do the same to the poor of another edge of London . . . by forcing quasi-intellectual food down their throats sugared with the awful phrase "it will do you much good . . . really it will".'

In 1929, Lilian Baylis was made a Companion of Honour. She expressed relief at not being made a dame, for she thought that with a handle before her name, she herself would be expected to pay out more than she could afford. On 6th January 1931, the new theatre opened, appropriately enough with *Twelfth Night*. John Gielgud, who was Malvolio, did not welcome the move from Waterloo Road. 'How we all detested Sadler's Wells when it was opened first,' he recalled. 'The auditorium looked like a denuded wedding cake and the acoustics were dreadful.'

Soon the first opera fortnight was given. Dame Nellie Melba, no less, had returned from retirement to appear at the Vic during the fund-raising period, and now here was a fully fledged company presenting a wide range of operas in English in their own specially built new home. In that first season alone, *Carmen, Faust, The Magic Flute, Il Trovatore, Pagliacci* and *Cavalleria Rusticana* were performed. The seat prices ranged from sixpence in the gallery to five shillings and ninepence, just under six shillings, for the

best seats. One night the novelist Hugh Walpole found himself almost alone in the five and nines at a performance of *Trovatore*. In the interval he met the Lady who said to him: 'It isn't very good dear, is it?' 'No', said Walpole, 'it isn't. If they had only filled the six shilling seats it would be better. And if the *performance* were better, they *would* fill the six shilling seats.' 'Yes', answered Lilian, 'it is a nasty roundabout, dear.'

The standard of performance, and the houses, rapidly improved, and on 15th May 1931 the first all-ballet performance was given. In the thirties I queued for the gallery to see Margot Fonteyn and Robert Helpmann week after week in a repertoire which included many of the earlier creations of Frederick Ashton, such as *Les Patineurs* and *Apparitions*, and memorable works by the ballet's director Ninette de Valois, notably *The Rake's Progress, Job*, to music by Vaughan Williams, and *Checkmate* with a score by Arthur Bliss.

Since there were no reserved seats in the gallery, the trick was to cycle to the theatre at the crack of dawn and purchase a stool ticket for the gallery queue. I could then return not less than an hour before the performance to claim my stool. These would be folded away by the queue attendant just before the doors opened, after which there would be a headlong dash up the stairs to get the best places.

I followed much the same procedure at the New Theatre in St Martin's Lane, where the Sadler's Wells Ballet Company established its headquarters during the war, after Sadler's Wells had been hit by enemy bombs. This was a vintage period both for the ballet company and the Old Vic Theatre Company which also took up residence at the New. It was possible to see Margot Fonteyn in *Swan Lake* one night, and Ralph Richardson as Falstaff or Laurence Olivier as Oedipus Rex on the next. Such was the calibre of those performances and the enthusiasm of the audience that air raid warnings were often ignored. Although a sign indicating that there was a red warning in progress would light up by the side of the stage,

Great celebrities such as Dame Nellie Melba appeared at the Old Vic to help raise funds for Sadler's Wells.

the evening would continue as though nothing had happened. Most of the audience chose to ignore the thumps and bangs outside, reasoning that if we had to go, we might as well go while we were enjoying ourselves.

When Sadler's Wells closed in 1940, the opera company ceased operations, to return in glory with the première of Benjamin Britten's *Peter Grimes* on 7th June 1945. An exciting period followed, with first performances of new operas by Lennox Berkeley, Richard Rodney Bennett and Malcolm Williamson, as well as the British premières of a number of works by Leos Janáček. But the backstage facilities at the Wells were beginning to prove a problem for a company whose ambitions were limitless, and in 1959, for the first time, they ventured into the West End when they took *Die Fledermaus* and *The Merry Widow* to the London Coliseum.

Marble, alabaster, mahogany and bronze come together to create the Coliseum's air of solid opulence.

With a capacity of 2358, the Coliseum is one of London's largest theatres. It was built by Frank Matcham for Sir Oswald Stoll, who foresaw that the bottom end of St Martin's Lane would be a highly convenient place for a theatre, close as it is to Charing Cross Station and its thousands of commuters. It opened on 24th December 1904 with a variety bill, sumptuously mounted on the first revolving stage in the country, incorporating three concentric revolves which could rotate independently. Stoll once organised a horse race with three horses running against the direction of the turntables, a scene typical of the theatre's spectacular fare in early days. The Coliseum still uses the area beneath the stage as a staff canteen and there is now a modern revolving system on the stage itself. Stoll put on rodeos, tennis matches and naval battles; he also housed Diaghilev's Russian ballet

and in 1912 gave a job to a child actor, Master Noël Coward in *A Little Fowl Play*. The musical comedy *White Horse Inn* had a very successful run at the Coliseum in the thirties, and after the war the Coliseum was home to a series of American musicals, notably *Annie Get Your Gun*. There was a period of seven years, from 1961 to 1968 when the Coliseum was a cinema, after which time it became the permanent base of the Sadler's Wells Opera. Six years later the company was renamed the English National Opera, and it continues to this day to attract huge, loyal audiences, presenting a formidable alternative to the Royal Opera at Covent Garden.

I first went to the Royal Opera House when it was a dance hall during the Second World War. After the war the Sadler's Wells Ballet Company was invited to reopen the theatre, and on 20th February 1946 the curtain went up on a spectacular new production of *The Sleeping Beauty* – an outstanding achievement by any standards. Although the company had already toured abroad, to Paris in 1937 and to Holland in 1940 (when they lost all their scenery to the invading Germans), it was *The Sleeping Beauty* at Covent Garden which really brought them into the international limelight. In the next few years their achievements were dazzling, and on 31st October 1956 the

Oswald Stoll's Coliseum is topped by a great globe (above, left) and even the foyer ceiling boasts some magnificent decorations (top). Stoll's mother, who often sold tickets in the Coliseum's box-office, still graces the lobby (above).

company became the Royal Ballet, with a junior branch, the Sadler's Wells Royal Ballet, still based at the theatre in Islington. Now the Sadler's Wells Royal Ballet is moving to the Hippodrome in Birmingham, although Lilian Baylis's pioneering theatre in north London will continue to be an important centre for the arts.

Of all the theatres I know, the one I love best is Covent Garden. Whatever its shortcomings backstage, the auditorium is very beautiful and it offers a welcoming warmth. When decorated for a grand gala event, such as the performance to mark the Queen's Jubilee in 1977, which I had the pleasure of introducing for television, it looks quite magnificent. For such occasions these days a royal box is set up in the middle of the grand tier, the better to see as well as be seen, but the royal box itself is by the side of the stage. It has its own private entrance and dining room and is now generally used for the entertainment of distinguished guests. Queen Victoria was a great opera-goer, and the gold chairs made for her and Prince Albert are still there, as is a settee against one wall, facing away from the stage. This was to accommodate the ladies-in-waiting, but the queen took pity on them and had a mirror put up on the opposite wall, so that at least they could see the stage in reflection.

The Opera House will close in the 1990s for a long period of refurbishment, but I hope nothing too drastic is done to

The royal box at Covent Garden, complete with the mirror that enabled ladies-in-waiting to watch the performance.

alter the interior. Most of the great opera singers and conductors of the world have appeared there, from Adelina Patti to Melba and Maria Callas, from Caruso and Chaliapin to Pavarotti, Domingo and Carreras. Gustav Mahler on his only visit to London conducted a performance of Wagner's *Ring* at Covent Garden in 1892, Sir Thomas Beecham directed many seasons there, and a long list of distinguished maestros since then has included Carlo Maria Giulini, Sir George Solti and the present music director, Bernard Haitink.

It is something for a person to be able to say that they have sung at Covent Garden, but this I am able to do. I once performed an immortal ditty called 'Two Little Sausages' by Lionel Monkton at one of the Christmas parties given in the theatre by the Friends of Covent Garden. I also carried the Prince of Wales's cello on to the stage during a fund-raising gala attended by the prince – the instrument was then auctioned in aid of the Opera House Development Fund.

Covent Garden was not primarily devoted to opera until it became the Royal Italian Opera House in 1847. Fire destroyed the theatre of that period, as it did so many others, and the admirable Gye, who was then manager, opened the present theatre in 1858. His achievements deserve recognition, and it is good to see that his statue is still in the foyer. It was found in a dilapidated condition in an antique shop and restored by the Victoria and Albert Museum before being erected in its present place of honour.

A statue of Frederick Gye, manager of Covent Garden when it reopened in 1858, still stands in the foyer.

Hogarth's 1732 print of John Rich's triumphant entry to the first Covent Garden Theatre. Rich is in the carriage; dramatist John Gay is on the shoulders of an admirer just under the arch.

Opera came to London in the wake of the revels of the Elizabethan era and the masques of the early seventeenth century. The first truly operatic presentation was Sir William Davenant's *The Siege of Rhodes* in 1656. In 1689 the first important English opera, Henry Purcell's *Dido and Aeneas*, was commissioned by the dancing teacher Josias Priest for his boarding school for young ladies at Chelsea. Subsequently Priest arranged the dances for a number of the semi-operas (plays with large amounts of incidental music) which Purcell and others wrote in the 1690s.

The vogue for Italian opera in London started in 1710 with Mancini's *Idaspe* at the Queen's Theatre in the Haymarket. The earliest theatre on the site of the present Her Majesty's was designed and built by Sir John Vanbrugh in 1704 and, following the huge success of Handel's *Rinaldo* in 1711, it became London's chief opera house. Its main rival for a time was the theatre at Lincoln's Inn Fields. There the gifted though illiterate John Rich, an excellent Harlequin, was manager for some fifteen years, and produced in 1727 John Gay's *The Beggar's Opera*, a satire on the conventions of Italian opera, and much else besides. Its success was said by the wits to have made Gay rich and Rich gay. Thus encouraged, Rich started a subscription to build a new theatre in Bow Street: this was the first Covent Garden Theatre, where, on the opening night in 1732, Rich made a triumphal entry, later immortalised in a print by William Hogarth.

The central figure in the musical life of eighteenth-century London was George Frideric Handel. Born in Halle in 1685, he served an apprenticeship in Italy before becoming kapellmeister to the Elector of Hanover at the age of twenty-five. However, he had long been attracted to London, and paid several visits to the English capital before deciding to settle there. In 1727, he became a naturalised Englishman. Meanwhile the Elector had succeeded Queen Anne as King George I of England, whereupon he conveniently overcame any feelings he might have had about the composer's dereliction of duty

in Germany to the extent that he paid him an increased pension and made him music master to the royal children. The production of the Water Music cemented their relationship still further, and under both George I and his successor, Handel was recognised as the dominating figure in London's musical life – apart from a few episodes when he fell out of fashion. For George II, Handel produced the superb coronation anthems which are still performed every time a monarch is crowned in Westminster Abbey, and the Music for the Royal Fireworks. On both occasions Handel almost upstaged his royal employer. The public rehearsal of the

Henry Purcell, composer of the first major English opera (above). The memorial tribute (top) is in Westminster Abbey.

Fire works Music at Vauxhall Pleasure Gardens is said to have caused the first traffic jam on London Bridge, and it was certainly more successful than the display itself in Green Park on 27th April 1749. The fireworks only went off in fits and starts, and the big central set piece went up in sheets of flame. The figure of the king giving Peace to Britannia (the event celebrated the Peace of Aix-la-Chapelle) 'dropped with its head ablaze into a cauldron of fire', wrote Handel's biographer, Sir Newman Flower. In fact the only man to emerge with credit from the affair was Handel.

One result of the death of Queen Anne was that the Queen's Theatre in the Haymarket became the King's, and here in the 1720s Handel poured out a succession of Italian operas under the auspices of a company he set up with business and musical associates called the Royal Academy of Music. This had nothing whatever to do with one of London's leading music colleges, which did not start operating until 1823. Handel's music was a great attraction to the public, though there was often also the added diversion provided by the fierce rivalry of two of the leading ladies he had imported from Italy, Faustina Bordoni and Francesca Cuzzoni. Encouraged by their respective groups of supporters, they finally came to blows on the stage during an opera performance in 1727.

Financial difficulties and the rivalry of other companies drove Handel to change direction in the 1730s, and in May 1732 his oratorio *Esther*, the first oratorio to be given in London, was produced at the King's Theatre. The Bishop of London had decreed that this biblical story should be performed without scenery or stage action, a decision made for religious reasons that had the commercial advantage of reducing the expense of putting the oratorio on. Handel therefore had come up with a rewarding new formula which was to result in the production of some of his greatest works. Later, to the shame of London, where Handel was going through one of his periodic bouts of disfavour, the immortal *Messiah* was first performed in Dublin. It did not find widespread favour in London until the 1750s, when Handel gave a series of charity performances in aid of the Foundling Hospital.

Handel was forced by problems at the Haymarket to put on a number of his operas and oratorios at John Rich's new theatre at Covent Garden. The oratorio performances in particular proved a great draw, not least because Handel himself would play organ concertos as interludes. This he continued to do even after he became totally blind in 1752. After a

25 Brook Street, where the blind Handel died in 1759.

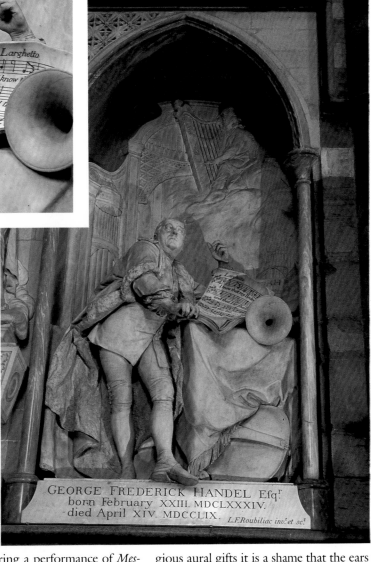

Roubiliac's statue of Handel in Westminster Abbey. The detail clearly shows one of the ears that belonged not to the composer, but to one Miss Rich.

fainting fit during a performance of *Messiah* in 1759, Handel died at his home at No. 25 Brook Street where he had lived for thirty-four years. Three thousand people attended his funeral in Westminster Abbey, and it was there, in 1784, that the first of a series of mammoth Handel commemorations was held. One of them was attended by another arrival from the continent who made a great impact on London's musical life, Joseph Haydn. The impression made on him by the splendour of Handel's music inspired him to write *The Creation*. In view of Handel's prodigious aural gifts it is a shame that the ears of his statue in Westminster Abbey are not modelled on his own. The sculptor Louis François Roubiliac thought them unsuitably large and modelled them instead on the ears of a young lady.

There was music in London's great religious establishments and at the Royal Court from a very early date. Westminster Abbey had an organ as early as 1304, and that important body of specialised liturgical musicians, the Chapel Royal, began to take shape at much the same period, during the reign of King Edward I.

Inside the Rotunda, Ranelagh Gardens, used for balls and musical entertainments. Mozart played harpsichord and organ here, aged eight, in 1764.

In the first half of the fifteenth century, John Dunstable was the chief composer of what is sometimes called the first golden age of English music; Dunstable's name was known in musical circles throughout Europe. In Tudor times too there were many important composers at work in London. Thomas Tallis and William Byrd were both gentlemen of the Chapel Royal, and in 1575, Queen Elizabeth I granted the two composers exclusive rights to print music in England; they made little money out of this pioneering venture in music publishing, but responded gracefully by producing a collection of Sacred Songs to which the composers each contributed seventeen items, one for each year of the queen's reign. The great lutenist and song composer John Dowland achieved fame on the continent before his true worth was recognised at home. It was a bitter disappointment to him when, in 1594, he failed to achieve an appointment at the court of Queen Elizabeth, so he took a job as lutenist to the king of Denmark. Not until 1612 did he achieve his heart's desire, a court appointment to King James I, after which he

spent the rest of his life in London, where his various collections of songs and lute pieces were published.

Alongside the music that could be heard in the Royal Court and Chapel Royal, and enjoyed by well-to-do citizens in their own homes, a good deal of popular music-making also went on in London. Ballad makers in Elizabethan times produced numerous songs on contemporary, often scandalous, themes, and sold their products in the street. The runaway success of *The Beggar's Opera*, for example, was to some extent due to the fact that it used traditional tunes that everyone knew.

In the seventeenth century, pleasure gardens began to multiply in London. At one time there were no less than 631 of these, and many of them made a feature of musical entertainment which drew large crowds. Charles I made Hyde Park accessible to the public in 1735, but it was after the restoration of the monarchy, which reversed the Puritan austerity of the Commonwealth, that the pleasure gardens really came into their own. One of the most famous was Ranelagh Gardens

IN MEMORY OF
THOMAS ARNE
MUSICIAN AND PARISHIONER
1710 - 1778
BAPTIZED IN THIS CHURCH
BURIED IN THIS CHURCHYARD

"RULE BRITANNIA"

LET US PRAISE FAMOUS MEN...SUCH AS
FOUND OUT MUSICAL TUNES
ECCLUS. XLIV 1.5.

Rule Britannia's composer is commemorated in St Paul's, Covent Garden (far left). He was born at 31 King Street (left).

Vauxhall Gardens, in about 1751. The gardens closed in 1859 and were eventually obliterated by houses and factories.

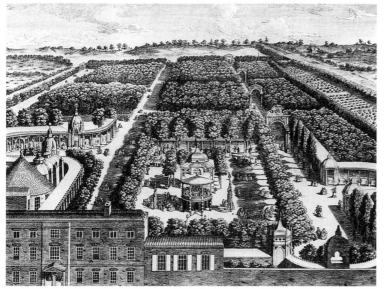

which opened in 1712, much to the annoyance of nearby Chelsea Hospital. Here an enormous rotunda was built in 1742 with an amphitheatre of supper boxes, and a wide promenade round a huge central stove which resembled a Baroque temple. As a boy of eight, Mozart played the organ and harpsichord at Ranelagh when his father brought him to London. Another immensely popular park was to be found at Vauxhall. The public rehearsal of Handel's Fireworks Music was one of the most celebrated events to take place at the gardens there, but other well known composers wrote for Vauxhall on a regular basis in the eighteenth century. The best known was Thomas Arne, son of an upholsterer, whose masque *Alfred* includes *Rule, Britannia*. He was an awkward customer

William Boyce. The anthem and march played at his funeral were his own compositions.

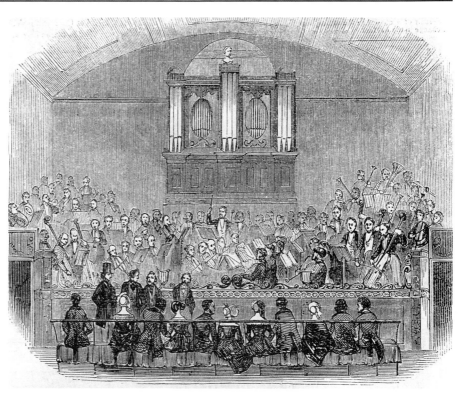

who quarrelled with David Garrick when he was engaged to write music for Drury Lane; he also fell out with another very fine eighteenth-century London composer, William Boyce, said to be one of the most agreeable of men. Boyce, who wrote a number of songs for Vauxhall, was appointed organist at the Earl of Oxford's chapel before becoming composer for the Chapel Royal in 1736 and Master of the King's Musick in 1757. He lies buried beneath the dome of St Paul's Cathedral.

The pleasure gardens presented a very wide variety of musical fare, much of it on the lighter side. The first serious public concerts seem to have been given in 1672 at the house of John Banister in Whitefriars, and six years later the coal merchant Thomas Britton began a series in the loft over his shop in Clerkenwell. This must have been an exciting period for music in London, dominated as it was by the genius of Henry Purcell, who started his brilliant but all too brief career as a chorister of the Chapel Royal.

The rapidly growing prosperity of London, and the likelihood of wealthy patronage, drew many celebrated foreign musicians to London. Johann Sebastian Bach's youngest son, Johann Christian, settled in London in 1762, becoming known as 'The English Bach'; with his fellow countryman Carl Friedrich Abel, he established a series of concerts at the Hanover Square Rooms, which became one of London's foremost musical venues for a century. Here, on 11th March 1791, Joseph Haydn gave the first of many concerts organised by the impresario Johann Peter Salomon. 'Haydn himself presided at the piano-forte', wrote an excited Dr Burney in his diary, 'and the sight of that renowned composer . . . electrified the audience' and awakened 'such a degree of enthusiasm as almost amounts to frenzy'. Haydn's two visits to London (he came again in 1794) were an unqualified triumph, and resulted in the composition of twelve of his 104 symphonies, the last of which has been known ever since as *The London*.

Haydn wanted Mozart to accompany him on the first of his London visits, but although Mozart was half his age, he was

Hanover Square Rooms was a major musical venue for over a century before it was, sadly, demolished.

The young Mozart at the fortepiano, with his father Leopold (also a composer) and older sister Maria Anna.

Thomas Hardy's portrait of Joseph Haydn, painted in 1791.

ill and exhausted and before Haydn returned he was dead. How London would have received him as a mature artist we cannot know. He would probably not have experienced the fashionable interest aroused by his visit in 1764, when his father put him on public exhibition as a child prodigy at their lodgings in Frith Street, Soho.

In the period when the Napoleonic Wars were bringing instability to continental Europe, these islands were relatively secure, and London became a major centre for music publishing and the manufacture of musical instruments. Beethoven loved the Broadwood piano sent to him from London, and the Royal Philharmonic Society, founded in London in 1813, commissioned his ninth symphony. Rossini was in London from 1823 to 1824, making a small fortune by attending the soirées of the wealthy, and in 1826 Carl Maria von Weber came to London to produce *Oberon* at Covent Garden, only to die seven weeks later at his lodgings at No. 103 Great Portland Street.

All through the nineteenth century major musical figures from abroad continued to visit London, including Berlioz, Liszt, Wagner, Dvořák and Gounod. Some, however, were not impressed by the great city. In 1848, Chopin came to London and was disgusted with the manners of the aristocracy in what he called 'this abyss of London'. One duchess asked him straight out how much he cost and, upon his reply, told him it was too much. But there were small consolations: he was delighted to hear Jenny Lind at Her Majesty's on a night when Queen Victoria (a great devotee of opera) was there, attended by the aged Duke of Wellington. But Chopin himself was not invited to perform at court, and left London to die, convinced that the royal family cared for no one except Mendelssohn. Felix Mendelssohn was indeed the darling of musical London and of the royal family at that time. He came to England no less than ten times and was entertained as a friend by Queen Victoria and Prince Albert at Buckingham Palace.

It was in Victorian times that Britain came to be regarded in continental Europe, not with entire justification, as 'the land without music'. The queen's own musical hero was the immensely popular Sir Arthur Sullivan, who scored an early success at Leipzig with his music for *The Tempest*, and could produce melodies every bit as appealing as Mendelssohn's. The queen's subjects flocked in their thousands to see the light operas Sullivan produced in collaboration with W.S. Gilbert; indeed she herself, although in lifelong mourning after the death of Prince Albert, commanded a performance of *The Gondoliers* at Windsor Castle. Sullivan entertained members of the royal family at his house at No. 58 Victoria Street, and the queen attended a performance of Sullivan's oratoria *The Golden Legend* at the Royal Albert Hall, after which she told him he ought to compose a grand opera. This must surely rate as one of the worst pieces of musical advice ever given, for Sullivan's *Ivanhoe* was not a great success. However, his achievement was such that he was buried in St Paul's Cathedral, and there's a touching memorial to him in the

Chopin left 4 St James's Place to give what was to be his last public performance – at the Guildhall, in aid of Polish refugees, in 1848.

Chopin, aged thirty-nine.

Embankment Gardens. In spite of his bitter quarrels with Gilbert, the memorial is inscribed with words by Gilbert from *The Yeomen of the Guard*:

Is life a boon?
If so, it must befal
That death, when'er he call,
Must call too soon.

But if creative music of the highest calibre was not being produced in nineteenth-century London, musical life flourished as never before. Sullivan enjoyed some of his earliest triumphs at the Crystal Palace, the giant glass conservatory built for the Great Exhibition of 1851 in Hyde Park and subsequently moved to Sydenham. The triennial Handel Festivals were held there in Victorian times, involving as many as 4000 performers. Music became a very much more democratic business than it had been in former times, thanks partly to the activities of an extraordinary Frenchman, Louis Jullien. The possessor of no less than thirty-six Christian names, he applied his grandiose ideas to musical life in London for twenty years, putting on, amongst

Sir Arthur Sullivan's monument (right) is in the Embankment Gardens behind the Savoy, and the memorial plaque (left) to his collaborator can be seen on the Embankment wall at Charing Cross.

other things, at least twenty-four seasons of promenade concerts at London theatres. The *Illustrated London News* of 9th November 1850 published his declared aim, which was 'to ensure amusement as well as attempting instruction, by blending in the programmes the most sublime works with those of a lighter school.'

Promenade concerts, however, did not start with Jullien – a series was given at the Lyceum Theatre in 1838 – and they did not become an enduring feature of London's musical scene until 10th August 1895, when Robert Newman, manager of the new Queen's Hall in Langham Place, gave the first of his summer promenade concerts with the Queen's Hall Orchestra. The conductor was a twenty-five year old Londoner, Henry J. Wood. At first the seasons ran for ten weeks every year, and every concert was given by the same orchestra and conductor. The programmes were very long by modern standards, and embraced all kinds of music, in the Jullien fashion, from classical masterpieces to popular ballads and cornet solos. While perfectly willing to leaven the musical fare with lighter material, Wood was a courageous pioneer. It was he who made

Wagner available to the musical masses (albeit in, as the musicologist Sir Donald Tovey described, 'bleeding chunks' from the operas), as well as introducing each season a large number of 'novelties' or new works by living composers, many of them British, which might otherwise have had little chance of performance. Prices were kept to a minimum, which was the reason why people like my father, who never earned more than a basic working man's wage, were able to go. He took me to the Proms twice, in 1937 and 1938, and I have never forgotten the experience. I recall how Henry Wood would go round the orchestra at the end of the Last Night shaking hands with the leaders of every section. He would make his final appearance wearing his overcoat and waving his hat, a sign that yet another season of Proms was really over.

The Queen's Hall was a perfect size and shape for such occasions, adequately large yet intimate. The colour scheme inside was gold, red and grey – a rather special grey which had to be exactly the same colour as the belly of a London mouse: one of the architects, T.E. Knightley, went so far as to hang a string of dead mice in the painters' workshop as

Queen's Hall, Langham Place, home of the first Proms in 1894.

Queen Victoria laid the foundation stone for the Royal Albert Hall in 1867, and it opened four years later. The organ there is one of the most powerful in the world, and has nigh on 9000 pipes.

a pattern. The hall was, from a musical point of view, one of the saddest casualties of the Second World War. It was destroyed by bombs in 1941, and there's a famous photograph of Sir Henry Wood standing on the ruins the next day. He was greatly in favour of rebuilding, but by then the Proms had been firmly established in their present home, the Royal Albert Hall.

Sir Thomas Beecham said of this great memorial to Victorian grandiloquence that it could be used for a hundred things, but music was not one of them. That was in the days before the notorious echo had been cured by the suspension of a number of large plastic saucers from the ceiling, with the effect that it is no longer true that Albert Hall audiences can hear two concerts for the price of one. The echo was discovered by the Bishop of London, whose concluding 'amen' during the opening ceremony on 29th March 1871 resounded round the hall and came back to him. The hall was declared open by the Prince of Wales, for his mother

Queen Victoria was too overcome by emotion to speak the necessary words. However, she was responsible for adding the words 'Royal Albert' to the existing name, the 'Hall of Arts and Sciences'. The addition was entirely appropriate, for the hall was first mooted as part of Prince Albert's scheme for a permanent cultural centre in South Kensington following the Great Exhibition of 1851. Sadly, by the time it opened, the hall had become a memorial to the prince, who died at the premature age of forty-two in 1861.

Able to accommodate around 7000 people, this great oval amphitheatre remains the perfect setting for great national occasions such as the Festival of Remembrance and the Last Night of the Proms. There it is always a joy to share in the enthusiasm of a new generation of young promenaders, who indirectly owe their introduction to music to Sir Henry Wood. In my mind, and no doubt this is true for many others, he shares with Lilian Baylis the glory of bringing great words and music within reach of the everyday Londoner.

Land of Hope and Glory has become an indispensable part of the Last Night of the Proms. Even before A.C. Benson's jingoistic words were fitted to it as part of a Coronation Ode for King Edward VII, Elgar knew he had a winner in the trio tune from his *Pomp and Circumstance March No.1*. Henry Wood had to give two encores the first time he played the march at the Proms – a unique honour. But it was another and much more profound work by Elgar which marked the end of the Victorian era in British music, and the return of these islands from what the rest of the musical world regarded as outer darkness. This was the *Enigma Variations*, first performed under the baton of the famous Austrian conductor Hans Richter at the St James's Hall in London on 19th June 1899. Not long after this, Elgar composed one of the finest musical evocations of London in his overture, *Cockaigne*, subtitled 'In London Town'. In it it is possible to hear snatches of street cries and parading military bands, and a quieter interlude as two young lovers take a stroll

through one of the London's parks and into a church.

Two other leading figures in the English musical renaissance of the early twentieth century wrote musical portraits of London. John Ireland's *A London*

The first manuscript page of John Ireland's A London Overture.

Overture, written in 1936, takes as its germinal idea the cry of a bus conductor as he calls out 'Piccadilly', while the *London Symphony* of Vaughan Williams, first performed in 1914, is a much more complex and poetic portrait of the capital. Like so many major twentieth-century British composers, Vaughan Williams was for a time a student of Charles Villiers Stanford at the Royal College of Music. This stands behind the Royal Albert Hall in Prince Consort Road and was one of the many cultural institutions in South Kensington which have given shape to Prince Albert's enlightened ideas.

Gustav Holst met Vaughan Williams while they were both students at the Royal College of Music, and they became lifelong friends. For much of his career, Holst was music master at St Paul's Girls'

10 Hanover Terrace, NW1, where Ralph Vaughan Williams lived from 1953 until his death five years later.

School at Hammersmith; there he had a special soundproof music room, and on Sunday mornings he would shut himself away in it to compose. His famous masterpiece *The Planets* was completed in this way. Two other distinguished students at the Royal College a little later on were Michael Tippett and Benjamin Britten, whose name has been adopted for the new opera theatre at the college.

How is it that in the course of the present century, London has ceased to be the philistine capital of 'the land without music' and become one of the most important of the world's musical centres? A succession of major composers has helped: apart from Britten and Tippett, names that come to mind include William Walton, Lennox Berkeley, Peter Maxwell Davies, Malcolm Arnold, Peter Racine Fricker and Harrison Birtwhistle. But there have been other contributory factors. The importance of the BBC in creating a widespread taste for good music from its earliest days can hardly be overestimated. This may have helped to account for the sudden outburst of interest in music during the Second World War; people seemed to appreciate its power to cheer and console, and the

Dame Myra Hess conducts Haydn's **Toy Symphony** *in the National Gallery, 1945 (below). The concert, to honour her, featured an orchestra of toy instruments.*

An audience of music lovers was attracted to the National Gallery during the Second World War thanks to Dame Myra Hess's lunchtime concerts (above and top).

orchestras attenuated by the loss of many members to the forces, were well attended. After the war, the establishment of the BBC Third Programme, very largely devoted to music, extended the audience for material outside the most familiar repertoire. Indeed, it has exercised very wide influence on Britain's cultural life.

Another factor was a rapid expansion in the number and quality of the capital's orchestras, to the extent that London now has more orchestras than any other city in the world. The oldest survivor is the London Symphony Orchestra, set up in 1904 by players who broke away from Henry Wood's Queen's Hall Orchestra to form a self-governing co-operative. In 1930 the BBC created its own symphony orchestra, with Adrian Boult as conductor. Sir Thomas Beecham, who might have expected the appointment, decided to form his own orchestra in 1932. This was the London Philharmonic, which attracted many of the city's best players and was described at its first concert as 'a miracle of fire and beauty'. After the war, in 1946, Beecham formed yet another orchestra, the Royal Philharmonic, which survived his benevolent despotism to run its own affairs.

famous series of lunchtime chamber music concerts organised by the pianist Dame Myra Hess in the sandbagged National Gallery were always packed with civilians and service people in uniform. Tickets for the ballet were hard to come by, and such concerts as there were, performed by

Beecham's contribution to London's musical renaissance was very considerable. He was an ardent champion of contemporary British composers, Delius foremost among them, though it has to be said that he was choosy in this respect: he once referred to Elgar's *Symphony in A Flat* as the musical equivalent of St Pancras Station, and was not at all sympathetic to Vaughan Williams. Beecham ran opera seasons of distinction at Covent Garden in the years between the wars, and as an orchestral conductor he set standards by which others are still judged in the eyes of British musicians – what is more he entertained them as no one else has done before or since.

In my early announcing days on the BBC Third Programme, I had to introduce a broadcast performance of Mozart's *Requiem* conducted by Beecham at the large Maida Vale studio just round the corner from my grandmother's house in Paddington. It was then that I had personal experience of Beecham's wit, and of his cavalier attitude towards broadcasting. After the second movement of the *Requiem* he sat down on his conductor's stool, looking quite exhausted. Sitting close to him at the announcer's table, I was worried that perhaps he might be ill. But he soon reassured me. Although the microphones were all live, he turned to me and said in a loud voice, 'I'm damn tired, dear boy. Why don't you say some more? Recite Macaulay's Lays for all I care!'

But Beecham was not the only creator of new orchestras in London. In 1945 the Philharmonia was set up by Walter Legge of EMI, primarily as a recording orchestra, and its quality was such that the world's leading conductors were happy to appear with it, pre-eminently, in the early years, Carlo Maria Giulini and Otto Klemperer. I have very happy memories of introducing a televised performance of Verdi's *Requiem* conducted by Giulini at the Royal Festival Hall, and also a series of Beethoven's symphonies with the Philharmonia conducted by Klemperer. By then he was an old gentleman whose beat was a little uncertain, but the players knew what a Klemperer performance was and the result was monumental.

In addition to the capital's large permanent orchestras, there are any number of smaller groups, concentrating on different aspects of the repertoire. The London Mozart Players, the Academy of St Martin-in-the-Fields, the Academy of Ancient Music, the London Sinfonietta and the Nash Ensemble are just a few of them. London also has a large number of concert venues. In 1951 the Albert Hall had a new rival in the Royal Festival Hall, built on a newly cleared site on the south bank of the Thames as the centrepiece of the Festival of Britain. Beecham was very rude about it. The hall was, he said, 'like a disused mining shack in Nevada. Frivolous and acoustically imperfect.' This was true: if the Albert Hall still had its echo, the Festival Hall was so dry that players had great difficulty in making their music cohere at all. Later, when the hall was refurbished and its appearance outside was changed, efforts were made to put the sound right. I remember describing the re-opening for television, clutching in my hand one of the so-called Helmholtz

Sir Thomas Beecham, one of the twentieth century's major musical figures.

Queen Elizabeth Hall, where my ingenuity was sorely tested when Her Majesty's arrival for its opening was somewhat delayed (above and below).

resonators which had been placed in the ceiling in a more or less successful attempt to correct the acoustics.

In 1967 the smaller Queen Elizabeth Hall and Purcell Room were opened on the South Bank. The Queen opened the hall named after her, and for some reason her arrival was delayed. Using the material I had prepared for just such an eventuality, I was able to 'fill in' during the delay, but I was greatly relieved when the royal party appeared. I had been reduced to talking about the aluminium used in the construction of the seats and the fact that the same material was used for the dust-carts of the Greater London Council.

Another very popular musical venue in recent years has been St John's Smith Square, formerly a church known as 'Queen Anne's Footstool' from the shape of its four towers; and for chamber music and recitals, there is the superb Wigmore Hall where most of the world's leading instrumentalists and singers have appeared at one time or another. A significant contribution to the creation of an informed chamber music audience has been the South Place Sunday concerts, held since 1929 at the Conway Hall, Red Lion Square. Prices have always been kept

The Baroque architecture of St. John's, Smith Square (above) wasn't to everyone's taste. Its eighteenth-century nickname was the 'footstool church', reflecting the opinion that Queen Anne must have designed it by kicking over her footstool and leaving it with legs in the air. Today it is best known as an excellent musical venue (left).

as low as possible, with the result that ordinary people could acquire a taste for Bartok string quartets for the cost of a pint of beer. In broader terms, younger audiences are still being educated by two continuing series of children's concerts, founded by those imaginative musical be-

nefactors Sir Robert Mayer and Ernest Read.

The most recent major addition to the concert scene in London has been the large concert hall at the Barbican, officially opened by the Queen in March 1982. By then the Guildhall School of Music

A modern-day footstool? The Barbican complex provides facilities for enjoying the fine, as well as the performing, arts.

and Drama, founded over a century ago, was already installed at the Barbican, where it continues a tradition of excellence that has produced Jacqueline du Pré and James Galway among its graduates.

The readiness of British musicians to tackle almost any repertoire with a minimum of rehearsal has helped to make London a major recording centre, both in the serious and popular fields. This is one reason why a number of the world's leading solo performers and conductors have made London their principal base. As for London's position in the sphere of popular theatre, the name of Andrew Lloyd Webber, son of a former director of the London College of Music, is up in lights in the major cities of every continent. The British Musical seems, at any rate for the time being, to reign supreme.

Beecham once remarked that 'British music is in a state of perpetual promise. It might almost be said to be one long promissory note.' Thanks in no small measure to his own ceaseless quest for the highest quality, that promise has to a considerable extent been fulfilled; indeed in the late twentieth century London has a strong claim to be the musical capital of the world.

The Barbican's concert hall seats 2000 and is the home of the London Symphony Orchestra.

POMP AND CIRCUMSTANCE

Farewell the neighing steed and the shrill trump,
The spirit-stirring drum, the ear-piercing fife,
The royal banner, and all quality,
Pride, pomp and circumstance of glorious war!

Othello William Shakespeare

Music and open-air drama are both part of the royal pageantry which has played a spectacular role in the life of London for centuries. I'm as vulnerable to the appeal of a big parade as anyone, and as a television commentator on a number of royal occasions, I've had a glimpse of the meticulous planning and rehearsal required to make such events appear effortless. I wonder if they worked as hard at these things in the days of Queen Elizabeth I? She was surrounded by elaborate ceremonial which must surely have been witnessed by William Shakespeare for him to give us the perfect phrase to describe such elaborate procedures: 'pomp and circumstance'. Elgar was certainly acquainted with the splendour of London's royal processions in Edwardian times when he used the poet's words as the title of five famous marches.

Most visitors who come to London do so in the hope of seeing something of the incomparable pageantry which surrounds the Queen in London, ranging as it does from the daily routine of Changing the Guard to more elaborately choreographed spectacles such as Trooping the Colour, the Opening of Parliament, and more infrequently, royal jubilees, royal weddings and coronations.

On a fine day, between 5000 and 10,000 people gather to watch the Changing of the Guard at Buckingham Palace whilst another crowd of spectators surges around the entrance of Horse Guards Parade in busy Whitehall to see the changing of the Queen's Life Guard by members of the Household Cavalry Regiment. The ever-popular annual Trooping the Colour ceremony has taken place on Horse Guards Parade on the monarch's official birthday since 1805. This recalls the earliest days of land warfare, when colours were used as a rallying point and, because they symbolised regimental honour, would be ceremonially carried down the ranks at the end of a day's march.

Coronations, royal weddings or a royal jubilee are events people will travel across the world to see. In these egalitarian days people can watch a royal show with a clear conscience, for it no longer represents the power of a repressive monarchy, but is rather a vivid expression of common traditions, a kind of living history. Buckingham Palace, where the royal standard flies whenever the Queen is in residence, lies at the heart of ceremonial London. It is the only royal palace named after a subject, standing as it does on the site of an earlier house owned by John Sheffield, Earl of Mulgrave. Mulgrave was created Duke of Buckingham by Queen Anne in 1703, though his haughty manner earned him the less attractive unofficial title of 'Lord Allpride'.

When the duke died, Buckingham House passed to his widow, an illegitimate daughter of James II. She, it seems, was even more haughty than her husband.

The familiar facade of Buckingham Palace, the monarch's official residence.

An early eighteenth-century view of Buckingham House, before Nash transformed it.

Marble Arch was moved away from Buckingham Palace to its present location when it proved too narrow for the state coach.

On her death bed she insisted that none of her ladies-in-waiting should sit down in her presence until the surgeon had pronounced life extinct. King George III purchased the house in 1762, but it was little used until his son, George IV, abandoning Carlton House as he thought it insufficiently grand, decided that it must be turned into a palace fit for a king. John Nash was engaged as architect and he designed a three-sided court, open on the eastern side, in front of which was to stand a marble arch, based on the arch of Constantine in Rome, to act as a grand entry. Unfortunately the arch proved too narrow for the state coach and was removed in 1847 by Edward Blore, the architect who succeeded Nash, to the western end of Oxford Street, where it still stands. The gates of Marble Arch are kept closed, except when senior members of the royal family, or the King's Troop, Royal Horse Artillery, wish to pass through them.

The facade of Buckingham Palace which is familiar to us today is an Edwardian remodelling by Aston Webb of the work of Blore; little of Nash's work is visible – except to garden party guests who can admire the west front. But that distinguished architect did make enduring changes to the area around the palace: he replaced Carlton House, whose columns were eventually to grace the National

Gallery, with Carlton House Terrace, rebuilt Clarence House, and remade St
James's Park, which had been bluntly
described by a visiting prince as 'a sort of
meadow for cows'. It was Nash who
turned the canal which once ran through
the park into an ornamental lake.

Prince Albert did not admire the
work of Edward Blore, who was so dis-
gruntled by the lack of royal approval that
he refused the knighthood that was offered him. He had been chosen by the

government partly because of his reputation for cheapness, and his efforts were no doubt vitiated by shortage of funds. Brighton Pavilion had to be sold to raise money, and Blore used some of the furniture and fittings to create a somewhat inappropriate series of Chinese rooms at Buckingham Palace.

Queen Victoria liked the palace in some ways, though not others. She cannot have been amused by the doors that would not close and the windows that would not open, nor by the disagreeable smells that arose from the ventilating system which was linked to the common sewer. Her son, King Edward VII, had things put to rights, and lived in Buckingham Palace in magnificent style, with all the clocks advanced half an hour to help

him comply with the old adage that punctuality is the politeness of kings. King George V made himself very much at home there, to the extent that he kept a pet macaw in the palace, which nearly had to go when a wave of psittacosis, or parrot's disease, swept the land and the import of parrots and related species was banned. However, the then Minister of Health saved the day by pointing out to the king that the ban applied to private owners only and that he could keep his bird if Buckingham Palace was classified as a zoo. The king did not object, so long as tickets were not sold to people 'who wanted to see the wild animals'.

The palace must sometimes appear to be a bit of a zoo to its inhabitants when it is invaded by thousands of visitors for a

garden party or investiture. When I was invited to attend an investiture, I was deeply impressed by the calm efficiency of the arrangements. By an entire coincidence, which seemed flattering at the time, as I walked into the ballroom with my wife and two sons the orchestra happened to be playing that old family favourite of ours, *Two Little Sausages*, in the course of a selection of music by Lionel Monckton. For a moment I thought meticulous research had revealed my affection for that song!

The impeccable ordering of most ceremonial occasions is the responsibility of the Lord Chamberlain, and in particular of the Comptroller of the Lord Chamberlain's office. He is based, along with a small team of assistants and secretaries, at St James's Palace. This was for some 300 years one of the principal royal residences in London, and ambassadors are still accredited to the Court of St James. The palace was built by Henry VIII on the site of a twelfth century hospital for the accommodation of fourteen 'leprous maidens'. Another grisly association recalls the name of the fifth son of King George III, the Duke of Cumberland, who had apartments in the palace. He had an affair with the daughter of his Corsican valet, a man by the name of Sellis, to whom the duke subsequently made homosexual advances. The outraged Sellis attempted unsuccessfully to murder the duke, after which he fled in panic and cut his own throat. His ghost is said to haunt the palace still, with its head lolling on one side, for it was almost severed from the body.

A rather more courtly anecdote concerns another resident of the palace, a certain Duke of Ormond. In 1746, realising that his last hour had come, he is said to have remarked to a stranger 'Excuse me, sir, if I make some grimaces in your presence, but my physician tells me that I am at the point of death.' With equal civility the stranger replied 'Do not, I beg you, sir, put yourself under any constraint on my behalf.'

Among numerous other annual responsibilities, the Comptroller of the Lord Chamberlain's office oversees some

St James's Palace: The Colour Court.

Built by Henry VIII for himself and Anne Boleyn, St James's Palace is now occupied by the Lord Chamberlain's office.

Claude, last of the College of Arms's feline mascots, appears on the balustrade under the windows in this painting of the College (below).

coronations and state funerals. The title of Earl Marshal of England has been hereditary in the Howard family since 1672 and is held by successive dukes of Norfolk. The incumbent who had to organise the investiture of Prince Charles as Prince of Wales in 1969 had a dry sense of humour as well as total command of his job. It is said that he first outlined the shape of the ceremonial at Caernarfon Castle by moving half a dozen flower pots around on the terrace at Arundel Castle. As a commentator I was present at a rehearsal arranged by the Earl Marshal one very cold winter's day in the garden of Buckingham Palace. The outline of Caernarfon Castle was taped on the grass, and members of the royal family and other principal participants went through all the motions under the duke's critical supervision.

The Earl Marshal's chief of staff is Garter King of Arms. His working home is the College of Arms in Queen Victoria Street, an elegant red brick house in the style of Wren which until recently had a black and white cat as a mascot. There was a long line of these animals, each of which wore a suitably heraldic collar around its neck; the latest of them was called Claude, and two paintings of Claude remain as a lasting tribute to him.

fourteen investitures each year and three Buckingham Palace garden parties attended by about 35,000 people. To cope with the rush of work this entails, additional people are employed in the office who are rather curiously known as 'permanent temporaries'.

Alone among annual royal events, the State Opening of Parliament is supervised by the Earl Marshall, who is responsible for such great occasional events as

There are two other kings of arms: Clarenceux and Norroy & Ulster; six heralds: (in order of precedence) York, Chester, Windsor, Lancaster, Somerset and Richmond; and four pursuivants: Portcullis, Bluemantle, Croix Rouge and Rouge Dragon. The heralds have been part of the royal household since the time of Edward I or earlier, and are still very active in the tracing of genealogies and the granting of armorial bearings. They still receive a stipend – originally established in Tudor times – which since the reign of William IV has amounted to the princely sum of £17.80 per year. As one of the heralds has put it, they have endured the longest pay pause in history, so it is just as well that they are allowed to act professionally on their own account. Many individuals and corporate bodies like to have armorial bearings: one herald was engaged as heraldic adviser to the Football League; another was kept busy for a time devising insignia to display the varying ranks of Maori chiefs. The heralds can be seen as a body at the State Opening of Parliament, when, dressed in their richly embroidered tabards, they precede the monarch in a procession led by the Earl Marshal and the Lord Great Chamberlain. Both of these gentlemen traditionally have to walk backwards, but nowadays (with the Queen's approval) they are relieved of this obligation as they descend the final flight of stairs after the ceremony is over. This change must have come as a great relief.

I was one of the hundreds of thousands of people who lined the pavements of the Mall to watch the Queen's coronation procession in 1953. We waited all the previous night and shared the general feeling of excitement when the morning papers came out with blazing headlines announcing the conquest of Everest by Sir Edmund Hillary and Sherpa Tensing, an announcement conveniently timed to coincide with the wave of patriotic coronation fever.

The great processional route, 115 feet wide, which runs from Buckingham Palace to Admiralty Arch, was constructed in 1903 as part of the national memorial to Queen Victoria. It runs

Outside the College of Arms, a herald stands resplendent in his ceremonial finery. The grand professional route of the Mall is another reminder of London's great ceremonial tradition (below).

along the route of the old Mall, a fashionable resort in the seventeenth and eighteenth centuries where, according to a contemporary account, the royal family would also take their exercise 'attended by only half a dozen Yeomen of the Guard' – an early version of the royal walkabout.

'Here used to promenade', recalled another observer, 'the whole British world of gaiety, beauty and splendour.'

Parallel to the Mall and just to the north of it is Pall Mall which takes its name from a croquet-like game which originated in Italy as *pallo a maglio*. Pall Mall was very popular with reigning sovereigns from James I to Charles II, who established his mistress Nell Gwynne at what is now No. 79 Pall Mall, the only house on the south side of the street which does not belong to the Crown. In 1676, the infatuated king had the lease conveyed to Nell's trustees after her complaint that 'she had always conveyed free under the crown and always would'. In the early nineteenth century, Pall Mall was the first London street to be lit by gas and people were so terrified of this wondrous innovation that they would not touch the lamp posts for fear of being burned. In more recent times, the conduct of a royal personage is said to have caused a curious incident in the Travellers', one

Pall Mall (above), first London street to be lit by the fearsome gas-lamps, and the Travellers' Club (right) at its spiritual heart. At one time, membership was open only to those who had travelled at least 500 miles from London in a straight line.

The decor of the Library in the Travellers' Club combines, somewhat appropriately, a mixture of Greek and Roman influences.

of Pall Mall's grandest clubs. The club is famous for blackballing anyone of whom it does not approve, and on the morning after King Edward VIII had announced his decision to abdicate, his portrait was found lying face down on the floor by the hall porter. The porter had been on duty through the night and insisted it could not have been placed there by any human hand. . .

There is always a sense of rising excitement among the crowd along a royal route when they hear the sound of a band in the distance and then catch glimpses of the gleaming helmets and cuirasses (breastplates) of a Sovereign's Escort of the Household Cavalry. This is the collective title of the two senior regiments in the British Army, the Life Guards and the Blues and Royals. Both regiments, which trace their origins back to the seventeenth century, have operational roles in the modern army, and they each supply a detachment of squadron strength to make up the Cavalry Mounted Regiment,

which is based in London and consists of some 350 men. These soldiers are given extended riding training, and their horses, all black with the exception of the mounts of the trumpeters (which are grey), are trained for four months before they are seen on parade.

Apart from their processional duties, the Household Cavalry provides the Queen's Life Guard in the front yard of Horse Guards Parade in Whitehall. This recalls the days when Whitehall Palace was the principal royal residence in London – in the time of Henry VIII, for example, the tilt yard of the palace occupied what is now the area of Horse Guards Parade. Today only the magnificent Banqueting House on the other side of Whitehall remains. The architect was Inigo Jones and Charles I commissioned Rubens to adorn the ceiling with a painting to commemorate Wise Rule. Alas, many of the king's subjects considered his rule disastrously unwise, and on 30th January 1649, he walked across the

Behind the scenes at the St John's Wood barracks of the King's Troop: the stables (top), the saddlery (above) and a farrier at work (above, right).

Palace Road on certain days and there they can see a selection from the seventy carriages of many different types. The Crown Equerry has to make sure that all are maintained in working order and, if necessary, he will conduct careful tests. One dark November night in 1976 the Gold State Coach itself was drawn by a team of horses to St Paul's Cathedral. It was to be used for the Queen's Jubilee Service seven months later, and there could be no doubt of its ability to negotiate a route that included the inclines of Fleet Street and Ludgate Hill.

The Gold State Coach, made for George III in 1762 and normally only used for coronations, is drawn by eight of the ten grey horses known as Windsor Greys which are stabled at the Mews, together with twenty bay harness horses. The coachmen, postillions and working grooms who look so impressive on parade

in their scarlet and gold or black liveries are the same men who have to cope with the daily chores of the stables.

For the State Opening of Parliament, the Queen uses the Irish State Coach, built in Dublin in 1852 and bought by Queen Victoria for that particular occasion. The procession makes its way to the Palace of Westminster via the Mall and Whitehall, to be greeted on arrival by a gun salute fired by the King's Troop, Royal Horse Artillery. The Queen enters the robing room before proceeding to the House of Lords. There, after the House of Commons has been summoned to the bar of the Upper House by the Gentleman Usher of the Black Rod, she reads the Queen's Speech summarising the government's intentions in the coming session. The ceremony is a reminder that although power has passed over the centuries from the monarch to the people's

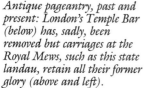

Antique pageantry, past and present: London's Temple Bar (below) has, sadly, been removed but carriages at the Royal Mews, such as this state landau, retain all their former glory (above and left).

elected representatives, ultimate authority in the land is still represented by the sovereign in Parliament.

London abounds in what the poet Milton called 'antique pageantry'. It is wrong to dismiss this as a mere colourful charade, for in most cases its roots go deep into the capital's history. Nor is public ceremony confined to royalty. The City of London, eager from early times to assert its power and independence, thrives on pageantry, and a small ceremony is still performed at the western boundary of the City whenever the sovereign wishes to cross it. At one time a barrier stood here known as Temple Bar – it was first described in 1293 when it consisted only of a chain between two wooden posts, but later a gate with a prison above it replaced it. Queen Elizabeth I passed through the gate on her way to St Paul's to give thanks for the victory over the Armada. She had to seek permission from the Lord Mayor before proceeding on her way, as does her successor Queen Elizabeth II to this day. At the site of Temple Bar, the Lord Mayor still offers his sword of state as a

demonstration of loyalty and thereafter it is carried at the head of any royal procession in the City to show that the sovereign is there by the Lord Mayor's permission and with his protection.

GOLD AND SILVER

During the Viennese carnival season of 1902, Princess Pauline Metternich decided to give a grand ball and engaged a military bandmaster called Franz Lehár to provide the music. It was a gold and silver ball: gold stars hung down from the ceiling, silver decorations adorned the walls, the women wore gold or silver dresses, and of course Lehár had composed a special Gold and Silver Waltz. Probably everyone was too busy talking or dancing to pay much attention when it was first played, but it created enough interest for Lehár to abandon the army and embark on a musical career which was to lead him to worldwide fame and fortune.

The creation of wealth, whether in gold, silver or any other form is the prime concern of the square mile of the city of London known as the City. Although I am as pleased to earn money as the next man, I have not the least idea how to make it, in the sense that City people do. The City therefore holds all the fascination for me of an impenetrable mystery, and an invitation to attend one of the City's innumerable ceremonial functions fills me with a mixture of wonder and apprehension.

When I was serving in the Royal Navy and subsequently in the Royal Naval Reserve, I never really learned how to handle a ceremonial sword correctly, and this proved a handicap when I was asked to take part in the Lord Mayor's Show. The Lord Mayor that year was himself an RNR officer and had decided to make a special feature of London's service affiliations. It was very pleasant to ride in an open carriage waving graciously to the assembled multitude, but not an easy task to alight from the carriage without getting my sword between my legs.

The Lord Mayor had a perfect right to command my participation in his show because, among his other functions, he is Admiral of the Port of London. He is the head of the oldest municipal corporation in the world, the holder of an office which dates back to the twelfth century. In 1215, before King John was persuaded to approve the more famous Magna Carta, he granted the citizens of London the right to elect their own chief magistrate, and since that time the Lord Mayor, as the embodiment of the City's jealously guarded rights and liberties, has occupied a position of great influence and distinction in Britain's national life. He signs himself with his surname only, in the manner of a peer; in the City he ranks before everybody except the monarch; he also has the right, when he wishes, to seek an audience with the sovereign through the Lord Chamberlain. At coronations it is his privilege to act as Chief Butler to the monarch, a role which requires that he provide himself with a special robe. This outlay occurs only at rare intervals, but each year the mayoralty involves very considerable personal expenditure on the part of the incumbent, in addition to the grant he receives from the City Corporation.

The authority of the Lord Mayor and Corporation extends over an area of 677 acres or slightly more than one square mile, from Temple Bar in the west to Aldgate and Tower Hill in the east, and from Smithfield and Moorfields southwards to the River Thames. Roman London must have been quite large, for it covered over half the area of the present City, and the wall around it, with six main gates, was three and a quarter miles in length. By the time William the Conqueror arrived in 1066, the citizens were powerful enough to warrant the building of the Tower of London just outside the eastern wall to keep an eye on their activities, while William also thought fit to placate them with a charter guaranteeing their rights.

The City emblem on a lamp-post signifies that you are within the Square Mile, one of Europe's major financial centres.

Sir Christopher Wren's Monument (below), tallest isolated stone column in the world, whose plaque (right) records the progress of the Great Fire of 1666.

From its earliest days, London was a centre of business activities, but a significant step for the City itself was the building of an exchange by Sir Thomas Gresham in the 1560s. Sir Thomas had been appointed King's Merchant at Antwerp, an office which virtually made him ambassador to Europe, and he was so impressed with the bourse in that city that he decided London should have a similar trading centre. On 23rd January 1570, Queen Elizabeth I dined with Gresham, and afterwards gave permission for the new bourse 'by an herald and trumpet to be proclaimed the Royal Exchange, and so to be called from henceforth and not otherwise'.

Two terrible events of the 1660s had a great effect on the subsequent shape of London. The first began at Christmas 1664, when a certain Dr Nathaniel Hodges 'was called to a young man in a fever who had two Risings about the bigness of a nutmeg, one on each thigh'. These swellings were the initial signs of a plague caused by Norwegian brown rats which in the course of the next eighteen months was to kill some 100,000 Londoners.

The second calamity was the Great Fire, later to be commemorated by Sir

Christopher Wren's Monument, the tallest isolated stone column in the world. The Latin inscription reads: 'In the year of Christ 1666, on 2 September, at a distance eastward from this place of 202 feet, which is the height of this column, a fire broke out in the dead of night which, the wind blowing, devoured even distant buildings and rushed devastating through every quarter with astonishing swiftness and noise. On the third day, at the bidding, we may well believe, of heaven, the fatal fire stayed its course and everywhere died out'. At the point where the fire was extinguished there's a less well-known memorial. High up on the corner of Cock Lane and Giltspur Street, which was once known as Pie Corner, there's a statue of a fat boy – it's a kind of pun in stone, since the flames spread from Pudding Lane to Pie Corner.

Fortunately for posterity, one of the greatest diarists of all time, Samuel Pepys, was a resident of the City at the time of the Plague and the Fire. Pepys sent his wife to Woolwich during the Plague, but his official duties as Secretary to the Admiralty compelled him to remain despite the fact that Parliament was prorogued because so many members had gone away. Walking down a deserted Drury Lane on 'the hottest day that I ever felt in my life', Pepys saw house after house shuttered and marked with the plague sign: a crude red cross on the front door. He recorded attempts to fiddle the mortality figures, such as when the parish clerk of St Olave's, Hart Street, told him: 'There died nine this week, though I have returned only six.' He also described the results of what may have been a disastrous decision on the part of the Lord Mayor: on the suspicion that animals might be spreading the disease, some 40,000 dogs, and, according to Pepys's calculations, perhaps five times as many cats, were destroyed within days. This made life easier for the real culprits, the rats, who carried infected fleas on their feet.

The Lord Mayor at the time of the outbreak of the Great Fire, Sir Thomas Bloodworth, did no better. When told of the fire, he went back to bed with the dismissive remark: 'Pish! A woman might

'Pie Corner', and the fat boy marks the point where the Great Fire was put out.

piss it out.' The next morning, according to Pepys, 300 houses, half London Bridge and several churches had disappeared. Pepys was bidden by the king to tell the Lord Mayor to pull down houses in the path of the fire, but Bloodworth was at his wits' end. 'I am spent, people will not obey me,' he told Pepys pathetically, 'I have been pulling down houses, but the fire overtakes us faster than we can do it.' While the navy was brought in to blow up streets with gunpowder, Pepys found a boat to remove his furniture downstream, and he managed to bury his wine and parmesan cheese in his garden. When the fire finally burned itself out, 87 churches, 44 livery halls and 13,200 houses had been destroyed, though astonishingly only nine lives were lost.

Kneller's portrait (above) of Sir Christopher Wren hangs today in the National Portrait Gallery. He rebuilt fifty-two churches after the Great Fire, proving that it's an ill wind that blows nobody any good. Martin Coles Harman's portrait appears, along with the puffins, on the currency he issued when he bought the island of Lundy (above, right).

One casualty of the Fire was Gresham's Royal Exchange. Another, of course, was St Paul's Cathedral. The thirty-one year old professor of astronomy at Oxford, Christopher Wren, had been asked to survey the old cathedral in 1663 and to suggest how to repair it. How badly it required renovation can be judged from Pepys's description of 'a miserable sight of Paul's church, with all the roofs fallen and the body of the quire fallen into St Faith's'. From the first Wren had wanted to rebuild the cathedral, and the Fire gave him the chance to create his masterwork. This extraordinary genius – scientist, mathematician and astronomer – who did not turn to architecture until he was thirty, left his mark on London in other ways too. He rebuilt a total of fifty-two City churches after the Great Fire, giving them an assortment of towers and spires which greatly added to the appeal of London's skyline – until the tower

blocks almost obliterated them. Wren's legacy to London could have been even greater if his master plan for the redevelopment of the City after the Great Fire had been accepted; but, along with another plan submitted by John Evelyn, it was rejected on the grounds that such schemes were inappropriate for a commercial city.

The air raids of the Second World War caused destruction on an even greater scale than the Great Fire and, when the war was over, the chance to re-plan the City was again missed. No coherent overall scheme was adopted, and the result is the architectural anarchy of today.

One of the New York-style skyscrapers houses the Stock Exchange. It has the largest number of securities listed in the world and its activities have been a major factor in making London one of the world's most important financial centres. The stresses of city life are not generally thought to promote longevity, but one member of the Stock Exchange in former times, John Rive, lived to be 118. Another of the many colourful characters in the history of the Exchange was Martin Coles Harman, who purchased the island of Lundy for £16,000 and issued coins with his own portrait on them. Alas his Rock Investment Trust went into liquidation and Harman ended his career in prison.

The deregulation of the Stock Exchange in 1986 led to far-reaching changes in the way business is conducted in the City. The old distinction between jobbers, who bought and sold shares on their own account, and brokers, who bought and sold shares for their clients through a jobber, making a commission on the deal, has been swept away, and the jobbers and brokers have been replaced by market makers who operate from large dealing rooms. The Stock Exchange floor remains but is now occupied primarily by the Trade Options Market.

Many other exchanges still remain in the City. The London Commodity Exchange, for example, still deals in such items as coffee, cocoa, sugar and wool, while the chief commodity of the Baltic Exchange is freight – it is a market in ship and air cargo space, and also arranges the sale of about half the world's ships. The London Metal Exchange is the market for six metals, each of which is traded by 'open outcry' in two five-minute sessions daily. Gold, however, is traded in a separate bullion market where twice daily five members meet to fix the price. Each holds

Dighton's impression of eighteenth-century jobbers at work in the Stock Exchange (facing page, above) makes them look a good deal more villainous than their present-day equivalents, the traders at the Royal Exchange (above). The sale of about half the world's ships is arranged at the Baltic Exchange (facing page, below).

a small Union Jack which he raises or lowers to indicate whether he is willing to deal at the suggested price.

Since 1982 the London International Financial Futures Exchange, housed in the Royal Exchange building, has played an ever-growing role in the market. No doubt its affairs are conducted with calm efficiency behind the scenes, but in the 'pit' on the floor of the exchange, chaos appears to prevail, with the traders yelling their orders (which is what 'open outcry' amounts to) and making a variety of hand signals whose meaning is only apparent to those in the know.

The City presents a fascinating contrast between the most advanced and sophisticated trading techniques and an elaborate respect for tradition. The events surrounding the election of the Lord Mayor on Michaelmas Day (29th September) are full of antique references. The chosen candidate is approved unanimously by the court of aldermen with cries of 'All'; the second in line is

consoled with shouts of 'Next year'. The Lord Mayor-elect must then seek the approval of the monarch and 'swear fealty', a procedure dating back to the charter granted to the City in 1215 by King John. Nowadays the Lord Mayor swears his oath of office before the judges of the Queen's Bench at the law courts in the Strand, and it is this ceremony which gives rise to the procession known as the Lord Mayor's Show.

For centuries the show has provided the cue for spectacular pageantry, not least in the days when the oath was taken at Westminster and the procession went by water – successive mayors vied with each other in the extravagance of the event. In 1612, five artificial islands were created in the river 'artfully garnished with all manner of Indian fruit trees, drugges, spiceries and the like, the middle island having a faire castle especially beautified' whilst, in 1602, after the Lord Mayor had returned to St Paul's Wharf, the usual procession to the Guildhall even included 'a lyon and a cammell'. There is a vivid description of the procession of 1575 which included a 'Pageant of Triumph richly decked' preceded by a 'set of hautboys playing and after them, certain whifflers in velvet coats and chains of gold with white staves in their hands'. The delightfully named whifflers were there to ensure nobody caused trouble.

It was traditional for the Lord Mayor to ride on horseback during the street procession until 1711, when Sir Gilbert Heathcote was unsaddled by a drunken flower girl. After that a coach was considered more becoming, and in 1757 the magnificent Lord Mayor's Coach we know today was constructed by Joseph Berry. It is now kept in the Museum of London, and brought out each year for the Lord Mayor's Show. Its panels are decorated with elaborate paintings

The Lord Mayor's Coach used today (left and facing page, below) was built in 1757. The print (above) is a view of Cheapside on Lord Mayor's Day 1761, and you can just about see the coach in the middle of the mêlée. The procession is still an excuse for having a jolly good time (facing page, above).

attributed to Giovanni Cipriani, and one of them presents in symbolic form the essential life style of the square mile: the Genius of the City is shown greeting Riches and Plenty, who are pouring fruit and money into her lap, and below, attended by Neptune, the Genius is receiving representatives of Trade and Commerce.

Nowadays, the Lord Mayor customarily uses the show to announce the 'theme' for his year of office and he or she is then in a position to draw the nation's attention to important issues and can often take the lead in raising large sums for charity. Recent themes have been 'Natural Resources and the Environment' and 'Leadership and Youth' and the first woman Lord Mayor, Dame Mary Donaldson, who was elected in 1983, chose the theme 'People that Matter'.

The custom of the Lord Mayor's Banquet goes back almost as far as the mayoralty itself and, for over 400 years, it

Fishmongers' Hall near London Bridge is the fourth hall to be built on the same site, and was opened in 1834. Playwright Ben Travers, famous for his Aldwych farces, was once Prime Warden of the Fishmongers' Guild.

has been held in the Guildhall. Much of the ancient structure of the building, including the medieval crypt, survived the fire caused by the Blitz in December 1940. It remains the centre of civic government, as it no doubt was in 1192 when the first mayor was installed in a building on the present site. In the hall itself, a pair of ugly nine-foot high limewood twins look down upon the hall and serve to recall history so ancient that it merges into myth. These are modern reconstructions of the giants Gog and Magog, around whom a variety of legends revolve. A twelfth-century historian related that Britain was once inhabited by a race of giants who were defeated in about 1200 BC by an army of Trojan invaders. The Trojan general, Corineus, was made ruler of Cornwall and, after killing every other giant in the district, he wrestled with the twelve-foot Goliath Gogmagog and succeeded in throwing him into the sea. In Elizabethan times, two figures called Corineus and Gogmagog were carried in City processions before Corineus somehow disappeared and Gogmagog was split in two. The story then arose that Gog and Magog were two giants captured by the Trojan general Brutus and made to

serve as door porters in his palace which stood on the present site of Guildhall. But the truth is that no one seems to know anything for certain about these two rather sinister figures, one armed with a spiked ball on a chain, and the other with a shield and spear.

When the Great Hall was completed in the fifteenth century it was larger than any other hall in the country with the sole exception of Westminster Hall. It was the scene of great events such as the trial of Lady Jane Grey in 1553, and it is here that the Court of Common Council meets to elect the sheriffs and the Lord Mayor. The court is composed of the liverymen of the City companies. These extraordinary institutions have demonstrated a remarkable talent for survival from their origins in the craft guilds of medieval times. Amongst the earliest companies were the Weavers, Clothworkers, Cordwainers, Fishmongers, Fletchers and Loriners. Nowadays it's a little known fact that the Cordwainers made articles out of Cordoba goatskin leather, that the Fletchers ruled the market in arrows, once they had broken away from the Bowyers, or that the Loriners made and sold bridles, stirrups, bits and other metal parts for harness. But

The plane tree marks the spot where seditious books used to be burnt behind Stationers' Hall.

Even today some companies exercise their ancient functions: thus all fish coming into London must first be inspected by officials of the Fishmongers' Company, while the Goldsmiths are still responsible, as they have been since 1248, for determining that the precious metal content of the coin of the realm does not fall below the legally prescribed minimum, an activity symbolised by the Trial of the Pyx (or Mint box) held annually in Goldsmiths' Hall. Other companies have lost their ancient monopolies. The Stationers' Company no longer has the sole right of printing outside the universities of Oxford and Cambridge, and the days are long past when seditious books were burned in the courtyard behind Stationers' Hall on a spot now marked by a plane tree. Nowadays all the City companies are involved in charity work of one kind or another, and many a socially useful project would not get started without their generosity.

After reaching a low point in terms of numbers and influence in the mid-nineteenth century, the companies have made a startling comeback, finding practical new roles in the twentieth century. Their total number now exceeds 100 and continues to grow, for new companies are still being formed reflecting modern crafts, such as the Air Pilots' and Air Navigators' Guild, composed entirely of professional airmen.

In medieval times, there were vicious quarrels over precedence among the companies: the Goldsmiths and Taylors became involved in a pitched battle in 1267, with Clothworkers and Cordwainers joining in, and in 1340 there was a similar set-to between the Fishmongers and Skinners. On both occasions the ring-leaders were hanged.

At one time all the companies would have had their own headquarters, but in the course of history many of these have disappeared and now only some thirty remain, many of great magnificence. Musical entertainments are often held in them, which is why I have had the chance to admire, among others, the splendours of Goldsmiths' Hall and the Fishmongers' Hall. Many halls had to be rebuilt after

the companies bearing these names today, and many others just as intriguing, such as the Horners and Pattenmakers, the Girdlers, Curriers and Upholders, are as active now as they ever were, often supporting research, development and educational projects in the modern equivalents of their ancient trades or 'mysteries'. To take one example, the Cordwainers support a technical college which bears their name and subscribe, as many other City companies do, to the City and Guilds of London Institute and the City University.

the ravages of the Blitz, but one which survived largely unscathed is that of the Vintners in Upper Thames Street. This company is particularly fascinating since it shares with the Dyers and the Crown the ownership of all swans on the Thames, and takes part in the annual swan–upping voyage in July when all cygnets on the river are numbered and some marked with nicks on the beak: the Vintners' swans are marked with two nicks, the Dyers' swans with one nick and those belonging to the Queen are left unmarked.

All the companies have individual traditions, and generally recall some aspect of the past. When the Vintners' Company walk in procession to the church of St. James's Garlickhythe following the election of their officials, a wine porter wearing a white smock and top hat goes before them sweeping the road clear with a broom – a tradition founded in necessity when the streets were full of mire and filth. The Clothworkers on the other hand have a drinking tradition which is entirely their own: the waiter will ask 'Do you dine, Sir (or Madam), with Alderman or Lady Cooper?' In fact he is offering a choice of brandy or gin, and the phrase recalls an incident in the eighteenth century when a certain Alderman Cooper dropped dead on his return home from a Clothworkers' dinner as a result, his wife considered, of drinking too much brandy. When Lady Cooper died, she left money in her will to provide gin for the company's guests, as she thought this preferable to the fatal brandy.

As my father was a plasterer by trade, I had the honour of being invited to become a liveryman of the Plaisterers' Company. Founded in 1501, its headquarters at one time was a hall designed by Sir Christopher Wren, but this was

There is more fine plate and jewellery at Goldsmiths' Hall (above and above,left) than there is anywhere else in the country. Another lavish showcase for the work of its guild's craftsmen is the Plaisterers' Hall, opened in 1972 and decorated with fine plasterwork (facing page, below and far right).

*Members of the Vintners'
Company on their way to
Garlick Hill in the 1930s.*

burned down in 1882 and the company is now housed in one of the finest of the modern halls. Opened in 1972, it is decorated, as might be expected, with particularly fine plasterwork.

Of all the quaint City company names, I particularly like the Gold and Silver Wyre Drawers. Their craft was the drawing of gold-coated silver wire thread through brocade fabric; it was also required in the making of uniforms, and is still in limited demand. But apart from its craft connections, the company, like all the others in the City, gives periodic banquets and I was once asked to speak at one of these, held in the grandeur of the Lord Mayor's official residence, the Mansion House.

Built in 1739, not long before the first performance of Handel's *Messiah,* the Mansion House has been described as 'a kind of Hallelujah Chorus in stone'. The public rooms are imposing, and the central Egyptian Hall is of palatial splendour, though its acoustic properties are far from ideal. On the second floor is the Ball

The eighteenth-century Egyptian Hall at the Mansion House (left), designed by the elder George Dance, and T.H. Shepherd's impression of a banquet there in the 1840s (facing page). I hope that none of the guests had occasion to sample the dubious comforts of one of the Mansion House's cells (below).

Room, originally known as the dancing gallery. Above the public rooms are the Lord Mayor's private apartments – though even these are used for entertaining during his year of office. His leisure time is very restricted, for he has an incessant round of engagements, organised by a small staff which resembles that of the royal household.

The Lord Mayor is also chief magistrate of the City, so the Mansion House serves as a police court. It is the only private residence in London to be equipped with cells, ten for men and one for women, which is known from its shape as 'the birdcage'. One Lord Mayor fell foul of the law during his term of office, at least according to his own estimation: in

1795, Lord Mayor Curtis, with Gilbertian severity, fined himself five shillings for failing to keep the streets clean, adding the rider that he hoped it would be a warning to himself.

Another offending Lord Mayor was Sir Robert Knollys who held office in 1346. During his year he, or according to some accounts, his wife, built a small bridge known as the fruit bridge across Seething Lane to connect two of his properties. Unfortunately he neglected to obtain the proper permission and was fined, in perpetuity, one freshly plucked rose. Each year, on the 24th June, the Lord Mayor is still presented with the Knollys Rose by Sir Robert Knollys's descendants.

Opposite the Mansion House is the fortress-like Bank of England originally designed by Sir John Soane in 1788 but substantially rebuilt in the 1930s. For almost two centuries, following the Gordon riots of 1780 when the Bank was threatened by a mob, the building was guarded every night by the 'Bank Picquet', usually drawn from the Guards detachments on duty in London. The officer and a guest of his choosing were allowed the privilege of sending out for their dinner at the Bank's expense – though other ranks had to bring sandwiches. The Guard was discontinued in 1973 and the premises have since been guarded at night by electronic scanners.

There's an interesting story about the Bank of England's security for it was severely threatened in 1836. The directors received an anonymous note from a man who claimed to have found a way into the bullion room, and sent papers to prove it. The note instructed the directors to meet him in the bullion vaults in the middle of the night and there, on the stroke of midnight, a flagstone lifted and a man emerged. He explained that, while working in the sewers, he had come across a small disused tunnel which led to the vaults. He was liberally rewarded for his honesty and the tunnel was filled in.

There are a number of other legendary figures in the Bank's history. The cashier Abraham Newland was so conscientious that he slept at the Bank every night for twenty-five years and signed every banknote in person. Then there was the director known as 'J.M.' who used to dress at night as a navvy and scour the

streets of Whitechapel hoping to catch Jack the Ripper. Kenneth Grahame, famous for his book *The Wind in the Willows,* was a secretary at the Bank for ten years, and Montague Norman, elected Governor of the Bank in 1920, is best known for meeting a curious end: he tripped over a sitting cow on the way home one dark night and sustained injuries which proved fatal.

The Bank's nickname of 'The Old Lady of Threadneedle Street' derives from a remark of Sheridan's in the House of Commons in 1797, when he referred to it as 'an elderly lady in the city of great credit and long standing'; but the Bank is also said to be haunted by two female ghosts, either of which could merit the title. One is a black-habited nun, and the other is Sarah Whitehead, sister of a man who was found guilty of forgery in 1811 and executed. Sarah was unhinged by the shock, and every day for twenty-five years she appeared at the Bank to ask for her brother. There is a statue of 'The Old Lady' holding a model of the building on her knees over the Threadneedle Street entrance of the Bank of England.

The Bank of England originated with an Act of Parliament in 1694 which set up the National Debt as a means of finding money for war. A sum of £1,500,000 was raised from 633 subscribers who were rewarded with interest paid by the government at the rate of eight per cent, the interest being derived from 'Rates and Duties upon the Tunnage of Ships and Vessels and upon Beer, Ale and other liquors'. The idea of an imposition of duties as a means of raising revenue occurred very early on to Britain's rulers. King

Ethelred levied the first known customs duty in AD 979, and in 1382 the first Custom House was built near the site of the present building, with its imposing 488-foot frontage facing the river in Lower Thames Street.

The fortress-like Bank of England (below), and the Old Lady herself (above, left) over the Threadneedle Street entrance. Kenneth Grahame (above) was a secretary there for ten years.

South view of the original Custom House, burnt down in the Great Fire, as it was in 1663.

Lombard Street (below, left) and the historic signs associated with the many banks there. The sign of the grasshopper (below) belongs to Martin's, first established in Lombard Street as a goldsmith's in 1563.

From Mansion House to Grace-church Street runs Lombard Street; it is almost entirely devoted to banks and each one displays the sign historically associated with it. There is, for example, the eagle of Barclays, the cat and fiddle of the Commercial Bank of Scotland and the artichoke of Alexander's. The grasshopper of Martin's is the sign for what is said to be the oldest of this group of banks, established in Lombard Street as a gold-smith's business in 1563. Sir Francis Child, who was Lord Mayor in 1698, is credited with being the founder of the banking profession since he was the first banker to abandon the goldsmith's craft and devote himself entirely to finance.

While some vestiges of the City's old banking traditions still remain, the importance of London as a financial centre today is perhaps best symbolised by the National Westminster Tower in Bishopsgate. Completed in 1980, its fifty-two storeys rise to a height of 600 feet, making it the tallest building in Europe at the time of its completion. Fortunately there were no fatalities during the construction of this huge edifice, but a building in the City's Philpot Lane has a carving of two mice on it which may commemorate the death of a workman. It's said that one craftsman accused another of eating his sandwiches and pushed him off the roof, only to discover that the thief was a mouse.

The City of London has been described as 'essentially one vast market place' but in the Blackfriars pub – whose name, like that of Blackfriars Station, commemorates a thirteenth century Dominican monastery destroyed in the Great Fire – there's an art

Art nouveau mosaics at the Blackfriars pub (left and below) welcome patrons with uplifting moral sentiments, while the carved mice (above) are reminders of the folly of jumping to conclusions.

nouveau mosaic with inscriptions, two of which comment neatly on the City's twin preoccupations with wealth and traditional pomp. One reads 'Finery is Foolery' and the other 'Contentment surpasses riches'.

BOW AND OTHER BELLS

The game of oranges and lemons featured at nearly every children's party when I was young, so we were all familiar with the various messages conveyed by the bells of the city churches in the old nursery rhyme.

When will you pay me?
Say the bells of Old Bailey;

When I grow rich,
Say the bells at Shoreditch;

Pray when will that be?
Say the bells of Stepney;

I'm sure I don't know,
Says the great bell at Bow.

I also became accustomed to the sound of Bow bells as an interval signal on the radio long before I had to put them on the air as a BBC radio announcer. It was therefore almost with a sense of home-coming that I went to the famous church of St Mary-le-Bow in Cheapside in the 1970s to take part in one of the popular lunchtime dialogues held there. There's been a church on the site since Norman times, and its close links with the very identity of London date back to 1492.

In that same year, a City mercer provided for the bells of the church of St Mary-le-Bow to be rung every night at nine o'clock and the tradition grew up that only those who could hear the peal deserved to be called a cockney – that is, a true Londoner. Nowadays the cockney spirit has come to be admired, but it was not always so. The word derives from the middle English *cokeney,* meaning a misshapen egg, and in earlier times it meant an effeminate person or a simpleton: country folk used the word to describe city dwellers because they considered them to be weaklings.

Whether admirable or not, cockneys have long had the sound of bells ringing in their ears – a notable enrichment of the London scene to those who agree with Charles Lamb that they offer 'the music nighest bordering upon heaven', or with Coleridge's more modest claim that bells are 'the poor man's only music'. Though some have taken the view that music in

church is an unnecessary and frivolous appendage, generally speaking it has been an integral part of Christian worship down the centuries, and London's churches, great and small, have long played a great part in the musical life of the capital. The church of St Sepulchre in Holborn Viaduct is known as the Musicians' Church, and although it has close connections with several City companies, among them the Cordwainers and the Cutlers, who hold annual services there, the chief association is with the Worshipful Company of Musicians. The festival dedicated to the patron saint of music, St Cecilia, is held here in November, with music provided by the combined choirs of St Paul's Cathedral, Westminster Abbey, Canterbury Cathedral and the Chapel Royal. Many of the kneelers in the church are embroidered with musical motifs, and some commemorate famous musicians such as Dennis Brain, Dame Myra Hess, Kathleen Ferrier and Sir Edward Elgar,

Gutted during the Great Fire of London (1666), the Church of the Holy Sepulchre retains its original Gothic walls but has a seventeenth-century interior.

St Sepulchre's – The Musicians' Church – honours Bach, Handel, Byrd and Purcell in one of its stained-glass windows (above), beneath which are buried the ashes of Sir Henry Wood (below).

The organ, once played by the founder of the promenade concerts (above), and kneelers (below) are further reminders of this church's rich musical tradition.

while the stained glass windows honour, among others, the memory of Sir Malcolm Sargent, John Ireland and Dame Nellie Melba. The ashes of the founding conductor of the Proms, Sir Henry Wood, are buried near the organ that he played when he first came to the church as assistant organist at the age of fourteen, and each year a special service is held in St Sepulchre's on the Sunday after the Last Night of the Proms.

The organ, a fine instrument originally built in the seventeenth century by Renatus Harris, was probably played by Handel and certainly by Mendelssohn. On the beautiful casing, the initials C.R. can be seen; they stand for Carolus Rex and were put there in the time of King Charles II, as were the carvings on the pair of mahogany pulpits, some of which are thought to be by Grinling Gibbons. The work of this astonishingly accomplished craftsman can be seen in a number of City churches, thanks to a long period of collaboration with Sir Christopher Wren which came about through an introduction from John Evelyn.

There can be no London school child who has not explored the acoustic mystery of the Whispering Gallery in Wren's supreme masterpiece. I certainly did, at a very early age, and I have never ceased to find St Paul's thrilling. The acoustic prop-

erties of the cathedral as a whole do present problems, but the glorious blur produced by its reverberations can actually enhance the effect of certain works. I'm thinking particularly of a televised performance of Berlioz's mightly *Requiem*, when four brass bands were played at the four corners of the building creating a truly shattering summons to the Seat of Judgement. And of course, as a setting for great state events, such as the wedding of the Prince and Princess of Wales in 1981 and occasions of national thanksgiving or mourning, the cathedral is unparalleled.

The history of St Paul's dates back to a roman temple to Diana that once crowned the top of what is now Ludgate Hill. Fire later destroyed two, and the Vikings the third, of three cathedrals which subsequently stood on the site before the arrival of the Normans. Built of Caen stone brought across the sea and up

Wren was paid (late) a miserly £200 a year for the privilege of designing – and supervising the construction of – St Paul's Cathedral. I visited the Whispering Gallery at a very early age.

Wenceslas Holler's 1656 depiction of the Norman St Paul's, the church destroyed in the Great Fire (above), and John Donne's statue which survived (right).

the Thames, the Norman building was larger and higher than the present cathedral and was topped by the tallest spire ever built. The precincts of the cathedral, which accommodated another church and chapel, a school and a law college among other buildings, were enclosed by a wall whose course ran along Creed Lane, Ave Maria Lane, Paternoster Row, Old Change and Carter Lane. Within the precincts was the Jesus Bell Tower whose great bell summoned the citizens of London to a compulsory assembly three times a year. The south-west tower of the present St Paul's houses that bell's successor, Great Tom, which sounds the hour and tolls the deaths of members of the royal family, bishops of London, deans of St Paul's and the Lord Mayor, should he die in office.

During the Reformation, the nave was used 'as a common thoroughfare between Carter Lane and Paternoster Row'. There was a fair in the middle at one stage, where horses were bought and sold, servants hired and lawyers met their clients. The tombs and font were used as shop counters, and it is said that a standard trading measurement, the foot, was taken from the carved foot of Algar, the first prebendary of Islington. Cromwell used the cathedral as a cavalry barracks and by the middle of the seventeenth century it was a near ruin.

The only statue to survive the Great Fire was of the poet John Donne and it now stands in the south choir aisle. After frightening the inhabitants of Ludgate Hill by using gunpowder to destroy the remaining fabric, Wren employed battering rams to complete the task that the Fire began. A royal warrant for the new cathedral was issued in 1675 on the basis of Wren's third design, though this was considerably modified in the course of the thirty-five years it took to complete the cathedral. During that time an impatient Parliament cut the architect's salary in half, and Wren did not receive his arrears until 1711, when he was nearly eighty years of age.

Although engaged in building over fifty City churches after the Fire, Wren made a point of checking on the progress at St Paul's at least once a week and, as the great dome neared completion, he was even hauled up to the lantern in a basket. The great architect, who died at the age of ninety-one, was one of the first people to be buried in the crypt of St Paul's and his epitaph there reads: *Lector, si monumentum requiris, circumspice* (Reader, if you want a memorial, look around you).

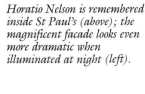

After lying in state in the Painted Hall at Greenwich, the body of Lord Nelson was also brought to St Paul's for burial. His imposing tomb was originally designed for Cardinal Wolsey but by order of Henry VIII it was never used

Horatio Nelson is remembered inside St Paul's (above); the magnificent facade looks even more dramatic when illuminated at night (left).

Westminster Abbey (above) has been the setting for the coronation of every British monarch since William the Conqueror.

until it was rescued from centuries of neglect at Windsor for the funeral of Britain's greatest naval hero.

A team of vigilant volunteers, St Paul's Watch, saved St Paul's from serious damage in the Blitz of the Second World War, though a bomb did destroy the high altar. The present altar commemorates the Commonwealth dead of both world wars and behind it is the American chapel, a memorial to the American citizens based in this country who died in the Second World War.

The other great ecclesiastical object of school outings in London is, of course, Westminster Abbey, and I was certainly taken there at an early age to gape at the tombs and monuments which commemorate so many of the great figures of British history. Since William the Conqueror was crowned in it on Christmas Day 1066 the abbey has been the setting for every royal coronation, but the royal connection goes back even further. King Sebert of the East Saxons is said to have built a church there in the seventh century on what was then a marshy area surrounded by ditches known as Thorney Island and a charter now preserved at the abbey records that, in AD 785, King Offa of Mercia granted land to 'St Peter and the needy people of God in Thorney, in this terrible place which is called Westminster'. In 1065 the new church, built by Edward the Confessor and dedicated to St Peter, was consecrated, but only eight days later he died and was buried before the high altar. After half a century he was canonised, and thereafter successive monarchs vied in their efforts to endow, enlarge and beautify the abbey created by the royal saint. One of the last major additions to the structure was the exquisite chapel built by King Henry VII in honour of the Virgin Mary, where the king himself lies buried with his queen. The fan vaulting here is of great beauty: the roof of the chapel, wrote Washington Irving, 'has the wonderful minuteness and airy security of a cobweb'.

The monastery was dissolved in 1540 at the time of the Reformation, but Westminster Abbey's royal associations saved it from wanton destruction. Some of the abbey's revenues, however, were diverted to St Paul's Cathedral, a transaction which is the origin of the phrase 'robbing Peter to pay Paul'. Later Cromwell's army camped in the abbey, broke down the altar rails and stood smoking tobacco around the altar itself.

Westminster Abbey is packed with monuments to royal and other notable personages and curious stories concerning them abound. King Edward I was buried in a very simple tomb chest so that his body could be taken out and the flesh removed, should his bones be required to inspire an army invading Scotland. The body of Edward I's first wife, Eleanor, was buried here after its journey south from Nottinghamshire where she died: each resting place was marked by a cross, the last of them at London's Charing Cross. From a hole in the tomb of King Richard II, a boy at Westminster School once removed the royal jawbone, though it was later restored.

Many statesmen, scientists and soldiers, actors, inventors and writers are

The last of twelve crosses – at Charing Cross – marks Queen Eleanor's punultimate resting place on her journey to Westminster for burial.

Among those remembered in Westminster Abbey are the Unknown Warrior (below), dramatist Ben Jonson, buried upright (below, right), and Elizabethan poet Edmond Spencer (bottom, right).

either buried or remembered by memorials in Westminster Abbey, but Godfrey Kneller is the only painter to be commemorated there, though his grave is elsewhere. 'By God', he said on his deathbed, 'I will not be buried in Westminster . . . they do bury fools there!' Ben Jonson, who lived in the abbey precincts, raised no objection to being buried near Geoffrey Chaucer in what became known as 'Poet's Corner', though he modestly considered a full-size grave unnecessarily large for him. 'Two feet by two feet will do for all I want', he told the dean and so Jonson was buried upright. He is one of a glorious company of writers remembered in Westminster Abbey which includes Milton, Wordsworth and Tennyson, Jane Austen, Thomas Hardy, T.S. Eliot and W.H. Auden.

One of the few foreigners to have a memorial in Westminster Abbey is Franklin D. Roosevelt; he has a plaque on the wall of the nave not far from the tomb of the Unknown Warrior, the most moving of all the abbey's memorials. In soil from the battlefields of the First World War lies an anonymous body, brought back from France and buried here as a symbol of the tens of thousands of ordinary people who perished in that appalling massacre.

Countless thousands of visitors stream through the abbey every day to wonder at what Joseph Addison called 'this magazine of mortality'. Whenever Edmund Burke entered the building he 'felt a kind of awe', and to him 'the very silence seemed sacred'. But a character in G.K. Chesterton's story *The Man Who Knew Too Much* was less favourably impressed. 'He was', wrote Chesterton, 'solidly dazed by Westminster Abbey, which is not unnatural since that Church became the lumber-room of the larger and less successful statuary of the eighteenth century'.

Chesterton, as a Roman Catholic, would have felt more at home in Westminster Cathedral, half a mile down Victoria Street from the abbey. Dispossessed of their ancient buildings by King Henry VIII at the time of the Reformation, Roman Catholics in Britain had to wait 300 years before diocesan bishops were again appointed to this country by the Pope. When the first archbishop of Westminster, Cardinal Wiseman, died in 1865, funds were raised towards the construction of a cathedral, though the fabric was not completed until nearly forty years later in 1903. The interior still remains

There are over 3300 graves and around 400 monuments in Westminster Abbey. These are in the nave.

The Italian-Byzantine style of Westminster Cathedral, by architect J F Bentley, is unique in all of London. Also remarkable is the 273-foot high campanile and lavish interior, complete with the widest nave in England.

unfinished though some parts of the brick structure are clothed in beautiful marble brought from quarries all over the world.

The music at both Westminster Abbey and Cathedral is of the very highest standard. In the abbey it is a peaceful and restoring experience to sit in the nave during evensong, when the movement of sightseers is stopped; and in the cathedral the sound of the choir is no less inspiring. Here Sir Edward Elgar conducted the first London performance of his oratorio *The Dream of Gerontius,* a setting of words by Cardinal Newman. The Grand Organ

is unique among cathedral organs in Britain, for a dual control system enables it to be played from either end of the building. The building lends itself to spectacle, and on grand occasions the ceremonial can have almost theatrical splendour. A friend of mine, a Roman Catholic priest, was sub-administrator of Westminster Cathedral for a time, and sometimes invited me to visit him in the clergy house at the rear of the building. When I asked exactly where to meet him, he would say 'Oh, come to the stage door'. When he died I was invited to read a lesson at his requiem mass, a moving and memorable experience.

The memory of St Edward the Confessor, who founded Westminster Abbey, is no less honoured at the cathedral. The campanile is dedicated to him, and the single bell, the gift of Gwendolen, Duchess of Norfolk in 1910, is even named 'Edward' – it bears the inscription 'St Edward, pray for England'.

The monks of Westminster Abbey used to work in their convent garden near what is now Trafalgar Square, and a small chapel was built for them in the eleventh century. On the site now stands the church of St Martin-in-the-Fields, sometimes called the royal parish church. It was built in 1726 by the Scottish architect James Gibbs, and King George II was its first churchwarden. In the eighteenth century St Martin's was the most fashionable church in London, with pews rented for the then large sum of ten pounds a year, and a London paper commented that St Martin's could produce 'as handsome a show of white hands, diamond rings, pretty snuff boxes and gilt prayer books as any Cathedral'. Writing in his journal on 25th July 1842, John Adolphus told a story rather at the expense of St Martin's, fashionable though it was: 'Opie was divorced from his first wife and Godwin was an infidel. They were walking together near St Martin's church. "Ha!" said Opie, "I was married in that church." "Indeed!" said Godwin, "and I was christened in it." "It is not a good shop," replied Opie, "their work don't last!" '

The design of St Martin's has been widely copied, especially in America, and

crowds come to admire it, as well as to take part in the numerous special services held in the church. It is dedicated to St Martin of Tours and one of his deeds of charity, that of sharing his cloak with a beggar, is depicted on the church door handles and on lamp posts in the vicinity. In recent years St Martin's has returned to the principles of its patron saint by losing its reputation as the resort of fashion in favour of providing practical help for London's poor and dispossessed. The Rev Dick Sheppard, who was vicar from 1914 to 1927, established a refuge for down-and-outs in the crypt which continued operating until 1945, and the spirit of his work has continued. Incidentally, it was from St Martin-in-the-Fields in 1924 that the first broadcast church service came.

The much-copied church of St Martin-in-the-Fields (left), whose crypt contained 3000 coffins – and their occupants – by the end of the nineteenth century. The coffins are now in Camden Town cemetery; the crypt is a community centre and restaurant (right). St Martin's (below) was the venue for the first broadcast church service.

Nowadays the parish church of the BBC is undoubtedly All Souls Langham Place. Designed by John Nash, it must be one of the most successful churches in London, as it is always packed for Sunday services. It offers a graceful setting on other occasions too, such as the memorial services for well-known broadcasters which are held there from time to time.

All Souls occupies a focal point in Nash's town planning scheme, laid out in the time of King George IV, which extends from Piccadilly Circus to the terraces in Regent's Park. The church has a tall, fluted steeple, an architectural feature ridiculed in the contemporary press, which published cartoons of Nash impaled on the spike at the top.

One 1824 cartoonist's idea (above) of a suitable end for the architect of All Souls, Langham Place (right). The cartoon's caption (not shown) reads:

Providence sends meat,
The Devil sends cooks –
Parliament sends Funds –
But who sends the
    Architects?!!!

St Paul's, Covent Garden (below), where Samuel Pepys's visit to the first Punch and Judy show on 9th May 1662 is recorded on a wall-plaque (above).

It was my grandmother who first took me to All Souls Langham Place. She also showed me the church in which she was married: St Anne's Soho. This seventeenth century church was almost entirely destroyed by bombs in the Second World War, but on the west wall of the tower, which remains, there is a tablet with a sculptured crown which records the nearby grave of the king of Corsica. He was a certain Theodore, Baron Neuhoff, a German soldier of fortune who in exchange for giving military help to the Corsicans in the 1730s, demanded that they acknowledge him as their king. For some time he lived on the island in affluence with a private army, but when his funds ran out he came to London where he was arrested and imprisoned for debt. He only managed to get out by forfeiting to his creditors all his effects, chief among which was his claim to the Corsican throne. Thereafter he made his way to Soho where he lodged with a kindly tailor until he died three days later. His funeral expenses were paid by John Wright, an oilman of Compton Street, who said that he would like, for once, to pay the burial expenses of a king. Horace Walpole contributed a verse to the memorial tablet which reads:

*The grave, great teacher, to a level
   brings
Heroes and beggars, galley slaves and
   kings;
Fate pour'd its lessons on his living head,
Bestow'd a kingdom and denied him
   bread.*

As one who was from a very early age attracted to the stage, I was gratified when I learned that actors, like musicians, have a church of their own. In fact I know of two in London that have close connections with the theatre, and they are St Paul's Covent Garden and St Leonard's Shoreditch.

St Paul's is the better known – indeed it became world famous when the east portico was used to provide the setting for the opening scene of Bernard Shaw's *Pygmalion*. Leading actors frequently read the lessons at St Paul's, and theatrical people often choose to be baptised or married there. David Garrick attended services in the church, the ashes

of Ellen Terry were interred in one of its walls, and memorials commemorate many theatrical luminaries of the remote and recent past. John Wesley loved to deliver a sermon in St Paul's: 'It is' he wrote in 1784 'the largest and best constructed parish church I have preached in for several years, yet some hundreds were obliged to go away, not being able to get in.' There's nothing more gratifying than a full house, whether you're a famous preacher or a poor player.

Wesley's praise for the building might have surprised the man who paid for it. Francis Russell, third Earl of Bedford, wanted as much expense as possible to be spared and told Inigo Jones who designed the church that 'he would not have it much better than a barn.' 'Very well then,' replied Jones, 'you shall have the handsomest barn in England,' and that's what he delivered for £5000.

The fine portico has never been used as an entrance to the church, for it is at the

Another church with close theatrical connections is St Leonard's, Shoreditch. Today's visitors are reminded of the original church's strong links with the theatre by a plaque (below)

The Clerk's House

Actors of yesteryear were often treated as little more than rogues or vagabonds, and the stocks at St Leonard's still bear testimony to their public humiliation.

east end, and the authorities insisted the altar must be situated there in its usual place. On 9th May 1662, Samuel Pepys saw 'an Italian puppet play' in the portico; this was perhaps the first Punch and Judy show and is commemorated by a plaque on the church wall. The church has continuing associations with puppeteers, who hold an annual service in St Paul's, and outside in the Covent Garden piazza the Punch and Judy Fellowship stage an October festival.

By contrast, in the churchyard at St Leonard's Shoreditch, there's a reminder that actors in the past were often regarded as little better than rogues or vagabonds and were often punished as such. Carefully preserved in the churchyard are stocks and a whipping post where it's thought rascally members of the profession may well have been chastised – along with other offenders.

The present St Leonard's was built by George Dance the Elder in the 1730s, but its predecessor stood not far from London's first playhouse, the Theatre, erected in nearby Curtain Road by James Burbage. Burbage lies buried in the churchyard, and his two sons Cuthbert, who built the Globe Theatre in Southwark, and Richard, the famous tragedian who first played Hamlet and Richard III, are commemorated at the church. Henry VIII's jester Will Somers and the Elizabethan comedian Richard Tarlton are buried there too. Among those christened at St Leonard's was Charles Bradlaugh in 1833, but the effects did not last, for he became famous as an atheist who, when elected Member of Parliament for Northampton, refused repeatedly to take the necessary oath.

The first London church to make an impression on me was St Augustine's Kilburn. It was not far from where my grandmother lived and we often used to walk past it. I was impressed by its lofty spire and ring of bells, but did not realise then that it was a classic of Victorian church architecture. It was built by the Gothic revivalist John Loughborough Pearson who said of his work: 'it is my business to think what will bring people soonest to their knees'. In the case of St Augustine's, what he thought of was a design based on the cathedral at Albi in

south-west France; for acoustic reasons it is nowadays very attractive to recording producers, and has been used for programmes of appropriate music in the promenade concert season.

London's places of worship are so many and so various that I shall make no attempt to mention more than the small number which have interested me in one way or another. I have yet to venture into the magnificent mosque in Regent's Park, though I have often admired it from the outside, and the same is true of the Spanish and Portuguese synagogue in Duke's Place, which is England's oldest synagogue, founded in 1657 and rebuilt on its present site in 1701. All kinds of belief, and most national communities, seem to

St. Augustine's, Kilburn impressed me at an early age, though I had no idea then of its architectural importance.

England's oldest synagogue (left, in an early eighteenth-century engraving) is reached via the archway of Biba House on Bevis Marks (below).

have their own churches in London. There is a Greek Orthodox Cathedral in Moscow Road, Bayswater, and a Ukrainian Catholic Cathedral in Binney Street, both without organs, for Byzantine practice forbids instrumental music in church. There is a Chinese church in Chiltern Street, rented from the Welsh Methodists, and a Danish church in Regent's Park with a window donated by Queen Victoria. Americans have their own church in Tottenham Court Road; the Dutch church in Austin Friars has, beneath the communion table, an altar stone which dates back to the thirteenth century; the Swedes have two London churches, one in the West End and another for seamen down the river in Bermondsey, not far from the Finnish church, which is also a seamen's mission and a home from home for Finns in London.

An unusual experience for me was to attend a memorial service at the Friends' Meeting House in St Martin's Lane. The long periods of silence observed by the Quakers were deeply refreshing, and I found to my surprise that I was moved to speak quite spontaneously, as others did,

London residence of the Archbishop of Canterbury, Lambeth Palace.

of our departed friend. In quite a different vein, I once took part in a charity fund-raising concert in Lambeth Palace, the home of the Archbishop of Canterbury. Its origins date back to the twelfth century but on that occasion history took a back seat, for we managed to persuade the archbishop to join us in 'doing the Lambeth Walk'.

Interesting associations with the past lend colour to many of London's churches. James McNeill Whistler, the American born artist who immortalised London's river at Chelsea, lies buried with his wife in Chiswick parish churchyard while St Paul's, in nearby Hammersmith, has a particularly fascinating bust of King Charles I erected by Sir Nicholas Crisp.

Old Battersea Bridge (below), as seen by James McNeill Whistler. The artist is buried in Chiswick Parish Churchyard (below, left).

Nicholas Crisp, seen here temporarily embellished thanks to a student prank (above), still pays homage to his monarch in St Paul's Church, Battersea (right).
In St Mary's, Battersea (below, right), tiger-slayer Sir Edward Wynter is remembered in verse (below, centre); Turner's chair (below, left) is in the vestry.

He was so ardent a royalist that he gave instructions for his heart to be buried beneath the bust, and removed from its urn once a year to be refreshed with a glass of wine. This extraordinary ritual was solemnly carried out until the middle of the eighteenth century, when the urn was finally sealed.

Continuing down the river, the chapel built in 1528 by one of the most distinguished of the Catholic martyrs, Sir Thomas More, survived the Blitz at Chelsea Old Church. St Mary's Church at Battersea on the opposite bank has a monument to the East India merchant, Sir Edward Wynter, who died in 1685 and whose achievements are commemorated in verse. Apparently he crushed a tiger to death in his arms and routed forty mounted Moors single-handed. At the west end of St Mary's there's a chair in which the painter J.M.W. Turner used to sit and admire the sunsets he saw across the river. Further down the Thames at

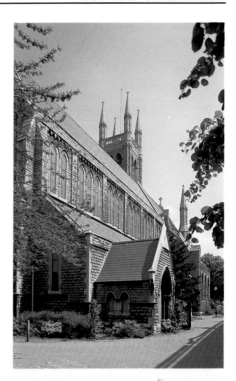

The tower of St Mary Magdalene's, Woolwich, is still there (left), though the semaphore signaller (above, seen in a 1796 engraving) is not.

Truncated caryatids with cast-iron cores (below) help support the roof of the Chuch of St Pancras.

Woolwich is the church of St Mary Magdalene which has close nautical connections: on top of the tower, in the days before the electric telegraph, there used to be a semaphore signalling apparatus. In a more mundane vein, St Mary's is said to have been the first church in England to install a restaurant and coffee bar within its walls.

Returning to central London, there's a reminder of the Acropolis at Athens in the Euston Road. Inspired by a fashionable passion for things Greek, father and son William and Henry Inwood designed the church of St Pancras in 1822. The tower is modelled on the octagonal Temple of the Winds in Athens, and the roof at the east end appears to be supported by caryatids (female figures) copied from the Erechtheum on the Acropolis. Henry Inwood made plaster casts of the originals which were turned into terracotta copies, but alas they proved too tall for the space they were due to occupy and a section had to be sliced out of their middles to make them fit. Furthermore, these truncated maidens could not support the weight of

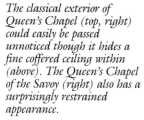

The classical exterior of Queen's Chapel (top, right) could easily be passed unnoticed though it hides a fine coffered ceiling within (above). The Queen's Chapel of the Savoy (right) also has a surprisingly restrained appearance.

the roof unaided: the terracotta was fixed in sections around cast iron columns running through their torsos.

Passers-by could not possibly fail to see the monumental church of St Pancras, but there are many quite tiny churches of great interest which could easily be passed unnoticed, among them two small royal chapels. The Queen's Chapel opposite St James's Palace was the first ecclesiastical building to be designed by Inigo Jones. Constructed between 1623 and 1627 for

Henrietta Maria, wife of King Charles I, this beautiful little church has a fine coffered ceiling and a fireplace in the West Gallery, which was originally the royal pew. The Queen's Chapel of the Savoy, near the Savoy Hotel, has since 1937 been the Chapel of the Royal Victorian Order, but in the eighteenth century it had a distinctly dubious reputation. In the 1750s the incumbent John Wilkinson performed illegal marriages there, advertising his services and pointing out to would-be clients that 'there were five private ways by land to this chapel and two by water'. Wilkinson married over 1500 couples and made nearly £2000 before the Watch arrived to arrest him. He fled from the chapel, discarding his surplice in flight, but was apprehended and sentenced to fourteen years transportation. Before the sentence could be implemented, however, he died of gout.

Most of the national press has now deserted Fleet Street, but the journalists' church, St Bride's, one of the finest achievements of Christopher Wren, remains. It was extensively damaged in the

Blitz, but this architectural tragedy provided a wonderful opportunity for archaeologists. In the crypt they discovered the remains of a Roman house and the skeleton of a Roman woman who had been given a Christian burial, as well as evidence that seven different churches had stood on that site between the sixth and seventeenth centuries. These were dedicated to St Bridget, whose feast day was the same as that of Brigit, the pre-Christian Celtic goddess of fertility. I wonder if Christopher Wren knew this when he designed the beautiful spire which was subsequently copied by a Fleet Street baker, Mr Rich, who thus invented tiered wedding cakes.

Another fascinating Fleet Street church is St Dunstan-in-the-West. Here Samuel Pepys, bored with the sermon, flirted with a girl who 'took pins out of her pocket to prick me if I should touch her again; which seeing I did forbear, and then fell to gaze upon another pretty maid in a pew close to me and did go about to take her by the hand, which she suffered a

Marble effigies of Knights Templar (top, facing page) testify to the origins of Temple Church, where they lie.

St Bride's, Fleet Street (far left), inspiration for Mr Rich's wedding cakes. Also in Fleet Street is St Dunstan-in-the-West (near left), proud owner of the only surviving statue of Elizabeth I. I rather like the sentiments quoted from Milton on the plaque (above), commemorating one of St Dunstan's organists.

Mendelssohn played the organ (above and below) in the Church of St Peter upon Cornhill in the 1840s.

little and then withdrew'. In a niche outside the church is what's said to be the only surviving statue of Queen Elizabeth I made in her lifetime.

The appointment of the Master to the Temple Church, not far away, remains the prerogative of the monarch. The church was originally built by the Knights Templar in the twelfth century, and it has been much altered since, by Wren among others, from its original circular form although this oldest part is still visible. One of the knights commemorated by Purbeck-marble effigies on the floor was Geoffrey Earl of Essex, although his body was not at first buried here. The earl had been excommunicated for bad behaviour, so his friends had his body encased in lead and strung up from a tree while awaiting absolution from the Pope. Standing as it does in the centre of the Inner and Middle Temple, this church now belongs to the lawyers, so much so that at one time they used to meet their clients in it. It also has a strong musical tradition for Sir George Thalben Ball was organist here for sixty years; and in former times the well known music publisher John Playford, who was clerk of the church, had a shop in the west porch were Pepys would go to buy the latest songs.

St Olave's, Hart Street, was Pepys's church and one of the few to survive the Great Fire. Its gateway is decorated – if that's the right word – by skulls and crossbones.

Another City church with musical associations is St Peter upon Cornhill, where Mendelssohn played the Father Smith organ in 1840 and again in 1842. Pepys' own parish church was St Olave's in Hart Street and he is buried with his wife in the nave. It used to have an outside stairway and a small gallery leading to the Navy Office in Seething Lane, so Pepys could go to church without getting wet. Charles Dickens, in his novel *The Uncommercial Traveller* gave St Olave's the name St Ghastly Grim because of the skulls and crossbones which adorn the gateway to the churchyard. Today, St Olave's, in common with other City churches, offers services and musical entertainments to office workers and others during weekday lunchtimes.

A great attraction which drew crowds of several hundreds for many years was the series of lunchtime dialogues held at the church of St Mary-le-Bow in Cheapside, whose bell began my exploration of London's churches.

At St Michael Paternoster Royal, where a mummified cat was found during restoration work (above) its benefactor Dick Whittington is commemorated in stained glass (right). Whether he's fact or fiction, Whittington's cat nevertheless has his own memorial (left).

Old Jimmy Garlick may be more than just another skeleton (below).

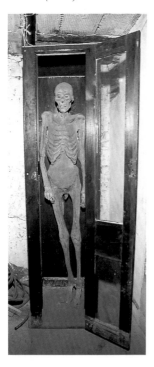

According to a legend that seems to have originated in a play of 1605 called *The History of Richard Whittington*, it was the message of Bow bells that made Dick Whittington 'turn again' and conveyed the promise to him that he would be 'thrice Lord Mayor of London'. In fact Whittington graced the office four times: in 1397, 1406 and 1419 on his own account, and once when he was nominated by Richard II to replace a Lord Mayor who had died in office. Whittington was a younger son of a landed family and thus unprovided for. He did indeed walk to London, where his commercial gifts made him extremely rich and successful. Dick Whittington's famous cat seems to have appeared either as a result of confusion with the French word for a trading exchange, *achat,* or because the kind of boat in which Whittington used to transport coals to London from Newcastle was known as 'a cat'. Mythical or not, this greatly loved feline, who is credited with guiding Dick to his great achievements, has his own memorial. In 1964 the figure of a cat was placed on the

stone on Highgate Hill which is said to mark the spot where Dick had second thoughts about leaving London. More mysteriously, the body of a mummified cat was found during excavations at the church of St Michael Paternoster Royal, where Whittington himself was a benefactor and is remembered in a stained glass window.

Whittington was reputedly buried at St Michael Paternoster Royal in 1423, but his tomb was destroyed in the Great Fire and the whereabouts of Dick Whittington's remains are still a cause for conjecture. Several medieval Lord Mayors were buried in the church of St James's Garlickhythe in Garlick Hill, and there, in the nineteenth century, the embalmed body of a man was found under the floor. The story goes that this was Dick Whittington himself, but no one knows for certain and so the mummy, now kept in a vault, is known as 'Old Jimmy Garlick'. Whoever he really is, several visitors have reported seeing his shrouded ghost standing on the tower steps . . .

MUSEUM PIECES

In his *Carnival of the Animals* Saint-Saens includes a musical picture of *Fossils*, a clever parody of his own *Danse Macabre*. The quality of the piece is admirably reflected in an introductory rhyme by the American humorist Ogden Nash which was adapted for a recording by Sir Noel Coward as follows:

At midnight in the museum hall
The fossils gathered for a ball.

There were no drums or saxophones
But just the clatter of their bones,
A rolling, rattling, carefree circus
Of mammoth polkas and mazurkas.
Pterodactyls and brontosauruses
Sang ghostly prehistoric choruses.
Amid the mastodonic wassail,
I caught the eye of one small fossil.
Cheer up, sad world, he said, and winked –
It's kind of fun to be extinct.

Children of all ages are fascinated by the glories of the Natural History Museum (left), which has its origins in collections amassed by Sir Hans Sloane. His tomb (below, in a detail from a nineteenth-century lithograph) is on Chelsea Embankment, near Chelsea Old Church.

Most children, and I was certainly among them, find the dinosaurs of the Natural History Museum irresistibly fascinating – the larger and more sinister the better. So whenever I was taken there by my grandmother or my parents, I would make a bee-line for *Tyrannosaurus Rex* and the brontosauruses. *Diplodocus Carnegii,* 85-feet long, was a family favourite, as were a vast blue whale, a mastodon from Missouri, the moa from New Zealand and the giant elk from the bogs of Ireland. Very small creatures such as the humming bird and the tiny British shrew mouse were also sources of wonder, but it was the unimaginable immensity that held me spell-bound and I occasionally had thrilling nightmares in which the *Diplodocus* made its heavy way up our garden path.

The Natural History Museum is strictly speaking a department of the British Museum and both had their origins in

Robert Smirke's British Museum, built in classical Greek style.

the extraordinary collections amassed by the Irish physician and naturalist Sir Hans Sloane. In 1712 he purchased the manor of Chelsea where his name is perpetuated in Sloane Square and Hans Crescent. When Sloane died in 1753 he suggested in his will that Parliament might like to buy his collections of antiquities, works of art and natural history specimens which had cost him £50,000 to assemble. Parliament agreed, and in 1759, after £30,000 had been raised by public lottery, the British Museum opened at Montagu House in Bloomsbury.

Manuscripts from the library founded by Robert Harley, first Earl of Oxford (the Harleian Collection) together with books and other objects from the Cottonian Library which had been assembled by the Cotton family, also formed part of the foundation collection which was soon augmented by the Royal Library of over 10,000 volumes. Acquisitions of all kinds poured in to Montagu House, including in 1816, the famous marbles removed from the ruins of the Acropolis in Athens by Lord Elgin. The material soon outgrew Montagu House and in 1823 a building programme began which resulted in the present imposing British Museum, designed in classical Greek style by Robert Smirke. In the 1850s the great Reading Room was added, and there, beneath the huge copper dome, many great writers have come to pursue their researches, from Thomas Carlyle and Bernard Shaw to Lenin and Karl Marx.

The new buildings were still too small to house the museum's natural history collection, so on land acquired at South Kensington with profits from the Great Exhibition of 1851, an impressive new museum was built. The architect Alfred Waterhouse decided that the wonders of the natural world would most suitably be housed in a building which resembled a medieval castle, but he did incorporate flowers and fauna into the decorative stonework.

To me as a schoolboy, the main British Museum seemed dull after the whales and dinosaurs of SW7; only the Egyptian mummies were able to offer competition in those days. Since then I have marvelled at so many things at the British Museum: the great dish from the Mildenhall Treasure, unearthed in 1942 on the borders of the fens and dating back probably to the third century, when Anglo Saxon raids were beginning to undermine Roman rule in Britain; the log book of Nelson's *Victory;* the last message of Captain Scott, written in his tent in the Antarctic wastes on 29th March 1912, with his two remaining colleagues, Dr Wilson and Lt Bowers already dead beside him. When I was presenting BBC Television's Arts magazine *Omnibus,* we made a programme about the Elgin Marbles controversy, and I spent a day filming in the special gallery built at the museum to house them. It was then that I became particularly fond of the horse of Selene, from the east pediment of the Parthenon.

In my young days, the Science Museum, just around the corner from the Natural History Museum, offered attractions which almost rivalled the dinosaurs. There I could walk through an invisible beam and a door would mysteriously open in front of me. Two other exhibits

particularly caught my imagination: the pendulum devised by the nineteenth century physicist Jean Bernard Léon Foucault which hangs freely in the stairwell, and by its movement over a calibrated scale on the floor demonstrates the gyration of our planet on its axis; and George Stephenson's *Rocket,* which in 1829 won a prize offered by the owners of the Liverpool and Manchester Railway for the most improved locomotive. It completed the prescribed 35-mile course, drawing three times its own weight, at an average speed of 14 miles per hour and was the forerunner of the steam-driven passenger train.

It's been said that most people visit the Science Museum three times in their lives: when they are nine years of age, when their children are nine and when their grandchildren are the same age. When I first went there in the thirties there was a special children's gallery with a dioramic history of the development of transport and power through the ages, and a lot of models that worked when a button was pushed. I would gaze up in wonder at the Vickers Vimy aircraft in which Alcock and Brown made the first air crossing of the Atlantic in 1919. Now there are jet engines and rockets to marvel at too.

Just as the Natural History Museum left home in Bloomsbury to grow independently in South Kensington, so the

Exhibits in the British Museum capture the romance of both ancient and modern history, and the horse of Selene (left), one of the Elgin Marbles, is a particular favourite of mine. No-one could fail to moved by Captain Scott's last message (above), a poignant reminder of his doomed Antarctic expedition.

One of Raphael's designs for the Sistine Chapel tapestries: a fragile miracle of survival.

Madame Tussaud's, where the Chamber of Horrors satisfied my boyish appetite for sensation.

Science Museum achieved independence from what is now the Victoria and Albert Museum over the road. The Victoria and Albert did not receive that name until Queen Victoria laid the foundation stone of the present building in 1900, in what was to be her last major public engagement. Much of the credit for the whole complex of museums and learned institutions at South Kensington must go to Prince Albert, for he wanted to give permanent shape to the aim of the Great Exhibition of 1851, which was to extend 'the influence of Science and Art upon productive industry'.

The forerunner of the V&A was the Museum of Manufactures which in the 1850s was transferred from Marlborough House to a new structure made of iron and glass in South Kensington which soon became known as the 'Brompton Boilers'. The name of the latest major gallery to be opened at the V&A, which houses examples of modern design, recalls those pioneering days: it is known as the Boilerhouse. Rapidly growing collections of many different kinds outgrew the original boilers, and just before Queen Victoria opened and named the new V&A, the decision was taken to separate science from art, and to move the scientific collections across the road. The building which houses them has grown in stages from 1913 onwards.

In spite of this separation of functions, the present collection at the V&A is vast and almost bewildering in its range. The best thing to do (as with other museums and galleries) is to go and look at a few objects at a time, otherwise weary confusion is likely to be the result. There are artefacts of every conceivable kind at the V&A, but I am always drawn to the tapestry cartoons of Raphael, a miracle of survival, for these designs for tapestries for the Sistine Chapel were painted in water colour on a fragile jigsaw of paper pieces glued together. Another miracle of art in the V&A is the tiny miniature painted by Nicholas Hilliard in about 1588 showing an unknown youth leaning against a tree among roses.

These things would not have appealed to me as a small boy. With my appetite for sensation I was more likely to be thrilled by the Chamber of Horrors at Madame Tussaud's. In this I shared the tastes of the Duke of Wellington, who visited the exhibition frequently and asked to be informed whenever a new horror was added to the array. In fact, Madame Marie Tussaud's own career was horrific in the early stages. She was drawing mistress to the children of Louis XVI of France, and during the French Revolution was compelled to make wax heads of many victims of the guillotine. She came to England in 1802, bringing some of those heads with her, and set up an

exhibition which toured the country until it settled in Baker Street in 1835, not far from its present site in Marylebone Road. No doubt she would have approved of the remark of Tweedledum (or was it Tweedledee?) in Lewis Carroll's *Through the Looking Glass* who said: 'If you think we're waxworks, you ought to pay you know. Waxworks weren't made to be looked at for nothing. Nohow!'

Millions of people from all over the world do pay to see Madame Tussaud's waxworks every year and they are rewarded with an ever-growing collection of astonishingly accurate effigies of the famous from all periods in history. When the effigy of Charles Dickens was replaced with a new one, the story goes that the discarded figure was placed in the Chamber of Horrors, lying face downwards, as a victim of the guillotine in the French Revolution exhibit. The figure of Cardinal Wolsey, which I particularly liked, used to provide a reminder of the unhealthy state of the London streets in Tudor times. He carried an orange, though not because he was in the habit of eating them in public; as his gentleman-usher explained: 'the meat or substance (of the orange) was taken out and filled up again with part of a sponge, wherein was vinegar and other confections against the pestilent airs; to the which he most commonly smelt unto, passing among the press, or

else when he was pestered with many suitors.'

There's another museum not far from Southwark Cathedral which would also have fascinated me in my ghoulish youth, had I known about it. This can be found in what is now the chapter house of the cathedral and was once the church of St Thomas in St Thomas Street. Until 1862 St Thomas's Hospital was situated here, and in the attic of the church – where the light was good – they set up the operating theatre for women which was in use for forty years. Bricked up when the hospital moved, it was rediscovered in 1957 and has been carefully restored, with an operating table of the period and a box of sawdust underneath to catch the blood.

I fear it was also the more horrific aspects of the Tower of London which chiefly interested me in my youth. In a book called *My Discovery of England* written in 1922, the Canadian humorist Stephen Leacock writes: 'I got to understand that when a Londoner says "have you seen the Tower of London?", the answer is "no, and neither have you".' But in fact it's quite hard to avoid visiting it, either as a press-ganged member of a school party or when called upon to show someone the sights of London.

Writing in the year 1610, William Camden described the Tower as 'a most

My ghoulish youthful imagination would have relished St Thomas's operating theatre (above, left), rediscovered practically intact almost a century after it was bricked up. Nearby is the apothecary's garret (above, right), where nineteenth-century pharmacists prepared their medications.

famous and goodly citadell, encompassed round with thicke and strong walles, full of loftie and stately turrets, fensed with a broad and deep ditch, furnished also with an armorie or magazine of warlicke munition, and other buildings besides: so it resembleth a big towne.' By that time the Tower had already been there for five centuries, keeping its 'silent watch and ward', as Gilbert puts in in *The Yeoman of the Guard,* over the city and citizens of London.

For a long period the Tower was the principal residence of the monarch, and when King Henry VII left it for his coronation in 1485, he did so attended by the newly formed bodyguard of the Yeomen of the Guard. Their number in those days included 'bed goers' who had to drive a sword through the royal mattress to make sure it contained no intruder, and 'bed hangers' who had to air and make the royal bed. They were also required to bring the monarch's food up from the

kitchens and taste it before their master or mistress did. These services are happily no longer required, but the eighty Yeomen of the Guard, with their characteristic uniform, still have an honoured place in the royal entourage. W.S. Gilbert confused them with the Yeomen Warders of the Tower of London, the so-called Beefeaters, who wear a similar Tudor uniform but are members of a junior organisation which was not set up until 1552!

It was in the Tower that the Order of the Bath, one of Britain's major orders of chivalry, had its origins. King Henry IV spent the night before his coronation in the Tower and selected forty-six of his followers as the first members of the order. They had to take a bath as a form of ritual cleansing, after which they spent the night in prayer.

The Chapel of St Peter ad Vincula contains the tombs of some of the illustrious figures who met their death at the

The Tower of London, in its time both palace and prison to Britain's rulers.

hands of the executioner whose block was set up on Tower Green. They include Anne Boleyn who became Henry VIII's second wife to the accompaniment of great celebrations at the Tower in 1533; three years later, accused of adultery with her brother and four other men, she was beheaded there. Sir Thomas More, the king's former chancellor, met his death at the Tower too, when he refused to accept the king's supremacy over the church rather than the Pope's. On the very day of his execution, the king commuted his sentence of being hung, drawn and quartered, to simple beheading, upon which More remarked: 'God forbid the king shall use any more such mercy on my friends'. The great Sir Thomas, who was canonised in 1935, seems to have retained his humour and philosophical temper to the last, remarking when he was taken to the Tower: 'Is not this house as nigh heaven as my own?' The Chapel of St Peter ad Vincula (dedicated to St Peter in chains) in its present form largely dates from the sixteenth century and was intended as a place of prayer and consolation from its twelfth century beginnings. It still draws considerable congregations, not least on account of its high musical standards.

London's sinister fortress has witnessed countless horrors, but the crime which gave the Bloody Tower its name

lives on as perhaps the most appalling. After the death of Edward IV, Richard, Duke of Gloucester, was appointed Protector. Declaring the boy-king Edward V and his brother the Duke of York illegitimate, he proclaimed himself king as Richard III, and was crowned at Westminster. A few weeks later the boys were murdered in what was then called the Garden Tower, on the orders of Sir James Tyrell. Almost two centuries went by before two skeletons thought to be those of the princes were reburied at Westminster Abbey.

The Tower of London has, apart from serving as a palace and prison, in its time housed the Royal Mint and the royal menagerie. Today it accommodates in the White Tower Britain's national collection of armour and arms, said to be the oldest museum in the country, and in the Wakefield Tower the Crown Jewels, which are displayed to immense crowds of visitors who often queue for some considerable time for the privilege of filing past them.

Another building on Tower Hill of great interest to me as a lover of the sea is Trinity House, though it is by no means a museum – it is the headquarters of the corporation responsible for all lighthouses around the coast of Britain, and until recently, for most pilotage. The origins of the corporation can be securely traced back to the early sixteenth century, but

Anne Boleyn died on Tower Green, and her tomb is in the Chapel of St Peter ad Vincula (above, left) in the Tower's grounds. The Tower also housed the Royal Mint for a time in the early eighteenth century (above, right).

While Trinity House (right) contains some nautical memorabilia, lovers of the sea like me can really indulge themselves at the National Maritime Museum in Greenwich. Among the exhibits there is a model (above) of one of the steamers in service on the Thames at the turn of the century.

tradition has it that a forerunner in the shape of a Guild of Mariners existed in the time of King Alfred the Great. The facade of the present building dates from the eighteenth century, although the rest of it had to be reconstructed after destruction by bombs in the Second World War. The interior houses, among other nautical objects and fine pictures, some interesting ship models.

I can spend hours gazing at such things, so of course the National Maritime Museum at Greenwich has to be high on my list of favourite London museums.

Some of the old ships still afloat on the Thames: **Kathleen and May** *(above),* **Robin** *(left), and* **Lydia Eve** *(below).*

Here there are steamship models in abundance in the New Neptune Hall (for some reason I've always found them more interesting than sailing ships), quite apart from a fabulous array of navigational instruments, and special collections commemorating two of Britain's great naval heroes, Captain Cook and Lord Nelson. Only a few of the real old ships can still be seen in various docks along the River Thames, such as the topsail schooner *Kathleen and May* at St Mary Overie's Dock, and the herring drifter *Lydia Eve* and the coaster *Robin* which are moored alongside Heron Quay in Docklands.

The elegant Arab Hall (below) at Leighton House in Holland Park Road, and (bottom) Leighton's great work **Cimabue's Madonna carried in Procession through the Streets of Florence.** *The painting is now owned by the Queen, and hangs in the National Gallery.*

Two museums which delight me for other reasons are both offshoots of the Victoria and Albert. These are the Museum of Childhood at Bethnal Green and the Theatre Museum in Covent Garden. I am drawn to Bethnal Green, once the poorest district of London, by the collection of puppets, model theatres and dolls' houses they have there as I have always found these small-scale dwellings endlessly fascinating. I'm not sure what it says for my character, but as a small boy of five I much preferred to be allowed to stay in the classroom during break and play with the dolls' house, than to go out and run around with everyone else in the playground.

It is the world of adult make-believe that draws me to the Theatre Museum. The basis of its extensive collection was the Gabrielle Enthoven archive consisting of thousands of playbills, photographs, engravings and other items relating to the stage and other forms of popular entertainment. You can also see a Sheraton dressing table which belonged to Sarah Siddons, mementoes of great theatrical figures such as Herbert Beerbohm Tree, Sir James Barrie and Harley Granville-Barker; and there's a major collection of material associated with the Diaghilev Ballet. During the 1970s the Theatre Museum was housed in an annexe at Leighton House. This was the residence of the artist Frederic Leighton, who was knighted in 1878 and became Lord Leighton a few days before his death in 1896, making him the only English painter to be raised to the peerage. The house is full of works of art by himself and his friends, notably William de Morgan. Some of Morgan's tiles are to be seen in the astonishingly elegant Arab Hall, along with ancient tiles from Persia, stained glass windows from Damascus and a mosaic frieze by Walter Crane.

One of the earliest of Leighton's works to attract attention was *Cimabue's Madonna carried in Procession through the Streets of Florence;* it was exhibited in the Royal Academy in 1855 and bought by Queen Victoria. Now it is on loan from the Queen and, newly cleaned, hangs over the main entrance of the National Gallery in Trafalgar Square where its bright colours and clarity of texture can still be admired.

The present National Gallery was built in the 1830s by the architect William Wilkins, and in its day caused as much disparaging comment as the proposals for a new extension have aroused in more recent times. Wilkins was forced to incorporate the columns that had been discarded when Pall Mall's Carlton House was demolished, and in a publication of 1862 the building as a whole was described in the following terms: 'This unhappy structure may be said to have everything it ought not to have, and nothing which it ought to have. It possesses windows without glass, a cupola without size, a portico without height, pepper boxes without pepper, and the finest site in Europe without anything to show upon it.'

Whatever its architectural shortcomings, I have, like most Londoners, 'grown accustomed to the face' of the National Gallery and would not want any addition to spoil or overwhelm it. I first went there during the Second World War to hear lunchtime concerts of chamber music organised by Dame Myra Hess and, like many music lovers, was sorry when they ceased after the war. Now I occasionally pop in for half an hour to look at one or two favourites and perhaps something new, though I could well exclaim with Logan Pearsall Smith 'How often my soul visits the National Gallery and how seldom I go there myself!'

Probably the most exciting collections of paintings in London is to be found at the Tate Gallery, whose official title is the National Gallery of British Art. When the fashionable sculptor Sir Francis Chantrey died in 1841 he left over £100,000 – a very large sum in those days – explicitly for the purpose of purchasing 'works of fine art of the highest merit

executed within the shores of Great Britain'. The collection which resulted, together with other acquisitions, was housed in South Kensington, while the great Turner bequest of 1856, consisting of 282 oil paintings and over 19,000 water colours, was accommodated at the National Gallery, though there was inadequate space for display. Then, in 1889, the sugar magnate Sir Henry Tate gave the nation sixty-five modern British paintings and £80,000 to house them, and in 1897 the Tate Gallery on Millbank opened. The great collection of Turners was transferred there in 1910, and is now displayed in the modern gallery named after the industrialist Sir Charles Clore.

*The National Gallery of British Art (facing page), more familiarly known as the Tate Gallery. Its restaurant is graced by **The Pursuit of Rare Meats** (right), a mural by Rex Whistler.*

With senses assailed by both music and fine art, visitors enjoy a Cushion Concert at Burlington House.

The Turners alone would make the Tate worth visiting, and I find it easy to lose myself in the romantic haze they create, but there are other pictures that excite me too. In 1923 Samuel Courtauld created a fund for the purchase of modern French paintings, which has resulted in a superb array of great works in addition to the much-admired collections of modern art and large sculptures. There is a powerful stylised head by Amedeo Modigliani which I find very haunting, though for me the greatest impact comes from the works of Picasso, especially perhaps the striking *Three Dancers* of 1925. The restaurant has its own work of art, an entertaining mural by Rex Whistler called *The Pursuit of Rare Meats*.

There was a fear in the 1890s that control of the new gallery's collections would remain in the hands of the Royal Academy – a fear, because at that time the Academy was identified with everything fustily conservative in art. However, the Tate gradually asserted its independence both from the Academy, which had had the responsibility of making purchases from the Chantrey bequest, and from the National Gallery.

For the first thirty years of its life the National Gallery building played host to the Royal Academy of Arts. This institution, with its rather complex origins in the eighteenth century, dedicated to the exhibition of works by established artists and the education of students, did not move to Burlington House in Piccadilly until 1867. In recent years it has provided the setting for a number of magnificent international exhibitions, but its most famous annual event is the summer exhibition of new work by artists of every stylistic persuasion. During this exhibition there is a remarkable merging of visual and aural art, for the Academy provides the setting for the annual Cushion Concerts, a most imaginative venture which greatly appeals to the rising generation. Perched on the cushions they pick up at the door, the predominantly young patrons get two artistic experiences for the price of one, and maybe an added stimulus from the counterpoint to the cool notes of Mozart offered by some violent contemporary canvas.

The very first public art gallery in London was the Dulwich Picture Gallery, founded in 1814. Its collection today is relatively small but very distinguished, including works by Rembrandt, Van Dyck, Rubens and Gainsborough. The building was designed by Sir John Soane, whose house in Lincoln's Inn Fields is one of the most original and fascinating of all London's museums. One of the rooms has walls which open out to reveal panel after panel of works of art. Soane acquired Hogarth's original paintings for *The Rake's Progress,* as well as the engravings themselves, and a huge and motley collection of antiquities including a big Egyptian sarcophagus which he bought when the British Museum turned it down. The acquisition so pleased him that he gave a party lasting three days so that his friends could admire it. This amazing house also contains a mock-medieval monk's cell and the drawings for Soane's most conspicuous memorial, the Bank of England.

Dulwich College Picture Gallery (left and below, left) contains a distinguished collection of fine pictures. It was designed by Sir John Soane, whose own house is one of London's most original museums (below, right: the Breakfast Room).

FRESH AIRS

'Architecture' said the German writer Friedrich von Schelling 'is frozen music', and there are many fine buildings in London which have the symmetry and grace of the more formal kind of music. But, much as I love music and fine architecture, there are times when a stroll in the park is more refreshing – and the temptation to wander into Kensington Gardens between a rehearsal and performance at the Royal Albert Hall often proves irresistible. There, a few hun- dred yards from the road, it's possible to find a spot where the rustle of leaves is louder than the roar of the traffic. It was the elder Pitt who described the parks as 'the lungs of London', and all my life I've felt grateful that the city has such an abundance of open spaces. They add up to a great deal more than, to quote the writer H.V. Morton, 'the rather pitiful patch of coun- try which the Anglo-Saxon bears with him like a captive' into many other British cities.

The large expanse of Hyde Park has been open to the public since the days of King Charles I, when it became very fashionable to parade in one's carriage or to watch horse-racing on the mile-long Rotten Row. It would appear that the air was not especially fresh even in those days: in April 1664, Pepys decided to go 'to Hide Park, where great plenty of gallants. And pleasant it was, only for the dust.' Thomas Brown, contributing to 'Amusements Serious and Comical' in 1700, echoed Pepys's comment when he wrote of Hyde Park as the place 'where horses have their diversion as well as men, and neigh and court their mistresses almost in as intelligible a dialect. Here people coach it to take the air, amidst a cloud of dust able to choak a foot-soldier, and are hinder'd from seeing those that come thither on purpose to show themselves.' These days the air is not much fresher, with the roads across and around the park often densely packed with traffic.

The monks of Westminster first enclosed the area in 1066, and subsequently Henry VIII took it for use as a royal deer park. After Charles I decided to share it with the public, Hyde Park did have one more brief period in private hands: it was sold during the Commonwealth to a private owner who instituted charges for admittance of a shilling for a coach and sixpence for every horse. This imposition was greatly resented, and it seemed like rough justice when the Lord Protector himself, Oliver Cromwell, was involved in an accident in the park. His horse bolted, flinging him to the floor of his coach, and a pistol went off in his pocket. But, according to Thomas Carlyle's account of the incident, 'his Highness got up again, little the worse; was let blood; and went about his affairs much as usual.'

After the Restoration in 1660 people and horses were once again admitted without payment to Hyde Park: it became once again a favourite place to rendezvous. But in those days a stroll in the park could also be dangerous, since many duels were fought there, including one between the Duke of Hamilton and Lord Mohum in 1712 when both combatants were killed. Thieves were very active too – in

1749 Horace Walpole, for example, was robbed in Hyde Park by the infamous highwayman McLean – and for a time a bell was rung at intervals to mobilise people who wanted to cross the park into protected convoys.

Not far from Marble Arch, on the north side of the park, there is a stone plaque on a traffic island which marks the

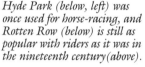

Hyde Park (below, left) was once used for horse-racing, and Rotten Row (below) is still as popular with riders as it was in the nineteenth century (above).

On a traffic island opposite the Odeon, Edgware Road, is this plaque (above) marking the site of Tyburn Tree. Squeezed in next door to Tyburn Convent is the smallest house in London (right).

site of Tyburn Gallows, or Tyburn Tree as it was known, where many a highwayman – among other offenders – met his end. One such criminal was Jack Sheppard, whose execution in 1714 was witnessed by 200,000 people. The tree, last used in 1783, stood twelve feet high and was triangular in shape, so that it was possible for eight people to be hanged at the same time on each of its three sides. Roman Catholics, persecuted for their faith, also perished at Tyburn and the nuns of the nearby Tyburn Convent still pray for their souls. Next door to the convent, incidentally, is the smallest house in London. Only three feet six inches wide, it was built to block a passage which the owner wanted to make private.

There was no threat from the criminal community when my grandmother first took me to feed the ducks on the Serpentine. We owe this attractive artificial lake which separates Hyde Park from Kensington Gardens to the imagination of King George II's consort, Queen Caroline of Anspach, who ordered it to be formed from the flow of the River Westbourne and had two yachts placed on it for the diversion of the royal family. They

The ducks on the Serpentine that my grandmother and I used to feed seem to be outnumbered now by Canada geese.

were living at the time in Kensington Palace, an elegant building in red brick graced with an orangery designed by Sir Christopher Wren and surrounded by gardens planned by Queen Anne's gardener, Henry Wise. If he'd had his way, the Serpentine would have consisted of a series of ten small lakes, and the Round Pond would have been oblong. This small area of water not far from the palace has long been a source of joy to lovers of model boats of all ages, and I have often stood gazing in envy as the owners of fine yachts or motor-driven craft hauled them ashore to make fine adjustments before sending them off again on voyages whose course seemed securely predetermined. They contrast with the small sailing boats such as my first one, which tottered away uncertainly from the shore changing course with every little breeze that blew, only to end up stationary and upside down in the middle of the pond, far from the possibility of rescue. Small boy departs in tears.

It was George II's wife Queen Caroline who first invited the public to use the gardens of Kensington Palace on Saturdays, when the king and court were spending the day at the lodge in the old deer park at Richmond. In the early nineteenth century, the gardens were accessible to the general public from spring to autumn, and it was then that the poet Shelley could be seen sailing paper boats made sometimes, it is said, out of bank notes, on the Round Pond. In Victorian times, the gardens were opened every day 'to all respectably dressed persons, from sunrise to sunset'.

Respectability has always been a keynote of Kensington Gardens, the traditional resort in the old days of uniformed nannies wheeling their perambulators along Broad Walk. The swings in the children's playground at the north end of the walk were a gift from Sir James Barrie, who lived for seven years in the Bayswater Road. While walking in Kensington Gardens with his large dog, Porthos, he used to see two small boys in red berets walking with their nurse, who also had a baby in a perambulator to push. The children were George, Jack and Peter

Llewellyn Davies, three members of a family of five boys who were to play a very significant part in Barrie's life. He already knew their mother and was to become an intimate friend of the entire family; it was they who provided him with the inspiration for *Peter Pan*, first produced in 1904. The bronze statue of

Kensington Palace's Orangery (below, and facing page, top, left) was never used to grow oranges but Queen Anne used to entertain her guests there regularly.

Kensington Gardens, where the statue of Peter Pan continues to delight visiting children (below and left). When William III first acquired Kensington Palace (top, right), the gardens only amounted to twenty-six acres. Now they extend to 275 acres.

Peter Pan, designed by Sir George Frampton, which stands near the upper end of the Serpentine, commemorates the play and its origins in Kensington Gardens. The statue was erected overnight, so that it could suddenly appear one morning and surprise the children. It remains a source of joy to children of succeeding generations, who continue to delight in stroking the fairies and animals which adorn the base of the bronze statue.

The Duke of Cambridge, when he was ranger of Hyde Park, must have been fond of animals, for in 1880 he obtained permission for his wife to bury her pet dog near Victoria Gate. This established a fashionable precedent, and over the next thirty-five years about 300 small tombstones were put up in what became known as the Dogs' Cemetery, inscribed to such canine friends as 'Wee Pet Monte', 'Sweet Baby Quita' and 'Darling Tsing'.

On the south side of the park, at Hyde Park Corner, stands Apsley House, formerly known as 'No. 1 London', when it was the home of the Duke of Wellington. In the eighteenth century an altogether humbler dwelling stood on the site, a hut inhabited by a former soldier called Allen who made a meagre living selling apples. One day, so the story goes, King George II was riding along the road when he spotted this figure in the tattered remains of a soldier's coat and stopped to talk to him. The king learned that Allen had fought at the battle of Dettingen, where he himself had led his troops into battle and, hearing that the poor soldier was about to be evicted from his hut, arranged for the freehold to be transferred to him. Allen's son grew up to be a prosperous lawyer and sold a lease of the

land to the Lord Chancellor, Lord Apsley. The stately house subsequently built on the site by Robert Adam was leased firstly to the Duke of Wellington's brother and then to the duke himself. In 1820 the nation bought the freehold and presented it gratefully to the victor of Waterloo.

Kensington Palace, which still has apartments used by members of the royal family, must be a relatively cosy residence. As Leigh Hunt wrote: 'Windsor Castle is

There are around 300 memorials to much-loved pets in the Dogs' Cemetery, near Victoria Gate.

Apsley House used to be the most westerly of a number of Mayfair mansions, but now it stands alone.

The Albert Memorial is a monument to Queen Victoria's Prince Consort (below), and to some of the age's skills and values: Commerce (left) and Manufactures (right) among them.

a place to receive monarchs in; Buckingham Palace to see fashions in; Kensington Palace seems a place to drink tea in.' George II's wife Queen Caroline certainly made herself at home there, brightening up the interior as well as the gardens around it, but after that it was more or less abandoned by successive monarchs. George III 'desired to be excused living in Kensington', and no sovereign ever resided there again, except the young Queen Victoria in the first three weeks of her reign.

Victoria's consort, quite rightly, is prominently remembered in Kensington Gardens. Opposite the Royal Albert Hall, in one of the most ornate of all Victorian monuments, sits a stone effigy, described by Osbert Sitwell as 'that gilded and pensive giant on his dais under the Gothic canopy, strewn with white mosaic daisies of a blameless life'. The figure of the prince is attended by statues representing the arts, manufacturing industry and aspects of learning, and in his hand is a catalogue of the Great Exhibition – quite appropriately, for not far away from Sir Giles Gilbert Scott's memorial stood the Crystal Palace which housed Albert's brainchild, the major national event of 1851. Scott received a knighthood for his work on the memorial, as did Joseph Paxton for his amazing edifice of glass and iron. It was a vastly enlarged version of the conservatory he had built for the Duke of Devonshire at Chatsworth House, where he was superintendent of the gardens.

The Crystal Palace, like the Great Exhibition, was unquestionably a great success for, in the space of 114 days, over six million people came to marvel at this entirely novel structure, in spite of early fears that it would collapse. The contents, consisting of 'the works of all nations', aroused a mixed response. The artist, designer and poet William Morris recalled that as a youth of seventeen he had 'stood aghast at the appalling ugliness of the objects exhibited, the heaviness, tastelessness and rococo banality of the entire display.' But Morris was ahead of his time, and no doubt the objects on view pleased and amazed the vast majority.

One of my favourite boyhood outings was to Crystal Palace (right: as it was in 1851) particularly because of the prehistoric animals there (below, left).

When the exhibition was over, the palace was moved to the summit of a steep hill at Sydenham in south London. There, with its twin water towers 282 feet high, it became the central feature of a park which offered one of my favourite outings as a boy. Very attractive to me were the huge plaster casts of prehistoric animals in the grounds, but even more alluring was the prospect of a magnificent evening firework display. These were held weekly in summer, but tens of thousands of people used to pack the terraces of the palace for 'Brock's Benefit', the prodigiously spectacular annual display. It recalled the name of Charles Thomas Brock, who in 1865 suggested a 'grand Competition of Pyrotechnists' at Crystal Palace and founded the pyrotechnic firm which bears his name. Brock, however, was not responsible for the fire which destroyed Crystal Palace in 1936, leaving only the water towers still standing – they too were removed in 1940, for they provided too obvious a landmark for enemy bombers. The National Sports Centre now stands on the site of Paxton's masterpiece.

On the northern heights of London, a counterpart to the Crystal Palace was created at Muswell Hill. This was Alexandra Palace, intended to provide, as its early proprietors put it, 'a Grand Institution

Dramatic firework displays used to be a regular summer entertainment at Crystal Palace.

North London's answer to Crystal Palace, the first Alexandra Palace was also destroyed by fire. Newspapers of the day pictured the fire from the north (above) and the south-west (right). The BBC erected a television mast on one of its remaining towers during early experiments with the TV transmission system developed by John Logie Baird (below).

of healthful recreation and elevating instruction, which will combine the solid advantages of the South Kensington Museums and schools of art with the lighter pleasures and pastimes of the Crystal Palace at Sydenham, thus giving effect to the large and enlightened views of the late Prince Consort.'

Alexandra Palace has, however, often been more of a liability than an asset to its owners. It burned down almost as soon as it opened in 1873, though it was soon rebuilt, and many attractions were staged to attract the crowds. In 1888, Professor Baldwin embarked on a number of parachute descents from a hot air balloon: a horse and trap were on hand to follow the courageous fellow and bring him back from wherever he landed. A year later, two 'daring American aeronauts', Williams and Young, raced each other by parachute, coming down near Southgate, some distance away. For much of the 1890s the palace was closed, but it re-opened in 1898 with, as the local paper claimed, 'every prospect of success'. Visitors on Easter Monday were promised 'two balloon ascents and a sensational race between *three* parachutists', a firework spectacle entitled 'The Last Days of Pompeii', and the opportunity to visit 'Captain Dreyfus in his terrible cage prison on devil's island'. Later on, during the First World War, the palace housed firstly Belgian refugees, and then German prisoners of war.

Run down and dilapidated, Alexandra Palace, or at any rate one corner of it, acquired new life when, thanks to its position 300 feet above sea level, the BBC erected a television mast on one of the towers and in 1935 began experiments with both the Baird and Marconi-EMI systems of television transmission. John Logie Baird is generally credited with the invention of television. Working in a garret in a back street in Soho, he managed to transmit a picture of a wooden doll; running downstairs in excitement he found a crippled boy, William Taynton, and persuaded him to sit in front of the camera. Taynton thus became the first human being to appear on 'the box'.

However Baird's relatively cumbersome system was dropped, and it was with the Marconi system that the BBC opened the world's first high-definition television service from Alexandra Palace in November 1936. Until the war, and for some time after it, the two tiny Alexandra Palace studios were home to the entire BBC Television service. In 1954 the studios were taken over by a new-born infant, BBC Television News, and there it grew and developed until its move to the Television Centre in Wood Lane, Shepherd's Bush in 1969. During all that time, and for years afterwards, I was one of the regular newsreaders, and Alexandra Palace became a home from home for me. A highly congenial village atmosphere prevailed, which could hardly have been

Home from home for me when I was a regular TV newsreader, Alexandra Palace (above) had become Britain's first television centre in 1936. Not far away, in Hampstead, is the famous old Bull and Bush (sign below), inspiration for one of the best known of all music hall songs.

expected to survive the rapid advance of television news into the realms of high technology.

Subsequently programmes for the Open University were made at Alexandra Palace, but eventually in 1981 the BBC finally departed. Under the supervision of the local authorities, the palace and its grounds have been extensively refurbished following yet another disastrous fire in 1980. The great hall has been rebuilt, the mighty Henry Willis organ, originally constructed in 1873, is being reassembled and a new hotel will occupy the area of the old television studios.

One of my routes to Alexandra Palace took me across Hampstead Heath, a place I have loved ever since I first went there on the No. 187 bus. Like thousands of other families we were drawn to the fairs held on the heath on bank holidays, and Hampstead has been a very popular outing with Londoners for generations. In 1914, the cockney comedian Albert

Chavalier wrote the words of a music hall song extolling its attractions:

Now if yer want a 'igh old time
Just take a tip from me.
Why 'Ampstead, 'appy 'Ampstead
is the place to 'ave a spree . . .
Oh, 'Ampstead's very 'ard to beat,
If you want a beano it's a fair old treat.

Another entertainer, Florrie Forde, wrote one of her most famous songs, *Down at the Old Bull and Bush*, at one of 'Ampstead's favourite pubs. Once a farmhouse – hence 'the Bull' – it was also for a time the country home of the artist William Hogarth, who is said to have planted a yew tree which contributed 'the Bush' to the pub's name.

On leave during the war and in the fifties, I often used to walk with friends across Hampstead Heath to one or other of its famous inns. Jack Straw's Castle, named after a leader of the Peasant's Revolt of 1381, was one objective. Charles

Jack Straw's Castle (above) was a favourite watering-hole of mine just after the war. Another was The Spaniards (below right), which looks remarkably as it did in the nineteenth century, though it has less of a rural air now.

Dickens liked it too, finding material for *Little Dorrit* in the tale of a fraudulent MP, John Sadleir, who poisoned himself nearby. Just down the road, The Spaniards was the setting of a scene in *Pickwick Papers*. The name of this sixteenth century house probably derives from the story of two Spanish brothers, joint landlords, who killed each other in a duel over a woman. The notorious highwayman, Dick Turpin, used to stay there, stabling his horse in the toll house on the other side of the road. But what appealed to me most about The Spaniards as a young man, apart from the welcome draught of cool beer after a long walk, was its link with Shelley, Keats and Byron. Indeed, for me, Hampstead owes its continuing appeal to an association with romantic poetry.

*Famous Hampstead houses:
Kenwood House (left),
remodelled by Adam in the
eighteenth century; Ivy House
(below, left), Anna Pavlova's
home for twenty years; Keats
House (below), where **Ode to
a Nightingale** was written;
Admiral's House (facing page,
top left), whose eighteenth-
century occupant did his best
to keep London safe from
invasion.*

Keats House in Keats Grove has been lovingly restored in recent years. Here, in the garden, he wrote what is without doubt my favourite poem, the *Ode to a Nightingale*. I first learned it by heart as a sixth-former, and the words coloured my Hampstead walks from then onwards. Keats first visited Hampstead at the invitation of Leigh Hunt, and the pair of them used to enjoy walking up Parliament Hill. It still offers a marvellous view of London – and it's an ideal place for flying kites.

Many a time I have walked across Hampstead Heath to Kenwood House, the former home of the Mansfield family which was elegantly remodelled by Robert Adam in the late eighteenth century. The house and the 74 acres immediately surrounding it were opened to the public in 1928 and both have since become very popular attractions. Concerts are often given in the house itself and on a specially constructed platform by the lake, where the surrounding slopes form a natural amphitheatre which is remarkably good for sound.

Two other houses in Hampstead appeal to me for quite different reasons. Ivy House, on the road that leads to Golders Green, was for twenty years the home of the great ballerina Anna Pavlova and whenever I see it I'm reminded of my great wish to have seen her as 'the dying swan'. Then there's Admiral's House, once the home of the eccentric eighteenth-century Admiral Matthew Barton. In the early morning he would stand in full uniform on the special deck he constructed above his house, looking out towards the sea across the roofs of London and firing his cannon to warn off potential enemies.

Hampstead has long been regarded as a place of escape from city life by Londoners. Many judges and lawyers set up shop there during the Great Plague, and not long afterwards the discovery of medicinal springs in what is now Well Walk helped to make Hampstead a fashionable resort. In the 1720s Daniel Defoe wrote that 'Hampstead indeed is risen from a little country village to a city, not upon the credit only of the waters, though 'tis apparent its growing greatness began there.' He also gave a somewhat exaggerated description of the 'very pleasant plain, called the Heath . . . on the highest part of the hill. But it must be confest, 'tis so near heaven, that I dare not say it can be a proper situation for any but a race of mountaineers, whose lungs have been so used to a rarify'd air.'

No climbing is called for on a day out to Kew Gardens, for the 163-foot pagoda erected there in 1761 is not open to the public. It was built to the design of the

Defoe said Hampstead Heath was high enough to present any but a mountaineer with a breathing problem. He might have said the same about the 163-foot pagoda at Kew Gardens.

architect, Sir William Chambers, who was fascinated by his travels to the Far East as a young man, and still remains a charming incidental attraction in the Royal Botanic Gardens.

Once the private gardens of a seventeenth century botanist, Sir Henry Capel, they were subsequently leased in part to the royal family, and only became public property when Queen Victoria presented them to the nation in 1841. For most of her reign, until the Diamond Jubilee of 1897, she retained the Queen's Cottage in the gardens for use as a summer-house. One of the glasshouses in the grounds, the Aroid House, was built originally as part of Buckingham Palace, but in 1836 it was moved to Kew where, with a temperature maintained at eighty degrees Fahrenheit, it houses specimens of plants from humid tropical forests.

The greatest of the Kew glasshouses, indeed at one time it was the largest in the world, is the Palm House, designed by Decimus Burton and built in the 1840s. In front of it is an artificial lake whose water supply comes from the Thames; it can only be replenished at high tide, preferably at the time of a new or full moon. Of great interest to children are the numerous carp which inhabit the lake; they are easily visible and squabble ferociously over any crumbs which may be thrown to them.

Though Queen Victoria presented Kew Gardens to the nation in 1841, she kept the Queen's Cottage (top, left) for her own use. The Aroid House (below), once part of Buckingham Palace, is now Kew's oldest glasshouse and home to plants from tropical forests (below, left).

The true business of the Royal Botanic Gardens is, of course, scientific. It was once estimated that if the gardens were closed to sightseers for a few years, the world's food supply problems could be solved by the scientists of Kew. Ironically, the destruction caused by the hurricane of 1987, when 500 of Kew's 9000 trees were brought down, has provided hitherto inaccessible material for research. One line of investigation, for example, has concerned the possibly valuable chemical properties of the fungi found among tree roots. The gardens have since been successfully replanted with a greater variety of species than was ever possible in London's more air-polluted days.

From Kew I have often walked along the tow path by the River Thames to Richmond, continuing, when I had the energy, across the wide expanse of Richmond Park. The park, incidentally, was appropriated briefly by King Charles I as a hunting area before being returned to the people of Richmond. However it's not necessary to go as far as Richmond or Kew to explore public parks which were once associated with the private pleasures of the royal family. Regent's Park, one of the most attractive in central London, is so named because the Prince Regent once planned to build a palace there, and the terraces, designed by John Nash and

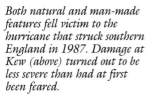

Both natural and man-made features fell victim to the hurricane that struck southern England in 1987. Damage at Kew (above) turned out to be less severe than had at first been feared.

Regent's Park (left) never got its palace, but the fine terraces (centre) were built for court favourites.

Decimus Burton, included houses at one time intended for court favourites. I once rather foolishly managed to capsize a small sailing boat on the Regent's Park lake in a sudden gust of wind, but my predicament was nothing compared with the disaster that struck there in the winter of 1866–7. The frozen lake was crowded with skaters when part of the ice gave way and nearly forty people were drowned.

It was the rapacious King Henry VIII who first enclosed the area of St James's Park and Green Park, but their present shape owes much to King Charles II's interest in horticulture. He engaged the French landscape gardener Le Nôtre to lay out St James's Park, with a central canal formed from a chain of pools. It was Le Nôtre who created Duck Island as a sanctuary for the water fowl which inhabit the lake in great numbers. There are also pelicans here, which I think add the final touch to what is surely one of London's most delightful parks. Alas, one of its charming features, an early iron suspension bridge across the lake, was replaced in 1956 by a concrete structure; this constitutes a busy thoroughfare for politicians and civil servants on their way to and from the Houses of Parliament or the government offices of Whitehall. From the bridge there is a fine view of the variegated pinnacles and domes of the Whitehall skyline which has been called 'the most romantic roofscape in London'.

In former times St James's Park was the scene of what must have been London's first milk bar. The guidebook *London in Miniature,* published in 1755, refers to 'stands of cows from whence the company at small expence may be supplied with warm milk', and ten years later a French visitor describes the scene in greater detail. 'The cows are driven about noon and evening to the gate which leads from the park to the quarter of Whitehall. Tied in a file to posts at the extremity of the grass plot, they will swill passengers with their milk, which is drawn from their udders on the spot and served with all the cleanliness peculiar to the English, in little mugs at the rate of one penny per mug.'

Near to St James's Park is London's most famous street, Downing Street,

which takes it name from Sir George Downing, the son of a London barrister, who was born in Dublin in 1623. In 1681 he bought some land in Whitehall and erected four houses on it 'fit for persons of honour and quality'. When Downing died in 1731, George II offered the houses as a gift to Robert Walpole, but it was decided instead that they should be allotted in perpetuity to the First Lord of the Treasury (an office customarily held by the Prime Minister) and the Chancellor of the Exchequer. Sir George Downing thus has a lasting memorial at the heart of London, though according to Pepys, who worked for him as a clerk, he was 'a perfidious rogue', changing his political allegiances with an eye to the main chance. Pepys did not stay with him long: 'he is so stingy a fellow,' he wrote, 'I care not to see him; I quite cleared myself of his office and did give him liberty to take anybody in.'

St James's Park: home of the first milk-bar in London (left), some pelicans on Duck Island (below) add the final touch to Le Nôtre's landscaping triumph (bottom).

Green Park has little to offer apart from a wide expanse of grass – its lack of flowers is said to be due to the fact that it was once a burial ground for lepers – but alongside the park are some of London's most interesting great houses. Lancaster House, in the stable yard of St James's Palace, was built by Benjamin Wyatt. Construction of the house began in 1825, but it was not completed until after the death of its intended occupant, the Duke of York, brother of George IV. Famous as the army commander who, according to the nursery rhyme, had 'ten thousand men', the duke ended up – away from his creditors it was said – on top of a monumental column where his brother's Carlton House once stood.

In this area rich in stately homes is Marlborough House, at the west end of Pall Mall, which also served as a royal home before it became the Commonwealth Centre in 1962. It was built by Christopher Wren for Queen Anne's friend Sarah, Duchess of Marlborough, who wanted it to look as little like her palace at Blenheim as possible. King Edward VII, Queen Victoria's eldest son, lived here as Prince of Wales and made it the most fashionable house in London; later it was to become home to his widow, Queen Alexandra, and to his son's widow, Queen Mary.

Further along Pall Mall is Schomberg House which, though rebuilt inside, retains its early eighteenth-century facade. It was for a time the home of the painter Thomas Gainsborough, but its most interesting occupant was Scottish 'doctor' James Graham, who in 1771 established his 'Temple of Health and Hymen' here. He used to charge barren couples a considerable sum for sleeping in his 'Magnetic Celestial Bed'. There, on a mattress made of springy hair from the tails of English stallions, and serenaded by music which came from the mouths of gilded nymphs, the customers were supposed to be ideally placed to conceive perfect babies. Graham, who was ultimately confined in a lunatic asylum, gave employment at one time to a fifteen year old girl called Emily Hart. Her job was to appear before the clients dressed in a see-through robe depicting the 'Goddess of Health'. Known to her friends as Emma, she became the wife of Sir William Hamilton and the great love of Lord Nelson.

Schomberg House (below, left), and 'Doctor' James Graham's Magnetic Celestial Bed (above) – complete with the 'Rosy Goddess of Health reposing thereon'. Also in Pall Mall is Marlborough House (below, right).

In contrast to the grandeur of Pall Mall, some of the most appealing of London's open spaces are relatively small. I very much like Soho Square, especially the Tudor-style toolshed in the centre – it was actually placed there in 1870. Few of the buildings around the square remain as they were when it was laid out in 1680, but the statue of King Charles II 'neatly cut in stone to the life, standing on a Pedestal', displaced for a time by the toolshed, is now back in the square where it belongs. A very welcome patch of open space near Broadcasting House is in Cavendish Square; it serves to conceal the presence of a large underground car park. In the square it's worth pausing to admire Jacob Epstein's *Madonna and Child* over the entrance to the Convent of the Holy Child which the sculptor called his 'passport to heaven'.

Just off Mecklenburgh Square, somewhat further to the east, there's an area where, for a change, adults are not admitted unless accompanied by a child. This is Coram's Fields, named after the remarkable eighteenth century philanthropist who, in 1742, established the Foundling Hospital. His aim was to provide care and accommodation for some of the unwanted children who were left to die in London's streets, and he was greatly assisted in his fund-raising efforts by distinguished artists of the time. Hogarth admiringly painted Coram's portrait which, together with other fine pictures displayed in the Governors' Court Room,

was an attraction to visitors and helped persuade them to subscribe to the hospital. Another notable supporter of Coram's work was Handel. He made the chapel of the hospital a very fashionable place of worship, and put on performances of *Messiah* which raised the large sum for those days of £7000 for the hospital funds. He also wrote a special Foundling Hospital anthem which has the Hallelujah Chorus as its climax. It is sometimes performed at the annual concerts given in the Court Room (now recreated in a modern building) to celebrate Handel's birthday.

Jacob Epstein's 'passport to heaven' (above): his **Madonna and Child** *at the Convent of the Holy Child.*

This Tudor gatehouse (left) is actually a Victorian toolshed in Soho Square.

Over 200 years after his death, Thomas Coram's name is still associated with children: adults can't get in to Coram's Fields without one (below, left). Handel raised funds for Coram's Foundling Hospital, and presented the organ (below) for its chapel. The Thomas Coram Foundation also has an original manuscript of Handel's **Messiah** *(below).*

COUNTER POINTS

My wife and I once went to Harrods and came out having bought a grand piano and a pair of kippers. This I think was perhaps the most enjoyable single shopping expedition I've ever had in London. I'm not one to linger in shops these days, but I used to find them fascinating as a boy: I particularly liked the old-fashioned haberdashery shops where the assistant at the counter would place the money and the bill in a small wooden cup which she would screw into a fitting on an overhead wire. By touching a lever, she would then propel the container along the wire at high speed towards a centrally placed cashier who would remove the cup, receipt the bill, replace it in the cup with any necessary change and send it zooming back to the customer at the counter. This added a great deal of interest to what otherwise might have been a very boring expedition in search of pillowcases or dusters.

Harrods, scene of one of the most enjoyable shopping expeditions I've ever had.

Going to Harrods to buy a grand piano is of course not the kind of shopping that has to be done every day and it felt wonderfully extravagant – even the kippers (bought rather more on impulse) had a touch of luxury about them; we took them away in a very neat little parcel lined with greaseproof paper and elegantly tied up with string. Our purchases that day were an indication of the extraordinary range of goods and services offered by the famous store in Knightsbridge: indeed it claims to be the most comprehensive shop in the world, with its own travel agency, estate office, funeral service and pet shop as well as the only circulating library in London.

The history of Harrods goes back to 1849 when Henry Charles Harrod, a tea merchant, took over a small grocery shop in what is now the Brompton Road from his friend, P.H. Burden. It had a turnover of £20 a week and employed two assis-

tants. Then, thanks to the Great Exhibition of 1851, Knightsbridge changed from an area infamous for highway robberies to a newly fashionable district and Mr Harrod's son, Charles Digby, was soon expanding the business. The way he coped with the situation after a fire destroyed the store, completely stocked for Christmas, on 6th December 1883, has passed into Harrods folklore. On the day following the fire, Charles wrote this letter to his customers:

I greatly regret to inform you, that in consequence of the above premises being burnt down, your order will be delayed in the execution a day or two. I hope, in the course of Tuesday or Wednesday next, to be able to forward it.
In the meantime, may I ask for your kind indulgence.
Your obedient servant,
C.D. Harrod.

A preservation order protects the mosaic tiles in the Meat Hall at Harrod's (right). Hamley's in Regent Street (below) is paradise for children of any age.

The first escalator in a London store was installed in Harrods in 1898 because the manager had an intense dislike of lifts but the new-fangled device was regarded with such alarm by some customers that an attendant had to be stationed at the top to dispense brandy to gentlemen and sal volatile to ladies who were overcome by terror. Construction of the present store began in 1901 and the original plaster ceilings can still be seen – the Meat Hall even has a preservation order on it because of its beautiful mosaic tiles.

The most popular store in London with children is unquestionably Hamley's of Regent Street, with its amazing range of toys and games. I remember emerging from it just before Christmas one year when my two sons were young, bearing an enormous stuffed elephant which had taken their fancy on an earlier visit – the taxi driver expressed no surprise. People have been tempted to indulge their own and other people's children with presents from Hamley's since 1760, when William Hamley opened a toy shop called 'Noah's Ark' in High Holborn. One new game they offered for sale was Cossima; it failed to catch the public imagination until it was renamed Ping Pong.

Another shop that was a great landmark in Holborn for many years was Gamage's. Known as 'The People's Popular Emporium', it was of great interest to children because it had a splendid toy department and a zoological department. The only problem in Gamage's was that it was a somewhat higgledy-piggledy place, thanks to the fact that its founder, A.W. Gamage, a farmer's son from Herefordshire, added a number of small old properties to his original shop. This was very tiny, but within a short while Gamage had fulfilled the motto he hung above the door: 'Great Oaks from Little Acorns grow'. He became official outfitter to the scout movement, and when he died in 1939 he is said to have lain in state in the cycling department.

A number of enterprising Victorian tradesmen felt it was part of the business to offer accommodation to their employees. The Bon Marché at Brixton, said to have been the first purpose-built department store in London, and founded in 1877 by James Smith out of the proceeds of successful punting at the Newmarket races, had a large residential block attached to it; 700 employees of Marshall and Snelgrove in Oxford Street not only lived on the premises but were offered the facilities of a library, sitting rooms, smoking rooms and reading rooms. One of the partners, James Marshall, another entrepreneur who made a great oak grow from a little acorn, lived in grand style at Mill Hill. When the Midland Railway wanted to run its line through his estate, Marshall allowed them to do so, provided he had the right to stop any train if it suited him.

I owe my first experience of London's large stores to my grandmother, who took me with her on many occasions to the shops in Kensington High Street where we visited Ponting's, Barker's and Derry and Toms. All three stores were owned by Barker's by that time, but each retained its own individual character. Ponting's, founded in 1873 by Tom

Ponting from Gloucester, offered the cheapest bargains. It was always busy and crowded and rather despised by my grandmother. Barker's was in the middle range – all right for school clothes and shoes – but Derry and Toms was really the only shop in Kensington fit for a lady. Thanks to an ample supply of water from artesian wells 400 feet below the street, the store had a magnificent garden on the roof extending over an acre and a quarter. Although the soil was nowhere more than thirty inches deep, the garden had 500 shrubs and trees, a stream complete with live flamingoes, and corners of special character such as the Dutch and Spanish gardens.

The imposing chateau-style facade of Marshall and Snelgrove (above), designed by Octavius Hansard contrasted vividly with Pontings in the late nineteenth century (below, left).

Derry and Toms, 'the only shop in Kensington fit for a lady', had its own garden – complete with Sun Pavilion (below).

WE HAVE EVERY PLEASURE IN ANNOUNCING THAT THE FORMAL OPENING OF OUR PREMISES—LONDON'S NEWEST SHOPPING CENTRE—BEGINS TO-DAY AND CONTINUES THROUGHOUT THE WEEK.

WE WISH IT TO BE CLEARLY UNDERSTOOD THAT OUR INVITATION IS TO THE WHOLE BRITISH PUBLIC AND TO VISITORS FROM OVERSEAS—THAT NO CARDS OF ADMISSION ARE REQUIRED—THAT ALL ARE WELCOME—AND THAT THE PLEASURES OF SHOPPING AS WELL AS THOSE OF SIGHT-SEEING BEGIN FROM THE OPENING HOUR.

SELFRIDGE & CO.
OXFORD STREET, LONDON, W.

A vivid example of the extravagant publicity that heralded the opening of Selfridge's in 1909.

The London Post Office directory of 1854 listed a Toy and Fancy Repository run by Joseph Toms. Eight years later he joined forces with Charles Derry and soon they had seven shops with 200 employees, all of whom lived in. The Derry and Toms I remember was built in 1933 and ceased to operate in 1973. To my mind it's one of the more regrettable losses from London's shopping scene.

Whiteley's in Queensway, Bayswater was another favourite store of my grandmother, and in the thirties seemed to fulfil the claim of its founder, William Whiteley, to be the Universal Provider, offering for sale everything from a pin to an

elephant. Whiteley came to London from Leeds in 1831 when he was twenty and ran a series of shops until, in 1851, that extremely fertile source of inspiration, the Great Exhibition, led him to conceive the notion of opening 'a vast emporium'. With the £700 he had saved, he decided to set up business in Westbourne Grove and by 1872 he had bought up most of the shops in the street. Whiteley continued to prosper in spectacular fashion until 1897 when a fire, started it's said by jealous traders, broke out in his premises, and burned for several days. He seems to have had a talent for arousing enmity, for on 24th January 1907 he was shot dead in his office by a man claiming to be his natural son.

The founder's death did not stop the progress of the firm, and in 1911 a magnificent new store in Queensway was opened. By the time I first entered it to visit Father Christmas in his grotto, the store was owned by a thrusting American from Wisconsin, Harry Gordon Selfridge, but it still retained its own leisurely and graceful character. During the eighties, Whiteley's was closed but it has been reopened as a smart shopping centre that once again reflects the grandeur of its beginnings as London's first department store.

Gordon Selfridge came to London in 1906, having established a meteoric buying and selling career in Chicago. He thought he could do better than the typical ingratiating London shopkeeper, and with the backing of Sam Waring of Waring and Gillow (given on condition that he would not compete with them by selling furniture), Selfridge leased 40,000 square feet at the western, unfashionable end of Oxford Street. In 1909 he opened his huge new store with a blaze of publicity such as London had never before known. The 130 departments were to include a bargain basement, reading and rest rooms, post office and roof garden; and there was an ice cream soda fountain which was a great attraction to the young – including Noel Coward who was taken there by his mother as a reward for successfully dealing with the part of a mussel in a play called *The Goldfish*. In all its aspects, Selfridge's was hugely impressive, particularly at Christmas time when its illuminations outdid those of any other shop (indeed that tradition is still maintained) and, for me, it was Selfridge's Father Christmas who gave the best presents. The enormous bronze lift doors always impressed me greatly, and as for the lifts themselves, the interiors in the thirties were so striking that they eventually found their way to the Museum of London.

A fine shop, which my family used to think too grand for us, was Swan and Edgar's. It used to occupy a large corner site in Piccadilly Circus but its origins were humble enough. William Edgar ran a haberdashery stall in St James's market and used to sleep under it at night; then he met Mr Swan and set up shop with him in Ludgate. The move to the bottom end of Regent Street came later.

An interesting history belongs to another of London's large stores, Liberty's in Regent Street. Famous originally for exotic fabrics, it now sells all sorts of things but has retained its artistically conscious image. Arthur Lasenby Liberty graduated from the oriental warehouse of Farmer and Rogers to found his own store in 1875, and from the outset he had close links with the aesthetic leaders of the day. Thomas Wardle, a friend of William Morris, produced for Liberty's block-printed designs on Indian silks – among their customers were Ruskin, Alma-Tadema, Burne-Jones, Rossetti and Whistler – and the 'costume department' was responsible for making the draperies of pre-Raphaelite paintings fashionable for women's clothes. Liberty's then received a further boost when in 1881 Gilbert ordered from the store the costumes for *Patience,* a satire on the aesthetic movement, and four years later it was partly the fashionable appeal of the Japanese fabrics sold by Liberty's that led him to produce the most successful of the Savoy operas, *The Mikado.*

The First World War brought Liberty's in touch with the march of modern history, for in 1914 they lost an order when the Archduke Franz Ferdinand was assassinated. Another order was automatically cancelled with the outbreak of the

Swan and Edgar (above), the store that used to dominate Piccadilly Circus.

Selfridge's (left), where Father Christmas really knew how to give a boy the right kind of present.

Russian Revolution: the new curtains ordered by the Tsar for his palace at St Petersburg were no longer required. In the twenties, Liberty's expanded into two large shops, one in Regent Street and the other in Great Marlborough Street, joined by a bridge over narrow Kingly

Liberty's, unlike many of its contemporaries, maintains an imposing and attractive presence in the West End.

Street. The timbered façade and interior of the Great Marlborough Street shop were constructed from the remains of two old men o'war, HMS *Hindustan* and HMS *Impregnable*.

In recent times the fashion-conscious young have not tended to look to Liberty's for their clothes; their fickle allegiance shifts instead from King's Road Chelsea, to Carnaby Street and Covent Garden, and back again. It was when I was living in Chelsea and enjoying the swirl of King's Road on a Saturday afternoon that I first began thinking about the extraordinary range of specialist shops that exist in London, some with equally extraordinary names. For example, there is Thomas Crapper and Co. Ltd, whose smart headquarters are in the King's Road. Crapper

came to London from Yorkshire in 1843 and made his reputation as a plumber and sanitary engineer. His firm became famous for its water closets, but he denied responsibility for giving currency to 'a rather vulgar verb'.

Some of the oldest specialist shops in London are to be found in St James's Street. For example, No. 3 is occupied by one of Britain's longest-established wine merchants, Berry Brothers and Rudd. There's an old set of scales in the shop dating from the days when they used to sell condiments; the scales were also used to weigh customers, including Lord Byron, Beau Brummell and a St James's character known as Fighting Fitzgerald. While he was being weighed, an acquaintance looked in at the door and remarked

he blood of an Irishman'. Fitz-
eputedly leapt out of the scales,
...s sword and cut off the man's
nos..., exclaiming: 'I'm damned if you'll
ever smell another!' The unfortunate visitor's remark was more pointed than it
might seem, for Fitzgerald used to drink
draughts of his own blood in the strange
belief that it would prolong his life for a
thousand years.

James Lock established his hatter's
business at No. 6 St James's Street in
1764 and amongst his customers were
Lord Nelson, who ordered a special hat
from the shop with a built-in eyeshade,
and Wellington, who came here to buy
the plumed hat he wore at the battle of
Waterloo. In 1850 a landowner called Sir
William Coke ordered a special hat for his
gamekeepers, designed to fit closely to the
head so that it would not fall off when

*Berry Brothers and Rudd
(above), one of Britain's
longest-established wine
merchants; and Lock's (left),
once hatters to Lord Nelson
and the Duke of Wellington,
and originators of the bowler.*

they were chasing poachers. Known in St
James's as a 'coke', it was popularly called
a 'bowler', after Lock's chief suppliers,
Thomas and William Bowler in Southwark Bridge Road.

A faded notice in the window of the
shop at No. 9 St James's Street reads 'Cobblers by special appointment to the Duke
of Edinburgh'. The notice dates from
1863, but its statement remains just as

true today, for the firm of John Lobb
holds royal shoefitting appointments to
the Queen, the Duke of Edinburgh and
the Prince of Wales. The connection began with the founder of the firm, the
Cornishman John Lobb; he had gone out
to Australia and done very well by making
a gold-prospector's boot with a secret
compartment in the heel to contain nug-
gets and dust. When he sent a pair of

'Cobblers by special appointment to the Duke of Edinburgh': Lobb's, St James's Street (above), and the 1863 notice proclaiming their royal connections (above, right). Footwear from Lobb's is more of an investment than an impulse-buy and a library of lasts ensures that handmade boots and shoes are produced to an exact fit (right).

boots back across the oceans to the Prince of Wales in 1862 he was rewarded immediately by a royal warrant. Lobb's handmade boots and shoes continue to be in high demand all over the world, though today a pair would cost not far short of a thousand pounds. It remains a cottage industry, with expert craftsmen working at home as well as in the St James's Street premises, and those who have the money to invest in Lobb footwear think it well worth waiting six months for delivery. Repeat orders are no problem, for there's a library of lasts in the shop which reproduce the shape of each customer's feet to perfection. Lobb's has attracted some remarkable customers: Caruso once sang an impromptu aria to the staff while waiting for his boots to be packed, and Lobb's experts were only momentarily nonplussed when a customer produced an elephant's ear out of a brown paper parcel and asked for his shoes to be made out of that.

Some of the customers of Willy Clarkson, who lived and died (in 1934) above his shop at 41-43 Wardour Street, were also noteworthy characters. He developed his father's wig-making business with such success that at one time he hired out some 10,000 wigs every Christmas. He was also patronised by leading members of the theatrical profession, so much so that when he set up shop in Wardour Street in 1905, Sarah Bernhardt laid the foundation stone and Sir Henry Irving the coping stone. But among those who consulted Willy Clarkson were people whose need for disguise was far from

legitimate, including it's said, the notorious criminals Dr Crippen and Charles
Peace. Clarkson's business is no longer in
existence, so when I was due to appear on
stage as Sir Arthur Sullivan, I consulted a
rather splendid establishment called
Theatre Zoo in Earlham Street. They ran
me up a set of very convincing and perfectly fitted whiskers in a matter of days.

Also in the business of deception is
Davenports, to be found in the underground concourse at Charing Cross Station. Claimed by those in the know to be
the best magic shop in the world, Davenports is notable for the fact that the assistants there will demonstrate any of their
tricks for you while you wait.

The scenic artist is catered for by
Brodie and Middleton at No. 68 Drury
Lane who sell stage paints and canvas,
whilst other artists might be directed to
L. Cornellissen and Sons in Great Russell
Street; they offer pigments and paint-
brushes and indeed most other things a
painter might need. Those who specialise
in calligraphy could find a visit to Philip
Poole, also in Drury Lane, very useful. In
the window there's a display of pen nibs
of all descriptions under the slogan *Vive
La Plume!*

I had a brief flirtation with a cello
as a schoolboy and, perhaps because of
that, I particularly like visiting J.P.
Guivier and Co. Ltd who have a charming
shop in Mortimer Street near Broadcasting House. The firm sells instruments of
widely varying value and age, from a do-
it-yourself violin kit from China which,
complete with bow and case, retails today
for £55, to cellos worth hundreds of
thousands of pounds. The company was
founded in 1863 by a French maker of
music strings, Jean Prosper Guivier. He

*Shops for specialists:
Davenports (top) offers magic
while you wait; Philip Poole in
Drury Lane caters for a
different kind of craft, and a
mosaic of pen-nibs (above, left)
is an unusual advertisement
for the shop's wares.
Everything the artist needs is
available at Cornelissen and
Son (above), Great Russell
Street.*

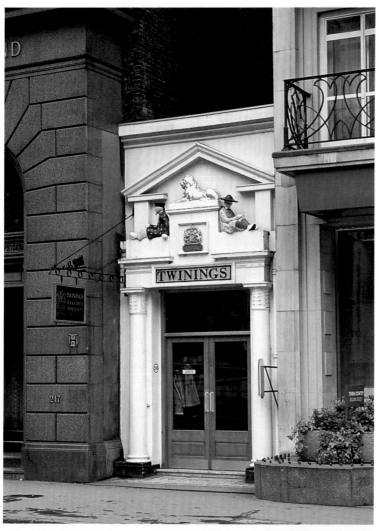

was killed in the Franco-Prussian war of 1870 and the business was purchased by an enterprising woman, Mrs Cohn – formerly Miss Hawkes – whose family was to become a major name in the music retailing business, as one half of the firm of Boosey and Hawkes.

There's a plaque in St Martin's Lane which recalls the work of one of Britain's greatest craftsmen in wood, Thomas Chippendale. In 1754 he and his partner James Rennie took out a lease on two houses in St Martin's Lane with work-shops and a yard (which still exists) at the rear; there they pursued their cabinet-making business, employing twenty-two workmen. Other people were able to copy Chippendale's elegant designs when he brought out a collection of engraved pla-tes showing Chippendale chairs, book-cases and other articles of furniture under the title *The Gentlemen and Cabinet Maker's Director*.

Another echo of eighteenth-century London is the doorway on the Strand embellished by two colourful models of Chinamen that leads into London's narro-west shop. Twinings', the tea merchant, is also the oldest shop in the city to stand on its original site and the Chinamen are a reminder that tea was imported from Chi-na long before Indian tea found favour in the nineteenth century.

A selection of bottles and old carboys containing coloured fluids of the kind that often used to be displayed in chemists'

Twinings' doorway in the Strand (above) is a reminder of China's long-standing importance as a tea-producer, and among the extensive stock at the Mortimer Street premises of J.P. Guivier (near right) is a make-it-yourself violin kit from the same country.

A commemorative plaque (above) marks the fact that Thomas Chippendale once had a workshop in St Martin's Lane.

shops is still to be seen in the window of Meacher, Higgins and Thomas in Crawford Street. This old pharmacy, which opened in 1814, has a splendid iron lantern projecting from the first floor and is a striking feature in a street which has retained, as a whole, much of its eighteenth-century elegance.

Sartorial elegance can be found at the tailors of Savile Row, and at the shirtmakers of Jermyn Street, but one of the most attractive shop fronts has more to do with the inner than the outer man. This is the famous cheese shop of Paxton and Whitfield, where some 250 carefully selected cheeses can be sampled in an historic setting – complete with sawdust on the floor – reminiscent of the shop's beginnings in 1797.

There are specialist shops of every conceivable description in London. Shops for collectors of coins and stamps, model enthusiasts, lovers of uniforms and militaria, connoisseurs of food, wine, fine art and antiquities, not to mention books of every description. I once worked for a time in the largest of London's bookshops, Foyles in Charing Cross Road, where I re-organised the shelves in the secondhand school-book department. I don't remember meeting any especially famous customers, but almost everyone

has been there at some time or another, including Walt Disney who was often seen browsing among the art books.

On a more practical note, I'm fascinated by Edwardes of Camberwell who surely have one of the oddest royal appointments. They are 'Suppliers of Mopeds to H.M. The Queen'. The Queen may not use too many mopeds personally, but they are said to be in demand by the

Cheese-purveyors Paxton and Whitfield (above, left) have been in business since 1797, while pharmacists Meacher, Higgins and Thomas (below) only opened in 1814, so are callow newcomers by comparison. The first floor lantern there is a further reminder of nineteenth-century elegance (above).

Edwardes of Camberwell (right) have been connected with the royal household since 1908 but, though they are official moped-suppliers to the Queen (above), I can't recall ever seeing her ride one.

You can find just about anything, and anyone, in Portobello Road's famous market (below and below, right).

staff at Buckingham Palace, and this firm, which has been selling bicycles, motorbikes and the like since 1908, is happy to provide them.

Those on the look-out for bargains in London have no need to go to the grand shops. There's a multitude of markets, some of them specialising in a particular line of goods. The Portobello Road, which took its name from the capture of Puerto Bello in the Caribbean by Admiral Vernon in 1739, is a mecca for antique dealers, but further north along Golborne Road pretty well anything is for sale from records to prams, books and plants and even, as I noticed in one shop, cut-price gold lamé suits. Portobello Road itself has become very fashionable, and the same is

Although the exterior of Covent Garden has not changed drastically (left), basket-carrying porters (below) have been replaced by visitors from all over the world.

true of Covent Garden. The latter is now a mass of small boutiques, cafés and restaurants, but for almost three centuries it was the home of London's biggest fruit and vegetable market. The lorries which transported supplies into the market created desperate congestion, and no doubt it was entirely sensible to move the market out to new premises at Nine Elms, but a wonderfully lively part of the London scene has vanished as a result. It was a great entertainment to see the porters skilfully moving around with great stacks of round baskets on their heads, and there was a stimulating contrast between the clamorous scenes in the market place and the plush elegance of the opera house, though sometimes, it had to be said, you had to wade through acres of rubbish to get there. That inconvenience was not a new one – complaints were registered on that score as early as 1666.

The present-day scene in Covent Garden is full of life and considerable crowds now gather to watch the buskers outside St Paul's Church or to wander in and out of the multitude of interesting shops. Among the shops is Segar and Snuff which, complete with its original interior, moved there from New Cavendish Street a few years ago. As the name suggests, it caters for the requirements of the smoker and snuff-taker and supplies

Smithfield market has been cleaned up, in every sense of the word, since the rowdy days of Bartholomew Fair (right). Meat may still be hung there (below, right), but the cattle are now slaughtered elsewhere.

New use for old: Covent Garden has been successfully converted into shops, such as Segar and Snuff (above), and restaurants (below).

specialist brands to customers from almost every country in the world. One day the proprietor hopes to welcome a visitor from the only country so far unrepresented, Rumania.

Another central London market that has remained in its original location is Smithfield. Everywhere in London it seems there are reminders of the Great Exhibition and here is another, for Horace Jones completed the main building in 1868 to a design inspired by the Crystal Palace. Smithfield is devoted to meat, and between 5 and 9am it is at its busiest. To cater for the thirsty workers certain pubs in this area open at the crack of dawn.

There's been a market at Smithfield, or Smoothfield as it was once called, since medieval times. For 400 years it was a place of public execution, and cattle were driven through the streets of London to be killed here until 1844. It must have been a horrible place in those days, to judge from the description in *Oliver Twist*. 'The ground was covered nearly ankle deep with filth and mire', wrote Dickens, who was choked by 'the thick steam perpetually rising from the reeking bodies of the cattle'. It was, he continued, 'a stunning and bewildering scene which quite confounded the senses'. More cheerfully, though often scandalously it seems, Smithfield was the scene of Bartholomew Fair from 1123 until it was banned in the nineteenth century for 'rowdiness and debauchery'.

Leadenhall Market, like Smithfield, was the work of the architect Horace Jones. Built in 1881, it stands on the site of a house with a lead roof and around this, in the fourteenth century, 'foreigners' (that is, people who came in from outside London) were allowed to sell their poultry. It remained a wholesale market for centuries, but now offers a great variety of meat, poultry, fish and game to the general public as well as some of the bars and eating houses that are so popular today with city workers.

The great attraction for market enthusiasts on a Sunday morning is Petticoat Lane. In fact there's no street of that name these days and the market extends over quite a wide area with Middlesex Street at the heart of it. The original name derived from an old clothes market which was already flourishing in the time of Queen Elizabeth I, and new and second-hand clothes are still to be found there. Large crowds surge around the stalls on Sunday mornings, as they did in Victorian times when Petticoat Lane was one of

London's most flourishing markets. Here, as at many of London's other markets and shops, customers are attracted just as much by the predominantly good-humoured bustle of the place as by the urge to buy something.

Though the present Leadenhall market (above) was built in 1881, there have been markets on its site since the fourteenth century. Unlike Leadenhall, Petticoat Lane (below) is open to the weather.

PASTYME WITH GOOD COMPANYE

'London' wrote Thomas Middleton in 1617 'is the dining-room of Christendom', and indeed there's little it cannot provide in the way of hospitality and social pleasure. Dining out in style is not a recent trend in London and, whilst I like good food and drink, I've neither the cash nor the capacity to consume the vast quantities required at one time by some of London's more notorious trenchermen. King Henry VIII was certainly among them, but it is perhaps less well-known that, when he was not busy acquiring possessions, disposing of those who stood in the way of his dynastic ambitions, or enjoying his sporting and social life, he was a great lover of music. In July 1517, he listened for four hours at a stretch to the organist of St Mark's Venice, Dionyses Memo; he employed about sixty court musicians; and was himself a notable performer on the organ, lute and virginals – as well as an enthusiastic singer. The King also wrote music and thirty-four of his compositions have survived. His most famous song expressed his relish for sociable diversions: it was called *Pastyme with Good Companye*; the tune however was almost identical to the melody of a chanson published in a French collection of 1529. But in those days most composers, monarchs or not, were great borrowers.

Henry's capital city, like the hills in a well known musical film, was 'alive to the sound of music'; it was also, then, as now, a great attraction to anyone who enjoyed the convivial life in all its forms. Dr Johnson, probably the best known of all London's *bon viveurs,* is said to have asserted that a tavern chair was the throne of human felicity; indeed the chair in which Johnson used to sit in the Old Cock Tavern is one of the treasures displayed at Johnson's memorial house at No.17, Gough Square. He lived there from 1746 to 1759 and compiled his famous dictionary in the garret with the help of six clerks. After Johnson had sent the last corrected proofs to his publisher, Andrew Millar, he asked the messenger about Millar's reaction. The messenger reported that the publisher had said 'Thank God I have done with him,' to which Johnson replied 'I am glad he thanks God for anything.'

When Boswell once suggested to Johnson that, if he stayed in the city for ever, he might grow tired of London, Johnson made the immortal reply: 'Why, sir, you find no man, at all intellectual, who is willing to leave London. No, sir, when a man is tired of London, he is tired of life; for there is in London all that life can afford.' It was in the company of

friends that Johnson was at his happiest; he was the acknowledged dictator of 'the Club', formed in 1763 by himself and Sir Joshua Reynolds, with Gibbon, Fox, Sheridan and Garrick among the members. Another member was Johnson's biographer Sir John Hawkins, but one wonders how much he contributed to the proceedings since Dr Johnson rather disparagingly referred to him as 'a very un-clubbable man'.

A sense of belonging must have been felt, however, by the select few invited to one of the oddest private parties ever given in London. It was held by the sculptor Adrian Jones who created the great bronze quadriga, a chariot drawn by four horses, which stands on top of Constitution Arch at Hyde Park Corner. Just before the unveiling of the quadriga in 1912, Jones gave a dinner for eight inside the monument.

I too had a distinct feeling of privilege when asked to dine as the guest of the officers of the Queen's Guard one night at St James's Palace. I am sure they are more than vigilant in their duties, but they also find time to dine well, inviting the occasional guest to join them. On the occasion of my visit, the Scots Guard were on duty, and we were serenaded through part of the meal by a piper who marched round and round the table. This did little to promote conversation. Another memorable occasion for me was when I dined as

17 Gough Square (below), where Dr Johnson lived and compiled his dictionary, is now a museum in his memory (above). His favourite chair from the Old Cock Tavern is on show there (bottom).

Constitution Arch provided an unusual setting for its sculptor's dinner party.

I enjoyed a lunch with the judges at the Old Bailey (below) undisturbed by any reminders of nearby Newgate Prison, noisome or otherwise. The 'condemned' cell (right: on the morning of an execution in 1828) was a far less pleasant place to be.

guest of a minister at the House of Commons, although towards the end of the evening I experienced a moment of disillusion. After an extremely good meal my host asked if I would like a liqueur. I decided on a Green Chartreuse, but I was brought a Crême de Menthe instead. Quite gently I asked the waitress, who I like to think was not a regular member of staff, if she would change the drink, to which she replied, 'Why? It's green, innit?'

No such anticlimax occurred when I was invited to lunch with the judges at the Old Bailey on one occasion. To me there's something faintly bizarre about sitting down to enjoy oneself in such surroundings, but I suppose there's no reason why the judges should not lunch in style even if the prisoners they are trying do rather less well in the cells down below. At one time such a party would probably have been ruined by the noisome smells which emanated from Newgate Prison, near to which the Central Criminal Court now stands. In 1750 the cells of the prison bred a horrible jail fever which killed the Lord Mayor, two judges, an alderman, an under-sheriff and fifty others. Ever since then, from 1st May to 30th September, the judges and their assistants have carried nosegays of sweet-smelling English flowers and the courtrooms have been strewn with fragrant garden herbs.

The name of one of Britain's most notorious judges is associated with two riverside pubs in the East End. Lord Jeffreys of Wem became known as 'the hanging judge' chiefly on account of his conduct during the so-called 'Bloody Assizes' of 1685; on circuit in the west country he tried the ringleaders of the abortive Monmouth rebellion against King James II, and sentenced 200 of them to be hung, drawn and quartered, as well as ordering a thousand more to be sent to the West Indies as slaves. The judge apparently liked to take a drink of an evening on the wooden balcony of The Prospect of Whitby which overlooks the river at Wapping Wall. From there he could look towards Execution Dock where the bodies of pirates were hung in chains to allow three tides to pass over them before their remains were cut down. One of the

oldest riverside pubs, The Prospect of Whitby started life in 1520 as an abode of thieves and smugglers known as the Devil's Tavern but its more respectable patrons included Pepys and, in later times, Dickens and the artists Whistler and Turner. In the early eighteenth century a sailor is said to have sold an exotic plant to a gardener he met in The Prospect, and that was how the fuchsia was introduced to these islands.

When James II fell from power in 1688, Judge Jeffreys attempted to leave the country but, while waiting to board a collier bound for Hamburg, he was recognised in another riverside inn, The Town of Ramsgate, by a man who had appeared before him. Jeffreys was threatened with lynching by the mob, but instead was arrested by a company of soldiers who removed him to the Tower of London where he died. There was rough justice in what happened to the 'hanging judge' in The Town of Ramsgate. In the cellars of the same inn, convicts were held in chains before being transported to Australia.

The more civilised aspects of the law are symbolised by London's four Inns of Court, and to be invited to dine in one of them is a pleasure not least because they are attended by many ancient traditional procedures. The Inns came into existence in medieval times as hostels and teaching institutions for legal apprentices, and the benchers of each Inn still hold the power of calling students to the Bar. The earliest records of Lincoln's Inn date from 1422, and one of its first known members was

The gallows on The Town of Ramsgate's terrace (above, left) is a reminder of 'Hanging' Judge Jeffreys' narrow escape from the lynch-mob.

Justice of a more civilised sort is associated with the Inns of Court, where a superb hammer-beam roof (top) presides over the oak table in Middle Temple Hall (facing page and above).

Sir John Fortescue, Chief Justice of the King's Bench in 1442; since then a number of Lord Chancellors and Prime Ministers have been members of the Inn, including Walpole, the younger Pitt and Lord Melbourne. Disraeli and Gladstone were both enrolled as students there.

On land once occupied by the Knights Templar, two Inns of Court are now accommodated, known as the Inner and Middle Temples. Every evening a horn is blown to summon members to dinner in their halls. The Inner Temple hall is a modern building which still retains a medieval buttery and crypt to serve as a reminder of the hall of the Knights Templar which once stood on the site. The Middle Temple hall was completed in 1573 and has a magnificent oak hammer-beam roof. The 29-foot long bench table was made from a single oak tree said to have been presented to the Inn by Queen Elizabeth I, who was so pleased with the way she had been received by the Middle Temple lawyers that she made them a Christmas pudding. Part of the pudding was saved and mixed into the following year's pudding as a continuing reminder of royal favour, and the ancient custom was recalled for one occasion in 1971 when Queen Elizabeth the Queen Mother stirred a special pudding for the benchers. The Middle Temple hall was often used to stage lavish entertainments and on 2nd February 1601, Shakespeare's *Twelfth Night* was performed there.

Another of Shakespeare's plays, *The Comedy of Errors,* was first performed in 1594 in the hall of Gray's Inn, where the playwright patron, the Earl of

Gray's Inn gardens, and the catalpa tree descended from Sir Walter Raleigh's American cuttings.

Southampton, was a member. Francis Bacon was treasurer of Gray's Inn and planted in the gardens a catalpa tree which grew from cuttings brought back from America by Sir Walter Raleigh.

In 1529 the benchers of Gray's Inn bought Staple Inn in Holborn and in 1586 added the façade with overhanging gables which is said to be the oldest example of Elizabethan domestic architecture in London. The Inn got its name from the Merchants of the Staple (wool merchants) who stayed there in medieval times, and a wool-pack is still to be seen on the wrought-iron gate of the garden. It was at Staple Inn that Dr Johnson wrote *Rasselas* in the space of a single week in 1759 in order to defray his mother's funeral expenses. Dickens described the place in *The Mystery of Edwin Drood* as 'one of those nooks turning into which, out of the clashing street, imparts to the relieved pedestrian the sensation of having put cotton in his ears and velvet soles on his boots.' The American writer Nathaniel Hawthorne had a similar impression. 'In all the hundreds of years since London was built,' he wrote, 'it has not been able to sweep its roaring tide over that little island of quiet.'

Members of the Garrick Club are the only ones allowed to retreat from twentieth-century London's noise into the 'snug' at the foot of the main stairs (above). Another haven from the 'roaring tide' is Staple Inn (left).

The atmosphere of a college or club prevails in London's time-honoured enclaves of the law – indeed there seems to be an endemic tendency among Londoners in general to form enclosed societies. Although I am, like Sir John Hawkins, not a particularly clubbable man, I do relish membership of the Garrick Club. Like most clubs it has curious idiosyncrasies: members dine in the Coffee Room (one of the most beautiful rooms I know,

Lyons Corner House in the Strand (above) in 1915: luxury at affordable prices. There was no self-service in those days: patrons were served by waitresses. These 'nippies' (top) were on duty at the Oxford Street premises.

The idea was to found 'a society in which actors and men of education and refinement might meet on equal terms' (as if the two categories were immutably distinct) and the style of the club remains to this day highly convivial. The Garrick was named after the most famous English actor of the eighteenth century, and it houses a number of items associated with the leading actor of a later age, Sir Henry Irving, including the chair in which he died while on tour at the Midland Hotel in Bradford. It's odd to recall that so revered a figure should have been black-balled when his name was first proposed for election.

One of the most successful journalists and war correspondents of the Victorian age was George Augustus Sala. In 1857 he decided, with a group of like-minded friends, to set up a society which would be a cross between a public house and a private club. The result was the Savage Club, to which I also belonged for some years. Perennially opposed to anyone who could be thought remotely self-righteous or pompous, the club took its name from a reprobate character of Dr Johnson's time, an actor and playwright called Richard Savage who killed a man in a brawl and was later imprisoned for debt. However there is nothing in the least sinister about Savages: their worst offence is what some might consider an excess of good humour. In my days with the club, I used to get great pleasure from a sociable session at the Savage bar at lunchtime, followed by half an hour of deep relaxation in one of the armchairs of the Constitutional Club, whose premises in St James's Street housed the Savage at that particular time.

When I first explored the streets of London as a boy, my grandmother pointed out some of these august premises to me, but the utmost height of our social ambition was to go for tea to a Lyons Corner House. The largest of these was in Coventry Street, where 4500 customers could be seated. There were others in Oxford Street, Marble Arch and near Tottenham Court Road, and there was one in the Strand. These great establishments bore a family resemblance to the picture

with its splendid array of theatrical portraits); there is a sort of 'snug' at the foot of the main stairs which only members are allowed to enter – their guests must not transgress an imaginary line across the entrance to this area; and until relatively recently ladies were not allowed to use the main staircase.

The club was founded in 1831 by a writer and art collector named Francis Mills with the Duke of Sussex as patron.

palaces of the thirties, in that they offered a sensation of grandeur and luxury to those whose normal way of life did not extend to such things. There were palm court orchestras in some of the corner house restaurants, and their music added to the sense of occasion. But a visit to a corner house was regarded as a special treat and more often we would go to an ordinary Lyons teashop. There were 260 of these at one time and prices were kept low, but there was none of today's queuing at a self-service counter. Patrons were served at their tables by a waitress known as a 'Nippy' in a black uniform dress with a tiny white apron in front, and were assured of a very good cup of tea for a penny.

One of the hotels pointed out to me by my grandmother was the Cavendish in Jermyn Street. With her interest in titled folk, she liked to think of its connection with the 'Duchess of Duke Street', even though the proprietor was not a real duchess at all but a society caterer called Rosa Lewis. I was taken to lunch at the

Cavendish not long before the death of the legendary Mrs Lewis in 1952. She still ruled the hotel personally, and guests had to do exactly as they were told. The food was not particularly good, being of the basic plain variety once in favour in upper class country houses, and indeed that was the appeal of the old Cavendish. It has now been replaced by a large modern hotel which still has features, such as the Sub Rosa bar, that are reminiscent of the old days. From her early beginnings as a kitchen maid to the Comte de Paris, Rosa Lewis built up an aristocratic clientèle and became the friend and confidante of King Edward VII in his days as Prince of Wales. She ran an apartment house at

A ragtime band provides a more upbeat tempo than the more usual palm court orchestra at the Oxford Street Lyons in 1916 (above).

Rosa Lewis (below), society caterer with friends in high places, celebrating her eighty-third birthday. She ruled the Cavendish in the days before the original hotel building was replaced by this modern one (left).

The Savoy Hotel (right: the lounge in 1904) was built by Richard D'Oyly Carte on his proceeds from Gilbert and Sullivan's light operas. **Patience** *(above) was the first to be staged at the Savoy Theatre, also built by D'Oyly Carte (below).*

No. 55 Eaton Square which provided him with a discreet rendezvous, and he often entertained in a private suite at the Cavendish after Rosa bought it in 1904 – no wonder it became the ultimate status symbol to give a party provided for by Rosa Lewis. But however grand her clients were, they had to win her approval: when the First World War broke out she hung a picture of the German Kaiser upside down in the servants' lavatory as she considered this to be 'the only throne fit for old Willie'.

One of the unusual features of the old Cavendish Hotel was that each suite of rooms was self-contained and featured an enormous bath. The fact that the Savoy hotel had seventy bathrooms was also thought to be one of its more extraordinary features. This hotel epitomising luxury was built by the impresario Richard D'Oyly Carte on the proceeds of the Gilbert and Sullivan operas and opened in 1889. However, not everyone approved of the efficient modern plumbing capable of filling a bath in twelve seconds. Oscar Wilde was one guest who considered running water vulgar: 'If I desire hot water,' he said, 'I shall ring for it like a gentleman.'

D'Oyly Carte was a great innovator and when he built the Savoy Theatre in 1881, it was the first public building in London to be lit by electricity. Some of the public were alarmed by this, so to allay their fears, Carte went before the curtain on the opening night to assure the audience that should the electricity fail, one gas light would be kept burning. The first Gilbert and Sullivan opera to be staged at the Savoy was *Patience* which was transferred in the middle of its run from the

Opera Comique. It was followed by *Iolanthe, Princess Ida, The Mikado, Ruddigore, The Yeomen of the Guard* and *The Gondoliers* in more or less swift succession, after which the prodigiously successful partnership began to crumble.

Meanwhile the D'Oyly Carte Opera Company was enjoying great success with the Gilbert and Sullivan operas in the United States, and American ideas were widely adopted in the new Savoy hotel. It offered 24-hour room service which could be commanded through speaking tubes installed on every floor, and it had the first electrically operated lifts in Europe. Known as 'ascending rooms', they were panelled opulently in red Chinese lacquer.

Wealth and celebrity have often gone hand in hand at the Savoy. There was the extraordinary Venetian party given by the Wall Street millionaire Alfred Kessler, when the forecourt was flooded and Enrico Caruso sang from a gondola surrounded by swans. Alas, the swans died from the chemical that had been used to turn the water blue. Alfred Krupps ordered a fountain that gushed champagne and the Sultan of Brunei kept two identical sky-blue Rolls Royces there, one at each entrance of the hotel. Frank Sinatra engaged fifteen rooms for himself and his court whereas Marlene Dietrich always slept in the oversize bed normally used by the ebullient reception manager, Claudio Buttafava. After the first night of his opera *Manon Lescaut* at Covent Garden, Puccini entertained Dame Nellie Melba at the Savoy, whose first chef Auguste Escoffier had already created Melba toast and Pêche Melba in her honour.

The Savoy has always taken great trouble to record and remember the tastes of its guests. Noel Coward, for instance, liked a large bed with five pillows, and the tables and chairs, his pills and water glass, all had to be placed in a particular position. Once these things had been disposed to the master's satisfaction, the arrangement was photographed so that it could be reproduced to the last detail every time he stayed at the hotel. The hotel staff are still very good at remembering visitors and this gives the Savoy, despite its grand associations, a warm and welcoming feeling. By the way, those who find themselves at a dinner party for thirteen at the Savoy will notice an extra guest at the table. He is Kaspar, the Savoy cat. This feline model, made by Basil Ionides, was a great favourite of Sir Winston Churchill when he dined at the Savoy, and traditionally he is given a complete place setting and a meal of his own.

Among my friends when I was young was an elderly lady who had been caught up in the literary circles which

One of the Savoy Hotel's 'ascending rooms', panelled in red Chinese lacquer (right). Guests descending to dine and finding themselves one of thirteen are joined at their table by Kaspar (below).

Aleister Crowley (above) – on this occasion without his black cloak – was a frequent visitor to the Café Royal (below). Allinson's painting (above, right) shows the original café, the haunt of many famous literary and artistic figures.

used to frequent the Café Royal, so from an early age I took an interest in the place. The present building, designed in the 1920s to fit in with the curve of Regent Street, preserves some of the atmosphere of the old Domino Room with its marble-topped tables and red velvet seats. From the 1890s until after the First World War it was the resort of many famous writers and artists, among them Augustus John, Walter Sickert, Max Beerbohm and Oscar Wilde. Marie Lloyd is said to have chased the head waiter round the grill room of

the Café Royal with a hat pin, and the necromantic Aleister Crowley would habitually walk to his table shrouded in a black cloak. On the only occasion when he was persuaded to take it off, he was seen to be wearing nothing underneath but a bronze butterfly, stolen from Epstein's nude statue of Oscar Wilde, where it had likewise been employed for modest concealment.

From the Café Royal it's no great distance to Soho where the restaurants which I particularly like – such as the Gay

Hussar in Greek Street – are to be found. However in my youth one of my favourite resorts was the pub then called 'The York Minster' but now, perhaps more accurately, is known as 'The French House'. The remarkable patron, Gaston Berlemont, and his hospitable son transformed it during the war into more of a French café than an English pub, at a time when wine had not entered into the British way of life to any popular extent. The York Minster was the forerunner of the innumerable wine bars which are now to be found in every part of London, and is an early example of the way the British pub has changed in style and opening hours to a much more continental pattern.

A favourite resort with people in broadcasting or the rag trade is a basement wine bar called 'The Lees Bag' (named after an article used in the manufacture of wine) at the Oxford Street end of Great Portland Street. With its upturned barrels and sawdust-covered floor, it seethes with keen wine bibbers at lunchtime and in the early evenings.

Favourite Soho haunts in my youth were the Guy Hussar (above) and The French House (top, right), one of London's first wine-bars. A popular wine-bar with broadcasting people is The Lees Bag (right).

One of the longest bars in Britain (below) is at the Cittie of York, Holborn. Given such a huge bar area, you shouldn't have too much trouble getting served there – but you might if you arrive at The Grenadier by car (below, right).

A taste for drinking table wines instead of beer has developed fairly recently among Londoners, but the call for a glass of port, or 'a small port and lemon', was often to be heard in old establishments such as Henekey's Long Bar in Holborn (now renamed the 'Cittie of York'). Originally built in 1430, it was reconstructed in the 1920s using some of the old materials. Some of the huge thousand-gallon vats from which Henekey's used to bottle their wines and spirits are still ranged above the bar, which happens to be one of the longest in Britain. It's reminiscent in some ways of the large gin palaces of Victorian London, but a measure of privacy is offered by a series of conversational boxes where lawyers, for example, can have a private discussion with a client. The famous Waterloo stove, made of cast iron, is also there and it is still in use, with an outlet for the smoke which runs under the floor.

A number of London pubs are famous for the ghosts that haunt them. The Grenadier in Old Barrack Yard, Wilton Row, formerly The Guardsman and until the year 1818 an officers' mess, is said to be haunted each September by the ghost of an officer who was caught cheating at cards and flogged to death. The Duke of Wellington is said to have played cards here, no doubt blamelessly. There's a sentry box outside The Grenadier and a curious notice saying that only those who have arrived on foot or by taxi will be served.

In 1982 an investigation was carried out to find the twelve most authentically haunted pubs in Britain, and one of them was the Asylum Tavern in Peckham, south London. It's the only pub to bear this name in England and is said to be frequented by the phantom of an old lady dressed in grey with her hair in a bun. I wonder whether an abstinent spectre or two hovers around a rather different place of liquid refreshment in north London. On the corner of Hanley Road and Crouch Hill is the former Friern Manor dairy with delicate frescoes portraying the process of getting the milk from cow to consumer.

One of London's most atmospheric restaurants certainly deserves to be haunted. This is Rules in Maiden Lane which was established at its present address in 1798. The walls are covered with reminders of the famous people who have visited in the past, many of them leading theatrical figures of their day. Lillie Langtry used to come here so often with King Edward VII when he was Prince of Wales that a discreet private door was made for them so that they could enter unobserved.

Contrary to common belief, great expense is not required to eat and drink well in London. I have a great weakness for Italian food, and there's a small Italian restaurant in Great Titchfield Street, the Monte Bello, which I think is a model of how to serve good food with speed and civility – despite the fact that it's always packed to overflowing. There's also an abundance of quick service snack bars all over London, most of which seem to be run by Italians, which offer an extraordinary number of instant dishes to take away or eat on the spot, as well as copiously filled sandwiches of amazing variety. As one who's often in a hurry, I like the friendly efficiency of these busy places.

There are no doubt plenty of people in London today who drink too much, but at one time intemperance was a scourge of city life. In 1859, the Metropolitan Free Drinking Fountain Association was set up with the idea of combating this evil and the spread of disease. After two years the association had set up eighty-five fountains and by 1886 the number totalled nearly 600. Many of them can still be seen today, including the association's first fountain at the Church of the Holy Sepulchre in Holborn Viaduct. The one in Lincoln's Inn Fields bears the inscription 'The Fear of the Lord is the Fountain

of Life'; Charles Barry's 'Woman of Samaria' fountain on Clapham Common dates from 1884; a Gothic fountain in Hyde Park was the gift in 1863, according to the inscription, of one Maharaja Meerza Vijiaran Gajapatiran Manea Sooltan Bhandoor of Vijianagram; and the elaborate fountain in Victoria Park in the East End was unveiled in 1862 before a crowd of 10,000 people.

It was perhaps fortunate that the arrival of the first free drinking fountain was preceded by the opening in 1852 of London's first public lavatory. Known euphemistically as a 'Public Waiting Room', it was established at No.95 Fleet Street by the Royal Society of Arts, at the instigation of Sir Samuel Merton Peto, who built Nelson's Column, and Sir Henry Cole who, among other distinctions, produced the first Christmas card. Admission to this unique haven of relief, however, cost twopence, a prohibitive sum in those days for the poorer classes and 'spending a penny' was not sufficient until the first municipal lavatory opened outside the Royal Exchange in 1855.

Not all the liquid refreshment available in London is based on alcohol. An altogether healthier substance was associated with the Friern Manor Dairy, where frescoes (above) portray the process.

Some of London's watering holes look like elaborate shrines to the virtue of temperance. These drinking-fountains are at Kensington Gardens (above) and Victoria Park (left).

MY KIND OF TOWN

The name of the Frank Sinatra song *My Kind of Town* seems to sum up my feelings towards London. They tend to be a little nostalgic and I can understand exactly what another American entertainer, Bette Midler, meant when she said 'When it's three o'clock in New York, it's still 1938 in London.' Some of the modern face of London I think I shall grow accustomed to: there seems to be a real chance, now that the London Pavilion has been refurbished, of having a Piccadilly Circus that London can be proud of, and now that the Underground is a cigarette free zone, the stations are far cleaner – one day perhaps the system will bear comparison with Singapore. Of the modern developments, I think Hay's Galleria near HMS *Belfast* on the site of what was once Hay's Wharf, is one of the most imaginative and attractive. But by and large it is not so much what is new or vast or imposing that I find attractive in London, but the odd corners and streets, certain areas and buildings that have a personal message for me. A quodlibet is, or was, a please-yourself assembly of musical bits and pieces from various sources that happened to interest the composer, and that is a fair description of the London that is 'My Kind of Town'.

There are certain landmarks in London I would be sorry to lose, though their architectural merit is debatable. Fortunately there is a preservation order on the Hoover factory, no longer used to make vacuum cleaners, on the Western Avenue near Perivale. The work of Wallis Gilbert and Partners in the early thirties, and decorated with a strange amalgam of Egyptian and Aztec motifs, it was con-demned as 'façadist' by the *Architectural Review*. Whatever that meant, one of the partners in the Hoover firm took it as an insult and is said to have visited the *Review*'s offices with a horsewhip threatening revenge; fortunately the editor was out at the time.

Just a couple of miles to the south of the Hoover factory is an architectural landmark which is beyond any critical

The Hoover factory was controversial in its time but stands today as a fine example of 1930s architecture.

Osterley House (facing page) is an impressive monument to architect Robert Adam's attention to detail. The position of the furniture is critical to the overall design in the tapestry room (far left) and in the state bedroom, where holes in the carpet mark the positions of the bed's feet (near left).

St Mary's Church,
Paddington (below), where
Sarah Siddons is buried. Her
statue (above) is by Sir Joshua
Reynolds. Plane trees (right)
are a familiar feature of
London's streets that I
particularly like.

mansions and terraces were built in the 1840s and 1850s. There are clusters of shops in Formosa Street and Clifton Road which help to give the district its air of a London village, and in Shirland Road there's a corner shop which was once the Warwick Farm dairy, built in 1886. When I was a boy it was called Welford's and I would buy a glass of milk there to consume on the premises, seated in the cool, tiled public part of the shop. Once there was nothing but farmland around Paddington, and in 1888 Lord Randolph Churchill put up a hard fight to save some of it for public use. The small recreation ground which survived has a running track where Sir Roger Bannister trained for his four-minute mile.

Another doctor, Alexander Fleming, discovered penicillin in Paddington, apparently quite by accident. He was working in a small laboratory, now incorporated in St Mary's Hospital in Praed Street, when a mould spore blew in through an open window on to a culture dish and dissolved the contents of the container.

The charm of Paddington Green has been virtually obliterated by an overhead motorway, but St Mary's Church still remains. Built in 1788 it's the oldest building still standing in Paddington and in the churchyard is the grave of the famous actress Sarah Siddons, whose funeral in 1831 drew more than 5000 mourners. Sir Henry Irving unveiled a statue on Paddington Green based on the portrait of the actress by Sir Joshua Reynolds. It was the first London statue to a woman other than a member of the royal family.

One of the great charms of these familiar streets to me is the abundance of plane trees in them. They are to be found, I know, in many a city around the world, but to me they belong in London. The sound of their gently rustling leaves on a summer afternoon does much to counter the mindless rush which is so often associated with city life.

One of my favourite places in London is the Royal Naval College, Greenwich. Wren's Painted Hall (left) is a magnificent setting for fine dining, while the Chapel designed by James Stuart (below) combines visual elegance with acoustic perfection.

It was in wartime that I first saw the Royal Naval College at Greenwich, and this marvellous complex of buildings is still one of my favourite places in London. The Painted Hall, whose walls, decorated by Sir James Thornhill, give the illusion that columns support the roof, is to me the grandest of all London's great rooms, and to dine there in the soft light of innumerable candelabra at tables set with the college silver, is a magnificent experience. Guests who can spare the time to take their eyes off their dinner can look up to see King William and Queen Mary handing Liberty and Peace to Europe on Thornhill's sumptuously painted ceiling.

I am almost equally fond of the chapel at the Royal Naval College. It's elegant to look at and has perfect acoustics. After the original chapel, completed to Wren's designs, was burned down, it was rebuilt according to the plans of James 'Athenian' Stuart and his work has a classical perfection. Benjamin West contributed a fine boxwood pulpit with scenes from the life of St Paul and also the painting above the altar showing St Paul at Melita (Malta).

Greenwich as a whole is, to me, one of London's most interesting villages. All the naval associations and the superb National Maritime Museum would make it so on their own. But there's the added attraction of the Greenwich Theatre, once Crowder's Music Hall, as well as many good places for eating and drinking ranging from the Trafalgar Tavern on the

Greenwich's attractions include the National Maritime Museum (ri... which reminds some A... ... visitors of Washington... ...ite House, and the twent... ... hour clock, a symbol ... London village's imp... ...ce as 'Time's Headquart... (below).

waterfront, dating from 1837, to Goddard's Eel and Pie House which has since 1890 supplied Cockneys – and others – with some of their favourite snacks. Daniel Defoe, in his *Tour through the Whole Island of Great Britain* published in the 1720s, described Greenwich as 'the most delightful spot of ground in Great Britain; pleasant by situation, those pleasures encreas'd by art, and all made compleatly agreeable by the accident of fine buildings, the continual passing of fleets of ships up and down the most beautiful river in Europe; the best air, best prospect and the best conversation in England'. One assumes the conversation must have been good when Dr Johnson strolled in Greenwich Park one day with James Boswell, though all that has survived is a terse oneliner from Boswell. Asked by Johnson if the park was not fine, Boswell replied: 'Yes sir; but not equal to Fleet Street.' I also like the journalist Norman Shrapnel's very neat description of Greenwich as 'Time's Headquarters'. At an international conference held in Washington in 1884 it was agreed that the meridian passing through Greenwich should be universally recognised as the line of zero longitude, and so it remains – unless or until it is moved, as a Swedish geographer has suggested it should be, to the centre of the Pacific Ocean.

Not far from Greenwich is Blackheath, on whose bleak heath centuries ago Wat Tyler assembled his ragged army prior to the Peasants' Revolt of 1381, and King Henry V was welcomed home after Agincourt. Since the late eighteenth century it has been regarded as a highly desirable residential area with its own 'village' centre and an intellectual and musical community which supports its own thriving festival. In 1829, the church of St Michael was built to serve the growing community of Blackheath. With its pinnacled spire, often called 'the needle of Kent', and its internal roof timbers shaped like the Bridge of Sighs in Venice, it is regarded as an extravagant example of the Gothic revival.

Two hundred years ago, a great attraction for well-to-do people in Blackheath was Jack Cade's Cavern. Accidentally discovered by workmen in 1778, the four connected caves became popular when 'a young woman, who had been to see the new-found subterranean cavities, a

St George's Church dominates Blackheath's skyline (above); its interior roof timbers are reminiscent, some say, of the Bridge of Sighs in Venice (below).

Jack Cade's Cavern (left), complete with gruesome carvings (above), was once a major attraction, despite its humble origins.

few minutes after she got in the air fell in a pit and expired in about half an hour'. The entrance to the cavern was enlarged and a bar, a chandelier and a new ventilation shaft were installed encouraging visitors during the day to see the winding passages and strange carvings on the walls. At night wild parties were held and by 1854

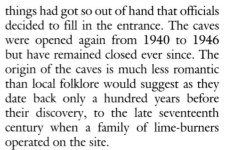

Canonbury Tower and King Edward Hall, where I used to perform with the Tavistock Repertory Company.

things had got so out of hand that officials decided to fill in the entrance. The caves were opened again from 1940 to 1946 but have remained closed ever since. The origin of the caves is much less romantic than local folklore would suggest as they date back only a hundred years before their discovery, to the late seventeenth century when a family of lime-burners operated on the site.

Moving to north London, many of my happiest times as a young man were spent performing with the Tavistock Repertory Company in the King Edward Hall, which was built in 1907 as a place of recreation for the residents on the Marquess of Northampton's estates at Canonbury. The hall is adjacent to Canonbury Tower, which was also leased by the theatre company for many years. There we rehearsed and held poetry evenings in two beautiful rooms with Elizabethan panelling whose names recalled two figures prominent in the tower's history. Sir John Spencer was one. He was Lord Mayor in 1594 and was responsible for embellishing and improving the tower, whose foundations go back to pre-Roman times. The other was the penniless Lord Compton. In 1599, so the story goes, Spencer's daughter, Elizabeth, was lowered in a basket from the tower to elope with Compton, disguised as a baker's boy. Spencer was furious and disinherited his daughter, but a reconciliation was engineered by Queen Elizabeth I. She commanded him to sponsor the child of an impoverished young couple, who turned out to be his own grandson. Sir Francis Bacon lived in Canonbury Tower for some years and it is still the headquarters of the society which considers him responsible for Shakespeare's plays. Oliver Goldsmith and Washington Irving were two other literary men who lived there, at the heart of a London village which, like Blackheath, has long been the home of writers and intellectuals.

The housing estates laid out by the Northampton family extended to Clerkenwell as well as Canonbury. The most famous of the medicinal wells which gave the area its name was undoubtedly the one exploited by Richard Sadler, now buried beneath the stage of Sadler's Wells theatre; but the original Well of the Clerks, named after the parish clerks of London who came to these parts to perform miracle plays in the Middle Ages, can still be seen and even sampled at No. 14 Farringdon Lane.

Clerkenwell is, for me, a fascinating area: Handel attended concerts organised by the coal merchant Thomas Britton in what is now Britton Street; and Clerkenwell Green, regarded by the locals as their village centre, was once a buffer between the nunnery of St Mary, founded in about 1160, and the priory of the Order of St John, whose great gatehouse built in 1504 houses the museum of the order. In more recent times, the green has been a rallying point for radical causes: the Char-

Distinguished visitors inspect the original Well of the Clerks, from which the district of Clerkenwell gets its name.

The gatehouse of the Order of St John's Priory, Clerkenwell which houses the Order's museum.

Clerkenwell Green (right) is known for its political connections but Bloomsbury, its neighbour, has literary claims to fame. Writers who lived there include Anthony Trollope, who displayed an early grasp of the importance of the written word when he designed the first post-box (far right) – he went on to become one of England's foremost men of letters – and Virginia Woolf (below), one of the original Bloomsberries.

tists started processions from here, and at No. 37A is the Marx Memorial Library, housed in a former Welsh charity school. William Morris spoke here and Lenin edited the magazine *Iskra* at the library in 1902-3.

Another great revolutionary to make his home in Clerkenwell was Giuseppe Mazzini who helped to make the district into London's 'little Italy'. In 1863, Italian immigrants built St Peter's Italian church in Clerkenwell Road; on its steps both Caruso and Gigli sang at different times to the assembled crowd, and in July each year it provides the starting point for a colourful street procession associated with the feast of Our Lady of Mount Carmel.

Adjoining Clerkenwell on the western side is Bloomsbury, which holds a certain magic for me on account of its

strong literary and artistic associations, not least thanks to the group of artists and intellectuals who assembled around Virginia and Leonard Woolf and became known as 'the Bloomsberries'. The Woolfs lived variously in Fitzroy, Brunswick and Tavistock Squares. Here in November 1851 Charles Dickens bought Tavistock House, which he described as 'decidedly cheap – most commodious – and might be made very handsome'. The property was later sold to Georgina Weldon, who so disliked it that she wrote a leaflet entitled 'The Ghastly Consequences of Living in Charles Dickens' House'. Another of the many literary figures associated with Bloomsbury was Anthony Trollope, who was born in 1815 at No. 6 Keppel Street. He entered the post office when he was nineteen and was responsible for the design of the first post box.

*Two great London characters:
the 'boy euphonium', Wee
Georgie Wood (above),
and Jeremy Bentham,
immaculately maintained
(right).*

The actor and poet-laureate Colley Cibber was born in Southampton Place in 1671 and to him it seems we owe the phrase 'perish the thought'. He was also famous for his short temper: he once fined a small-part player five shillings for fluffing his lines and, upon being told that the poor man's weekly wage hardly amounted to that, Cibber retorted 'Very well, pay him ten shillings a week but fine him five!'

In more recent times an altogether more congenial theatrical figure lived in Torrington Place. Wee Georgie Wood, four foot nine inches in his socks and crushingly described as a midget by his mother, was a wonderful raconteur who held the stage in the bar of the Savage Club for many years whenever he was not appearing on the boards. Put on the stage at the age of five, he was at first described as 'the boy phenomenon' until one theatre billed him by mistake as 'the boy euphonium'. He achieved great success but by his own account was often unhappy, so much so that in 1940 at the height of the London Blitz, he deliberately went out for a stroll hoping Hitler's bombs would end his misery. 'But all I got', recounted George in that inimitable cracked little voice of his, 'was a piece of grit in my eye.'

At the heart of Bloomsbury is Russell Square, designed in the early nineteenth century by James Burton for the fifth Duke of Bedford, who is commemorated by a statue in the gardens of the square. He seems to have been an unattractive

The attractive statue of the Duke of Bedford in Russell Square hardly reflects the man's disreputable character (right). One of my favourite London Streets: Lamb's Conduit Street (below).

character for he is reputed to have made a man eat a live cat in order to win a wager. Nor did he know how to dress: in spite of his attempts to remain in the height of fashion, he was once stopped in the street by Beau Brummell, who looked at him in horror and exclaimed, 'Bedford, do you call this thing a coat?' Nearby, at University College in Gower Street, a very strange figure can be seen, apparelled in dress of approximately the same period. It is a fully-clothed skeleton of the law reformer Jeremy Bentham, who sits in a glass case in a cloister of the college with his embalmed head held between his legs. Not surprisingly, Bentham's ghost is said to have been seen quite frequently around the college.

On the fringes of Bloomsbury is one of my favourite London streets, Lamb's Conduit Street. The name recalls a certain William Lamb who, in 1577, restored an ancient dam in one of the tributaries of the Fleet river and provided 120 pails for the use of poor women. There's a statue of a lady with an urn at the top of the street and a plaque which reads: 'Lamb's Conduit, the property of the City of London. This pump is erected for the benefit of the publick'.

A short walk away is Gray's Inn Road, where in the early nineteenth century the master builder Thomas Cubitt set up workshops and craftsmen in all trades were employed for the first time on a permanent basis. Cubitt had plenty of work for them, for he radically altered the appearance of parts of Bloomsbury and virtually created large areas of Belgravia and Pimlico, including Belgrave Square, Lowndes Square and Chesham Place.

It was from Cubitts that one of the most successful of Victorian artists, Sir John Millais, bought the site of his mansion in Palace Gate for the then very large sum of £8400. That was in 1873, well after he'd abandoned the lofty principles of pre-Raphaelitism in favour of the popular style exemplified by the celebrated *Boyhood of Raleigh* and *Bubbles,* for which Admiral Sir William James was the model as a boy. The floor of the hall in Millais' house was covered in Sicilian marble and on the landing water spouted

from the mouth of a black marble seal in a marble basin.

I love the grand houses of south-west London, very few of which are now inhabited, as they once were, by single families. They were built in the days when domestic servants were cheap and easy to come by, and a community of eager tradesmen set up shop in the little streets off the great squares. Kinnerton Street, just off Wilton Street and Wilton Crescent, was created for this purpose. In 1854, it offered the services of a cowkeeper, a saddler, two tailors, a plumber, a wheelwright and two dealers in asses' milk, which was thought to have valuable therapeutic properties. Nowadays the small houses of Kinnerton and other similar streets fetch huge sums: they are pretty rather than grand, and their inhabitants have charming 'village' shops and pubs near at hand, such as The Horse and Groom near Eaton Square.

Thomas Cubitt was responsible for the creation of Eaton Square and Eaton Place, where for a short time I had a bedsitting room. However I felt more at home further along the King's Road, Chelsea, in Beaufort Street. Chelsea is oozing with prosperity now, but reminiscent draughts of interesting decadence can still be felt. What was it that attracted the fashionable world in droves to Dr Dominicetti's Fumigatory Steam Baths at

No.6 Cheyne Walk in the middle years of the eighteenth century? They may have been attracted to the street in the first place by the coffee house at No.18, where a former servant of Sir Hans Sloane offered a range of curiosities to interest his customers, including 'A necklace made of Job's tears' and 'Pontius Pilate's Wife's Chambermaid's Sister's Hat'.

Most of London's grand houses have changed their function: No. 2 Palace Gate, once home to Sir John Millais, is now the Zambian Embassy (above, left). The shops in Kinnerton Street, however, still remain, though the cow-keeper is long gone (above).

James MacNeill Whistler lived for twelve years at No.96, painting the famous riverside 'nocturnes' which prompted John Ruskin to accuse him of flinging a pot of paint in the public's face. A great one for matching colours in interior decoration, Whistler is said to have dyed a rice pudding green in order that it should blend with the walls of his dining room. Dante Gabriel Rossetti lived at No.22, sharing the house with a white bull which chewed up the garden, a white peacock, a kangaroo, a racoon and a wombat. The wombat, thought to have been the model for the dormouse in *Alice in Wonderland,* was fond of eating ladies'

hats. One guest was greatly incensed when she lost her headgear in this way, but all Rossetti said was 'Poor wombat. So indigestible!' Apparently, there's still a clause in the lease of No.22 forbidding tenants to keep wombats.

Thomas Carlyle, or 'the sage of Chelsea', lived at No.24 Cheyne Row. There he held court 'singing his great sentences, so that each one was the stanza of a narrative ballad' according to the American writer Margaret Fuller. But Carlyle found time for his neighbours too. He exchanged visits with Leigh Hunt who lived in poverty at No.22 Upper Cheyne Row and when Hunt called on

22 Cheyne Walk, where wombats are most definitely not welcome.

Carlyle, he would always find a guinea left on the mantelpiece. By unspoken agreement, Hunt was expected to pocket it before he left.

Leigh Hunt's hard existence was softened, or so he said, by the fragrance of the lime trees outside his house, and many a London Street is made congenial in this way. There are streets in Kensington and Chelsea which look like orchards of cherry blossom in the spring – no wonder artists have found this part of London so attractive.

But it is to the Thames that I return as I near the end of this exploration of London. The artist William Hogarth moved to what was then the riverside village of Chiswick because he needed a country residence. In the garden is the mulberry tree from which he is supposed to have fed the village children, and in 1780, a visitor came across 'a rude and shapeless stone, placed upright against the wall'. It was inscribed by Hogarth in memory of his pet bullfinch with the words 'Alas, poor Dick! OB 1760 aged 11.' A grander fugitive to the Chiswick countryside was the third Earl of Burlington who in the 1720s created a magnificent country villa modelled on Palladio's

There are streets in Kensington and Chelsea which remind me of orchards in the spring.

Hogarth's country residence now stands in the heart of built-up Chiswick.

Chiswick House (above), where the high-minded can discover rooms adorned with souvenirs of the third Earl of Buckingham's Italian travels. Those searching Chiswick for pleasure of a less elevated sort may find them at The City Barge (below).

Villa Rotunda at Vicenza. To Chiswick House came all the wits of the day, including Pope, Swift, Handel and John Gay, and the rooms were adorned with souvenirs in paint and marble of the earl's travels in Italy.

But, fascinating though Chiswick House is, the chief attraction of Chiswick for me is the riverside village of Strand-on-the-Green. In the centre of a very attractive row of old houses stand two

pubs. One is The City Barge, so named because the Lord Mayor's barge used to be moored here in winter. Perhaps the finest of these barges was the Maria Wood, built in 1816, painted blue and gold and capable of carrying 200 people on the upper deck. In an inn on the site of the second pub, The Bull's Head, a few yards away, Oliver Cromwell is said to have held a military court, and during the eighteenth century the comic actor Joe

Miller was a regular patron. He was illiterate but that didn't stop him from learning, with the aid of his wife, thirty or so parts in plays by Shakespeare and other writers.

Among the many famous inhabitants of Strand-on-the-Green was the artist Johann Zoffany who lived from 1790 to 1810 at what is now Zoffany House. Zoffany had had an adventurous life before he settled in Chiswick, earning great sums of money at the court of an Indian ruler; in London he was greatly in demand as a portrait painter, and in his *Last Supper* which hangs in St Paul's Church Brentford, he used local fishermen as models for eleven of the Apostles and painted his own portrait as St Peter.

I'll cross the river for two final glimpses of London. There's a block of offices in Black Prince Road with a façade in decorative terracotta which is a survival from the vanished empire of Sir Henry Doulton; he owned a huge terracotta factory which once extended from Lambeth Bridge to Vauxhall Bridge on the south bank of the Thames. There, as a young man fresh from the country air of Lincolnshire, my father worked, and I salute him when I pass through Battersea, where he lodged.

In nearby Clapham too, there are surprising reminders of the countryside.

The name means 'village or homestead on the hill', and it started to become fashionable in the wake of the Great Plague in the seventeenth century. Samuel Pepys lived in Clapham for a time, the historian Macaulay was born there, and William Wilberforce, the central figure of an in-

*Painter John Zoffany lived at this house in Strand-on-the-Green from 1790 to 1810 (above, left). His **Last Supper** (left) now hangs in St Paul's Church, Brentford.*

Two hidden reminders of London's great industrial heritage: the former base of Sir Henry Doulton's terracotta empire (below) and the quiet back garden of a nineteenth-century railway worker's cottage in Clapham (below, right).

fluential evangelical group, the Clapham Sect, was also a resident. The elegant Clapham of those days must have been totally overwhelmed by the arrival of the railways, and the construction of what was, at one time, the busiest railway intersection in the world, at Clapham Junction. Around it grew a bustling sprawl of shops, pubs and places of entertainment, and to go 'up the Junction' meant a rowdy Saturday night out among the flaring gas lamps of a thousand market stalls.

However, for those who worked on the building or running of the railway junction, rows of cottages were built which, in the manner of modern London, have now become desirable residences. Urban and yet quiet, these little back-streets offer access to the great metropolis and a retreat from it at the same time. In the gardens at the back, you might well be in the countryside of Kent.

So there is my London. It's not everyone's London of course; there are as many Londons as there are people who live in it or come to look at it. There's plenty to dislike about it: the traffic and the noise, the heartless concrete and the threat of crime on the vandalised tube trains. 'I don't know what London's coming to,' said Noel Coward, 'the higher the buildings, the lower the morals.' Alexander Pope anticipated him when he expressed the motto of London thus: 'Get money still, and then let virtue follow if she will.' And George Mikes put it more bluntly when he said 'London is chaos incorporated.'

Well, I know all that. But I'll go along with Arthur Symons who, when writing about London in 1918, said: 'The appeal of London is made by no beauty or effect in things themselves . . . but by the atmosphere which makes and unmakes this vast and solid city every morning and every evening with a natural magic peculiar to it.'

INDEX

ACKNOWLEDGMENTS

The majority of illustrations in this book were specially
commissioned; others supplied to us or requiring
acknowledgment are listed below.

8 By kind permission of T F Bryan, G W R Museum 9 Reproduced by permission of the Trustees of the Science Museum 10 *top* Raymond Mander and Joe
Mitchenson Theatre Collection 11 Royal Albert Hall 14 Thames Line 16 *top left* By gracious permission of Her Majesty the Queen 17 *bottom right* London
Borough of Richmond Upon Thames 20 *top right* Royal Botanic Gardens, Kew; *bottom* Museum of London 21 Tate Gallery 27 *top left* Guildhall
Library 28 Hulton-Deutsch Collection 31 *top right* Guildhall Library; *bottom right* Peter Jackson Collection 32 *top* Guildhall Library 33 *top* Folger
Shakespeare Library/ET Archives 34 *top left and right* Popperfoto 35 *bottom* National Maritime Museum 36 *top right* Guildhall Library 37 *top left* Guildhall
Library; *top right* By kind permission of the Dean and Chapter of Westminster 39 *bottom left* Popperfoto 40 *top* National Maritime Museum 44 *top and
bottom* Museum of London 45 *bottom* Popperfoto 46 Guildhall Library 48 *top and bottom* Popperfoto 49 *left* Peter Jackson Collection 50 *left*
Popperfoto 51 *bottom* Museum of London 52 *top* Museum of London 53 *top* Museum of London 54 Hulton Picture Library 58 *right* By kind permission
of Kumagai Gumi UK Ltd 60 *bottom left* Raymond Mander and Joe Mitchenson Theatre Collection 61 *top right* Raymond Mander and Joe Mitchenson
Theatre Collection 62 *top and bottom right* Raymond Mander and Joe Mitchenson Theatre Collection; *bottom left* Royal Commission for Historical
Monuments 63 *top* Allen Eyles 65 *top* Allen Eyles 66 *top right* By kind permission of the Friends of Highgate Cemetery; *bottom* Reproduced by permission
of the Trustees of the Science Museum 67 *right* Hulton-Deutsch Collection 68 *top left, bottom left, bottom right* Raymond Mander and Joe Mitchenson Theatre
Collection; *top right* Allen Eyles 69 By courtesy of the Board of Trustees of the Victoria and Albert Museum 70 *top* Popperfoto 72 *top* Courtesy of the
National Theatre 74 *left* Society of Antiquaries, London 75 *right* Raymond Mander and Joe Mitchenson Theatre Collection 76/77 By kind permission of the
Theatre Royal, Drury Lane 79 *top* Raymond Mander and Joe Mitchenson Theatre Collection 85 *top* Guildhall Library 87/88 By kind permission of the
London Coliseum 90 *bottom* Mansell Collection 91 *top* By kind permission of the Dean and Chapter of Westminster; *bottom* Reproduced by courtesy of the
Trustees of the British Museum 93 By kind permission of the Dean and Chapter of Westminster 94 Museum of London 95 *bottom* Guildhall Library 96/
97 Royal College of Music 99 *top left* Royal College of Music 100 Royal Commission for Historical Monuments 101 Royal Albert Hall 102/103 Royal
College of Music 104 *bottom* Hulton-Deutsch Collection 105 *bottom* Popperfoto 106 Hulton-Deutsch Collection 108 St John's, Smith
Square 110 Barbican Centre 111 By kind permission of the Kings Troop, Royal Horse Artillery 113 *top* Guildhall Library 115/116,117 *top* Reproduced
by gracious permission of Her Majesty the Queen 117 *bottom* By kind permission of Mr and Mrs H C Bowering and the College of Arms 118 *top* Adam
Woolfit/Susan Griggs Agency Ltd 122/123 By kind permission of the King's Troop, Royal Horse Artillery 124 *top left and right* Libby Turner; *bottom*
Museum of London 129 *left* National Portrait Gallery; *right* Courtesy of the Deputy Master of the Royal Mint 130 *top* Guildhall Library 131 London
International Financial Futures Exchange 132 *top* Guildhall Library; *bottom* Museum of London 136 By kind permission of the Worshipful Company of
Goldsmiths 137 *top* Guildhall Library; *bottom right* By kind permission of the Plaisterers' Company 138 *left* Angelo Hornak Photography; *right* By kind
permission of the Corporation of London 139 Guildhall Library 140 *top right* Eileen Tweedy 141 *top* Peter Jackson Collection 147 *top* Guildhall
Library 151/152 By kind permission of the Dean and Chapter of Westminster Abbey 155 By kind permission of the Vicar and Churchwardens, St Martin-in-
the-Fields 156 *left* Guildhall Library 161 *top* Guildhall Library 162 *bottom right* Tate Gallery 163 *top left* By kind permission of the Vicar and Parish of St
Paul's, Hammersmith 164 *top right* Guildhall Library 165 *left* Reproduced by gracious permission of Her Majesty the Queen 166 *left* By kind permission of
St Bride's Church, Fleet Street 167 *top left* By kind permission of Temple Church 170 *right* Royal Borough of Kensington and Chelsea Library of Art
Services 172 *top* The British Library; *bottom* Reproduced by courtesy of the Trustees of the British Museum 173 *top* By courtesy of the Board of Trustees of
the Victoria and Albert Museum 176 *right* Museum of London 177 *top* National Maritime Museum; *bottom* By kind permission of Trinity
House 179 *bottom* Reproduced by gracious permission of Her Majesty the Queen 181 *top* Tate Gallery; *bottom* By kind permission of Youth and
Music 182 *bottom right* By courtesy of the Trustees of Sir John Soane's Museum 184 *top* Guildhall Library 186/187 *top left* By gracious permission of Her
Majesty the Queen 190 *top* By courtesy of the Board and Trustees of the Victoria and Albert Museum; *bottom right* Roger Spencer, London Borough of
Bromley 191 *top* Mansell Collection; *bottom* Hulton-Deutsch Collection 193 *bottom left* Mansell Collection 194 *bottom right* Reproduced by permission of
the London Borough of Camden from the collections at Keats House, Camden 195 *right* Royal Botanic Gardens, Kew 196 Royal Botanic Gardens,
Kew 197 *top* Royal Botanic Gardens, Kew 198 *top* Museum of London 199 *top* Peter Jackson Collection 203 *bottom* By kind permission of Hamleys,
Regent Street, London 204 *top* Marylebone Library; *bottom left* Guildhall Library; *bottom right* Peter Jackson Collection 206 *top* Royal Commission for
Historical Monuments 214 *bottom* Popperfoto 215 *top right* Mansell Collection 218 *top and bottom right* By kind permission of the Trustees of Dr Johnson's
House 219 *top* Museum of London 223 *top* Museum of London; *bottom* Royal Commission for Historical Monuments 224 *top* Royal Commission for
Historical Monuments; *bottom right* Hulton-Deutsch Collection 225 *top* Raymond Mander and Joe Mitchenson Theatre Collection; *centre* Royal Commission
for Historical Monuments 227 *top left* Hulton-Deutsch Collection 234 Popperfoto 236 *bottom* Woodmansterne Ltd, Watford 238 *centre, bottom left* By
kind permission of the Marquis du St Empire 240 *top* By kind permission of the Clerkenwell Heritage Centre 241 *top right* Crown Copyright; *bottom* Mansell
Collection 242 *left* Raymond Mander and Joe Mitchenson Theatre Collection; *right* By kind permission of University College, London

The publishers wish to express their gratitude to the
many individuals and organisations whose help or
specialised knowledge was invaluable in the
preparation of this book. Many thanks particularly to
Joanna Cherry, Anne-Marie Ehrlich, Georgina Harris
and Peter Jackson for their tireless efforts in the
production of this publication.

Barrow Hill

Battle

170

118

Hole Bourne

West Bourne

115

136

121

106

Bourne

Bayswater

94

67

47

Notting Hill

93

Hyde Park

28

Westminster

Campden Hill

Ford

120

34

Thorney

Kensington

Pimlico

Bridge Creek

Chelsey

Ne

Ke

25

Batters ey

Stockwell

Waverley Brook

Fulham

45

62

77

Falcon Brook

Putten Heath

53

103

Brixton Hill

191

173

105

Streath Hill

R. Wa